Th‌e ... kit

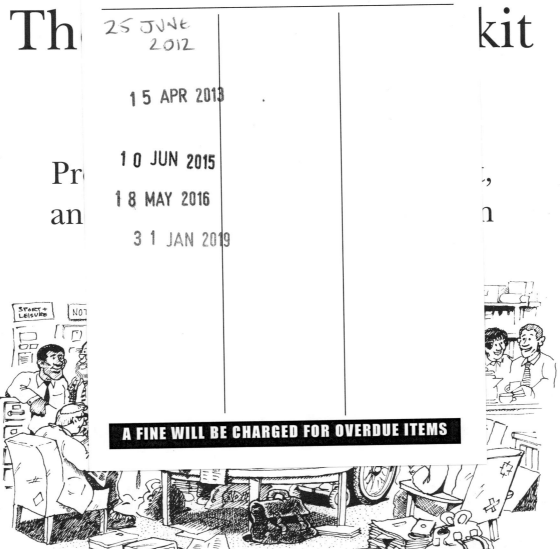

Paul Ginnis

Illustrations by Les Evans

Crown House Publishing Company LLC
www.CHPUS.com

243 669

The Teacher's Toolkit, Volume 1
Promoting Variety, Engagement, and Motivation in the Classroom

Grades K–12

© 2005 by Paul Ginnis. Reprinted 2007 and 2009.
Originally published as part of *The Teacher's Toolkit: Raise Classroom Achievement with Strategies for Every Learner*
(Crown House Publishing Ltd., Bancyfelin, Carmarthen, Wales, UK)
© 2002 by Paul Ginnis

Printed in the United States of America

ISBN: 9781904424581

Published by:
Crown House Publishing Company LLC
6 Trowbridge Drive, Ste. 5
Bethel, CT 06801
www.Crownhousepublishing.com
Tel: 866-272-8497
Fax: 203-778-1900
E-mail: info@CHPUS.com

Editing (of this edition): Melanie Mallon
Design and typesetting (of this edition): Dan Miedaner
Cover (of this edition): Benjamin Hight

Library of Congress Cataloging-in-Publication Data

Ginnis, Paul.
　　The teacher's toolkit / Paul Ginnis ; illustrations by Les Evans.
　　　v. cm.
　　"Originally published as part of The teacher's toolkit: raise classroom achievement with strategies for every learner, Crown House Publishing Ltd., Bancyfelin, Carmarthen, Wales, UK, c 2002."
　　Includes bibliographical references and index.
　　Contents: v. 1. Promoting variety, engagement, and motivation in the classroom, grades K-12.
　　ISBN 1-904424-58-9 (v. 1 : alk. paper)
　　1. Effective teaching.　2. Teaching—Aids and devices.　3. Activity programs in education.　　I. Title.
LB1025.3.G513 2005
371.102—dc22

2005003100

We should be as concerned with how we teach as we traditionally have been concerned with what we teach.

—John Bruer, *Schools for Thought*

Dedicated to those closest to me:

Sharon, Helen, Steven, Clare

Contents

**Section 3: Tools for Managing Group Work,
Behavior, and Personal Responsibility**

Acknowledgments

My deepest appreciation goes to my family and friends, without whose love and support I would not have written this book. They waited patiently while *The Teacher's Toolkit* took time and energy I should have given to them: my wife, Sharon, beautiful and intelligent, my companion and coworker, who has given so much to see this project through; my three multitalented children, Helen, Steven, and Clare, to whom I wish all the happiness in the world; my mother, Jean; stepfather, Cliff; sisters, Trish and Debs; brothers-in-law, Andy, John, and John; nieces, Nicola, Amy, and Megan; nephew, Daniel; mother-in-law, Monica; sister-in-law, Mary; my inspiration, Donna Brandes; and my dear friends Peter Batty and Steve Munby.

Thanks to all at Crown House and the Anglo-American Book Company, and to David Bowman in particular, for their persistent faith in the *Toolkit*. Thanks to Veronica Durie and Melanie Mallon for their skilled and enthusiastic editing. Thanks to Professor Robert Sylwester for his helpful and very generous advice. Finally, thanks to Joanne Clarke and Jayne Cotton for keeping me on the road and in clean shirts.

Foreword

It is always a pleasure to be asked to write a foreword to a book by a person whose writing I have admired for a number of years. It is also a pleasure to act as a "go between" for an English writer as he projects one of his best books into the American market. As a former headmaster of an English secondary school (in England a job involving teaching and administration) who lived and worked for four years in Washington D.C., and whose three sons were educated both in English and Virginian secondary schools, I'm proud to share with my American colleagues this most thoughtful and helpful book.

Some years ago a skeptic at one of my lectures on new research into the ways in which humans learn commented, "I don't know what all the fuss is about. Surely we humans have been using our brains to think for as long as we've been using our stomachs to digest food. Both are perfectly natural activities. There is nothing new in any of this." Unwittingly, this person gave me the most perfect opportunity for a powerful response. "That's true," I said, "but consider this. Over the past thirty or forty years medical science has taught us so much about the chemistry of food, and the nature of the human digestive system, that most of us, by taking sensible notice of this information, are eating more sensibly, and exercising more regularly. Not only are we very obviously healthier, we are living considerably longer than our grandparents simply because we have a better 'user guide' to the human stomach."

"The same is just starting to happen to human learning," I told my audience, "because of recent findings in cognitive science, neurobiology, developmental psychology, and especially evolutionary psychology, we are fast building up the better user guide to the human brain."

With such knowledge—with such guides—I believe that within a generation we will be able to do for the human brain what over the past two or three generations we've been able to do for our bodies—use them more effectively. That's exciting.

Note, however, that I said "more effectively." I did not say "efficiently." That was intentional. We are living in a highly utilitarian world, and there is a tendency, when considering education, to think of utility. We ponder how the skills that we can now teach more effectively will improve a youngster's life prospects. Here we have to be careful; we are in danger of submerging the glorious inquisitiveness of young people into too many formal structures—too many of the "right way of doing things." Fortunately Paul Ginnis recognizes this danger. Human learning is the most gloriously "messy" activity. Once our inquisitiveness is fired up our learning can take us into a multiplicity of different directions. As always, education—human learning—is about both strong roots and healthy wings. It's about rigorous discipline and active imagination. It is about not accepting any boundaries to human learning. It is about thinking well beyond the classroom walls, and well beyond the ideas that a teacher can transmit. It's about going with confidence into places that earlier you would not have had the confidence to approach.

This is an excellent toolkit to take on a journey; it's a toolkit that teachers can share with their students as the young people take increasing responsibility for directing their own learning. I commend it warmly.

John Abbott, President, The 21st Century Learning Initiative

Preface

I have packed into *The Teacher's Toolkit* (this volume and the forthcoming volume) almost everything I know about teaching and learning. Educators have been trying to raise student achievement for years. Given that the challenge is still on to pursue excellence day by day, often in testing circumstances, it seemed like a good time to gather my favorite practices and share them.

Teachers want practical ideas. There are loads of them in this book, but that's not all. In my experience, the quality of teaching and learning improves most readily when practice and theory inform each other. It is helpful for us to know why things work or don't; to have principles to guide the design of lessons; to know how students learn so that we don't always operate unthinkingly from expediency or unquestioningly from political directive.

Consider the old saying:

Insanity—doing the same thing the same way and expecting a different result!

Making the same point, Frank Zappa once said:

Without deviation, progress is not possible.

We have to do things differently if we want greater student achievement. But what? Fortunately, we no longer have to depend on guesswork, trial and error, ideology, or flights of philosophical fancy. We can now rely on some fairly secure truths about the learning process. It seems that there are natural laws of learning, some givens, some universal principles that provide a firm foundation for effective practice. These provide us with compass directions to follow, indicating the best, though not necessarily the easiest, ways forward.

Where have they come from? In recent years a huge amount of scientific information about the brain has become available, thanks to new neuroscanning technologies. This has been popularized in accelerated learning and through the wealth of print and Internet material on brain-based approaches (see the recommended resources, on page 225, for details). What is impressive, and reassuring, is the extent to which this new information affirms and refines earlier practices based on the principles of humanistic psychology, holism, cooperation, and democracy. Many educational theorists of the past, who held only quasi-scientific notions about teaching and learning—John Dewey, John Holt, and Carl Rogers, for example, whom we shall meet later—have been proved largely right. This current convergence of thinking from various old and new sources—neuroscientific, psychological, sociological, and moral—suggests that the main thrust of national and state policy should be rethought. It seems to be barking up the wrong trees.

Be that as it may, the principles that underpin the *Toolkit* are sufficiently down to earth for individual teachers such as yourself to adjust your practice no matter what the big wide world outside your classroom is up to. The practical techniques inspired by current thinking are sufficiently self-contained to be conducted within the confines of your own four walls. In some cases the strategies of yesteryear belonging to the older, recently reaffirmed thinking can be dusted off and reused with confidence.

Classroom techniques created in the days of active learning, student-centered learning, drama across the curriculum, flexible learning, and supported self-study are found to be compatible with the latest findings of neuroscientists. These ideas always were effective, and now we know why. They just got buried under the pile of prescriptions from federal legislation and state standards. So, where is this particular collection of ideas from?

Over the 25 years that I have worked in schools—as a teacher, a department head, an advisory teacher, a staff development tutor, and a freelance trainer—I have learned my craft from many remarkable people. Without doubt the deepest and most pervasive influence has been Dr. Donna Brandes, the internationally renowned student-centered educator. Donna brought into my young professional life—at a time when, I am ashamed to say, students called me Hitler—a coherent person-centered philosophy and skill set. The ideas stretched me to the limit but resonated strongly with the deep values of my theological training, and so they created the kind of congruence in my teaching that I had been seeking. Over the years that we worked and wrote together, she taught me how to trust students, how to be myself in the classroom, and how to pursue the goals of self-esteem and personal responsibility above all and let everything else fall into place. An expert practitioner herself, she showed me the power of optimism, unconditional regard, and self-belief. Donna's insights continue to influence my work, fundamentally, day by day.

The second greatest influence on my thinking has been my good friend Professor Roland Meighan. Roland taught me to see the big picture, to understand what is happening socioeconomically and politically within and beyond schools. He showed me the true nature of democracy and cooperation, the value of unconventional and free-spirited thinking, and the place of pioneering action. He continues to model the winning combination of hard-hitting analysis, humane values, sharp wit, and genuine warmth.

Then there is my wife, Sharon. She taught me how to use drama, how to trust intuition, how to think laterally, and how to be daring in the classroom. She showed me what it's like to have a learning style and intelligence profile that don't fit the system, what it's like to be on the outside, and what happens to self-esteem and life chances when teachers do not have the will or the skill to meet individual learning needs. I aspire to her creativity and spontaneity.

The fourth, but by no means least, significant influence is my close friend and colleague Peter Batty, the ultimate reflective practitioner and man of integrity. Peter has taught me to slow down—to make room for learning, not just teaching. He has shown me how to trust the process, how to value reflection and review, how to let principles be the guide to practice, and how to live a little.

You will no doubt get to know these characters as you read between the lines of the pages that follow. Beyond them are countless teachers, principals, advisers, and trainers who have taught me, often unknowingly, crucial lessons. Therefore, many of the ideas in the *Toolkit* are not mine. Credit is hard to apportion, though, as many strategies have their origins somewhere in the mists of time, so forgive me if you read something that you thought you'd invented! The ones that *are* mine have been fashioned from experiences in thousands of classrooms in hundreds of schools of all types. In fact, every practical suggestion has been thoroughly road tested, often with difficult classes and always in a variety of subjects and with different age groups. In the hands of skillful teachers, they have almost always had positive effects on motivation, discipline, and the quality of learning. Ideas that didn't work have been ditched.

By the way, don't use the ideas slavishly; the intention is to stimulate your own creativity. Don't underestimate the power of enthusiasm; it lifts lessons to a higher plane, and your enthusiasm will always be greatest for ideas that you invent yourself. I hope you enjoy using *The Teacher's Toolkit* as much as I have enjoyed writing it. Now, at last, I can get back to listening to my jukebox and going to some home team soccer games.

—Paul Ginnis

SECTION 1

Design Tools

Why?

In his best-selling book *The Seven Habits of Highly Effective People,* Stephen Covey (1989a, 47–48) suggests that a habit is formed whenever a person knows *what* to do, knows *how* to do it, and has a good reason for doing it—in other words, knows *why.* Understanding why helps to create motivation. Covey (1989b) says, "A habit is the overlapping of *what* to do, or knowledge, *how* to do, or skill, and *why* to do—want to or attitude. Where they overlap you'll see a habit."

Knowing *what* to do = awareness

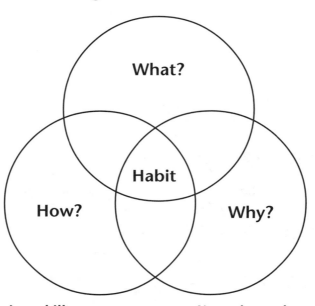

What?

Habit

How?   **Why?**

Knowing *how* to do it = skill   **Knowing *why* to do it = motivation**

Those who work in the field of professional development, or whose job it is to manage change, know the truth of this. Simply exhorting people to alter their ways doesn't work. Telling them what they should do differently, without giving them the necessary skills, leads to feelings of frustration and failure. Nor does it work in the long term to give people new techniques without a convincing rationale. Innovation is then short lived. On the whole, new practice is not sustained unless people have

- a motivation to keep doing it, which comes from conviction; and
- an understanding of the principles that underpin the practice so that the new methodology can be continually refreshed and reinvented.

Much of this book is about *how.* This, I hope, makes it attractive to teachers and trainers who are understandably eager for new practical ideas. The risk, though, is that it provides no more than a box of chocolates. Once the chocolates have been enjoyed, the box is likely to be thrown away and a fresh one demanded. The more taxing but ultimately more productive intention of the *Toolkit* is for readers to internalize the recipe, so that they can make their own chocolate when this particular selection runs out.

So this first section is about *why*—the rationale. Why push the boat out and do things differently? Why not just carry on as usual? My basic premise is that learning in schools is likely to be at its best when teachers follow the natural laws of the learning process. This idea is true in education around the world and is presented strongly by the Scottish Consultative Council on the Curriculum (1996) in the introduction to their excellent "Teaching for Effective Learning:" "Some would argue that teaching is a different job depending on where you teach and whom you teach. Obviously there are differences but [we] believe that the basic principles of learning apply no matter where you teach and no matter what the needs or the age of the learners you teach" (1).

The title of Mike Hughes's (1999) book *Closing the Learning Gap* says it all. In the past, teaching tended to be hit or miss, because as a profession we were less certain about learning. Even now, the way many teachers teach is out of step with the way most learners learn. The task of the modern, aware teacher and school administrator is to bring teaching methods increasingly in line with the learning process. Herein lies the real solution to the apparent problems of under-attainment (measured narrowly) and underachievement (measured broadly).

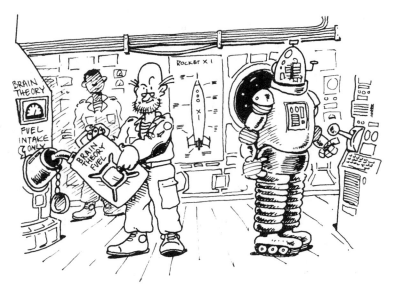

Fueled by the latest ideas, their journey began. Instinctively they knew...the future wasn't what it used to be.

The difference between attainment and achievement is more than semantic. In *Effective Learning in Schools*, Christopher Bowring-Carr and John West-Burnham (1997, 28) stress "that learning must have a consequence for the learner. By 'consequence' we mean that by learning x, the learner will see the world in a slightly different way, will alter his or her behavior or attitude in some way. If the 'learning' that has taken place is merely capable of being reproduced at some later date in answer to the demands of some form of assessment which replicates the original problem, and the context for that problem, then what is being learnt is 'shallow learning' only."

Deep learning involves the development of an increasingly sophisticated personal reality, with matching competencies and disciplines. The *Toolkit* attempts to provide some of the means of arriving at deep learning (achievement), even within a culture concerned largely with shallow learning (attainment).

Behind all this is biology. For the last couple of decades, neuroscientists have been telling us with increasing confidence about the workings of the brain. This confidence and knowledge is a direct consequence of advances in scanning technology, particularly functional magnetic resonance imaging (fMRI) and positron emission tomography (PET), which allow us to see the brain in action to a precise degree.

Learn More about Learning Theory

Many excellent books provide surveys of modern learning theory.

- Ideal starting points: Alistair Smith's *Accelerated Learning in the Classroom* (1996), *Accelerated Learning in Practice* (1998), and the myth-busting *The Brain's Behind It* (2005b); Colin Rose and Malcolm J. Nicholl's *Accelerated Learning for the 21st Century* (1997); and Robin Fogarty's *Brain Compatible Classrooms* (1997).

- *The Learning Revolution* (1999), by Gordon Dryden and Jeannette Vos, is a recognized classic.

- The many books by Eric Jensen, especially *The Learning Brain* (1995a), *Teaching with the Brain in Mind* (1998), and *Brain-Based Learning* (2000a), provide crisp, readable, and, above all, applied insights into recent research.

Nowadays the brain is thought of as dynamic, not as some sort of computer crunching its way through billions of inputs per second. It is considered to be a flexible, self-adjusting, unique, ever-changing organism that continually grows and reconfigures itself in response to each stimulus. Early in the 1990s, researchers such as the neurobiologist Karl Friston and the psychologist Stephen Kosslyn were instrumental in formulating this new paradigm (cited in McCrone 1999). They realized that the brain operates rather like the surface of a pond. New input provokes a widespread disturbance in some existing state. The brain's circuits are drawn tight in a state of tension, and when a pebble is thrown in (a sensory input), there are immediate ripples of activity. New pebbles create patterns that interact with the lingering patterns of previous input. Then everything echoes off the sides. Nothing is being calculated. The response of the pond to the input is organic, or more accurately, *dynamic.*

Aware of the vitality and fluidity of the brain, all made nakedly apparent by imaging, John McCrone suggests that a complete understanding of consciousness can be achieved only by combining insights from a number of disciplines: "Scanning technology has already had the beneficial effect of forcing the beginnings of a marriage between psychology and neurology. . . . But if the human mind is a social as well as a biological phenomenon, then yet further marriages are required with the 'soft' sciences of sociology and anthropology, and their many sub-disciplines" (1999, 309). Therefore, in our rush to embrace the main messages from brain science, it is vital that we do not bypass more established cultural and socioeconomic insights as if they were now old hat. The classic perspectives of Ivan Illich (1971) and Paulo Freire (1970), along with the popular works of John Holt, most crucially *How Children Fail* (1969), and Neil Postman and Charles Weingartner's *Teaching as a Subversive Activity* (1969), may be middle aged and unfashionable, yet they combine to present a powerful agenda for personal, social, and ultimately political empowerment that is entirely relevant to our modern needs. In assessing Illich in *The Trailblazers* (1998), for example, Professor Edith King concludes: "As the educational issues that Ivan Illich espoused now seem familiar at the close of the 20th century, teachers and parents can find strength . . . from his writings in their advocacy of the democratic school and alternative educational futures" (10).

What Next?

Revolutionary insights into the brain are only part of a more general overhaul of thinking that has gathered momentum in the last 15 years. An increasing number of commentators are now weaving global social, economic, commercial, and technological "megatrends" with modern insights into the brain to present us with new visions of the future. Dryden and Vos's "16 major trends that will shape tomorrow's world" (1999, 37–83) provides as good an overview as any, and Charles Handy, the internationally renowned business and social commentator, established some time ago that change is now discontinuous. He said, "the success stories of yesterday have little relevance to the problems of tomorrow. . . . The world at every level has to be reinvented to some extent. Certainty is out, experiment is in" (1996, 16). Guy Claxton's reflective *Wise Up: The Challenge of Lifelong Learning* (1999) makes the persuasive case for major shifts in our thinking about learning, schooling, training, and parenting. He argues that the ultimate life skill for the 21st century is the ability to face difficult and unprecedented challenges calmly and resourcefully.

Worldwide, ordinary people are increasingly understanding and using information and communications technology (ICT). This brings two major positive benefits to learning. First, teachers are gradually being released from having to be the main transmitters of information, ideas, and skills, enabling them instead to concentrate on the facilitation of learning, on being learning coaches. Second, students are being empowered to learn independently. They have access to most of the information they need and often whole courses, on CDs or online. Learning, even of regular examination subjects, can take place in the school's learning center, at home, or in the local cyber café, meaning that students can control when and where they learn, and often how. The visual and interactive nature of most high-tech resources makes them appealing to learners who struggle with academic routines. ICT is free of time, space, and tradition constraints. All students need to do is learn how to learn.

Don Glines, director of the California-based Educational Futures Project, has argued for years that "there is only one overriding issue facing educators today: the transformation to communication age learning systems" (1989, 49). The 21st Century Learning Initiative (www.21learn.org) sums up the situation in its vision: "New understandings about the brain; about how people learn; about the potential of information and communications technologies; about radical changes in patterns of work as well as deep fears about social divisions in society, necessitate a profound rethinking of the structures of education" (2004).

Such thoughts raise important questions—two in particular. In this day and age, what should be the purpose of education? And how should it be organized?

Learn More about the Brain

- For those who are not familiar with all the parts of the central nervous system, visit Eric Chudler's fresh and frequently updated website Neuroscience for Kids: http://faculty.washington.edu/chudler/neurok.html.

- For more advanced technical stuff about the structure of the brain, with lots of photographs and diagrams, go to the Virtual Hospital, The Human Brain, at www.vh.org/adult/provider/anatomy/BrainAnatomy/BrainAnatomy.html. Alternatively, familiarize yourself with Susan Greenfield's work. She describes the inner secrets of the gray matter in readable texts such as *The Private Life of the Brain* (2000b), *Brain Story* (2000a), and *The Human Brain: A Guided Tour* (1998).

- If you're ready for a detailed and fairly technical account of shifts in brain research from the 1940s to the present day, read John McCrone's *Going Inside: A Tour Round a Single Moment of Consciousness* (1999).

Education and the Economy

Over recent decades a view has crept to dominance in the industrialized world that education exists primarily to serve the economy. This premise drives almost all current education policy. The economy has become the politician's first and foremost, and unquestioned, reason for pursuing high quality in education, but where does such functionalism lead?

Even education theorists in the learning-to-learn camp often argue their case on economic grounds—they say that people are often required to learn on the job and will inevitably have to retrain at least once in their working lives, so they need the skills to do it. It's true, companies increasingly expect employees to learn, and employees increasingly expect companies to provide for their learning. Many companies do pay for employees to further their education in work-related skills and knowledge.

Clearly, education and the economy are in a mutually dependent relationship: Each needs the other, and this will remain so. Individual livelihoods and the continuance of national life depend on it. But there are two issues to debate. First, the *prominence* of the economy in a nation's thinking about education: Currently it dominates and dictates. National education and training goals are set explicitly to improve competitiveness. The second debate concerns a nation's understanding of what the economy needs from education. According to Abbott and Ryan (2000, 35):

> Today's social and economic needs argue for a new model of learning that entails:
> 1. mastery of basic skills;
> 2. the ability to work with others;
> 3. being able to deal with constant distractions;
> 4. working at different levels across different disciplines;
> 5. using mainly verbal skills, and;
> 6. problem-solving and decision-making.

By contrast, most political thinking about education is driven by an out-of-date understanding of business needs. In most cases, current education policy is way behind the times, serving the old factory age, not the new information age. Attendance, punctuality, compliance, acceptance of the "manager's" decisions, an understanding of one's place in the pecking order, a sufficient general knowledge, and the ability to use a few basic skills make up most current curricula (as they did a hundred years ago), whereas businesses are crying out for flexibility, responsiveness, creative problem solving, teamwork, self-management, and sophisticated communication skills. The reason for the yawning gap is clear. The modern business agenda chimes with the modern learning agenda, and there's a deep-seated stubbornness about accepting modern educational ideas, even those grounded in the most credible neuroscientific research. Why? Because they resemble the progressive child-centered practices that have been so successfully discredited in the popular mind.

Compounding the problem is the simplistic idea that educational outcomes can be fundamentally altered by changing the curriculum and its content. This, of course, is nonsense. The kinds of changes required for modern economic success, for a healing of social ills, and for personal fulfillment are rooted in the *way* learning is conducted, not in *what* is learned. In other words, changes to teaching and learning methodology and to educational structures are required. No wonder John Bruer, a cognitive scientist, said that "we should be as concerned with how we teach as we traditionally have been concerned with what we teach" (1993, 53).

Take creativity for example. Teachers tell us that creativity is crushed by the continuous focus on preparation for mandatory tests, and we see the natural learning processes of childhood—free play and random exploration, for example—abandoned by zealous teachers and parents in their desperate attempts to give children an "advantageous" start. Schools are using increasingly bizarre bribes (such as offering tickets to a rock concert or checks students can use at the school store) to get students to attend (Toppo 2002). The chronic teacher shortage and high turnover suggest that adolescents are not the only ones who don't want to go to school anymore. How long will this position be tenable in a society that still harbors deep divisions and signs of serious disaffection (the turnout for every election is always shockingly low), and in which we now know enough about learning to address these issues successfully? The snag is that politicians get stuck. Once they've declared their course, they can't backtrack. They fall prey to a common habit: If something doesn't work, do it harder and more often (in other words, test, test, and test some more). Politicians are simply not allowed by the media and the public to learn from mistakes and adapt to fresh evidence—what a role model for a "learning society"!

Once free of the Earth's gravitational pull, many things became possible.

Those who break with the economy-driven view of education and propose fundamentally different purposes are few and far between. Tom Bentley, director of the independent think tank Demos, said: "A sustained transformation of the education system needs a guiding purpose. I have suggested that this goal should be creativity, at the individual, organizational and societal level" (2000, 62). Bowring-Carr and West-Burnham "see the development of the mind as the overriding purpose of education" (1997, 25). Professor Clive Harber, on the other hand, speaks strongly of education for democracy that is "as much about the *way* in which people think and behave, *how* they hold their political opinions, as it is about *what* they actually think" (quoted in Ginnis 1998, 11). He quotes Carl Rogers, the inventor of client-centered counseling and student-centered learning: "People who can't think are ripe for dictatorship" (11).

If we are to break from the shackles of shallow learning, navigate these uncertain times, and fashion a morally sound and fruitful future for all, then purposes such as "the development of the mind" and the "preservation of democracy," or others such as "the creation of an inclusive and egalitarian society" or "the fulfillment of the whole person" will have to become driving rather than half-hearted concerns. As I hope you will come to recognize, these intentions underlie the practical strategies presented in sections 2 and 3, as well as in volume 2 of the *Toolkit*.

Educational Organization and Purpose

Then there is the question of how education should be organized. It all depends on the dominant purpose, of course. If education were supposed to secure acceptance of the social order and working habits of the past, then we'd probably want the kinds of schools we have now. Writing a few years ago, Anita Higham, former principal, puts this point strongly: "My thesis is that we are in the death-throes of secondary schools as we know them because we are attempting to educate adolescents of the late 20th Century within the style and structure of the late 19th Century school and its teachers' contractual conditions" (1997–1998, 1). We have never shaken off the idea that schools are primary agents of socialization; we've stuck with them because they do this job rather well. Sadly, as Bill Lucas and Toby Greany put it: "Schools as we know them are fast becoming an anachronism. . . . Their very traditions and structures mean that they are educating young people for a world which no longer exists" (2000, vii)

In a foolish attempt to cling to what they had left behind, they religiously prepared the young for a world they would no longer inherit.

If instead the primary purpose of education were to meet learners' individual needs, we would follow the lead of Valerie Bayliss, director of the Redefining the Curriculum project: "Implicit in these [modern] ideas is a greater emphasis on the individual. A competence-led curriculum, together with the liberating capacity of technology, has the potential to open up much more individualized learning" (1999, 18–19). If the primary purpose were to help people learn how to learn, we'd be asking serious questions along with Christopher Ball: "Is it going to be possible to adjust traditional school education to satisfy [students]—or should we think about replacing it with something altogether different? The true learning society we all seek will require a new breed of teachers— more like guides than instructors, more part-time than full-time, more philosophers than pedagogues" (1995, 6). If the purpose were to *promote democracy,* we'd have democratic schools, as in Denmark, for example (Powell 2001). It is significant that calls for fundamental change are no longer being made by radicals alone, but increasingly by mainstream, and in many cases establishment, figures.

Part of the reason for sticking with what we have is that there are no large-scale models to copy. Individual examples of reconstructed schools include Ted Sizer's mainstream Coalition for Essential Schools, with its 1,000-plus member schools (www.essentialschools.org); schools redesigned along the lines of multiple intelligences; the chain of schools modeled on Daniel Greenberg's Sudbury Valley School, in Massachusetts (www.sudval.org); Arthur Andersen's School of the Future in Alameda, California—these are just some of the welcome experiments.

These schools are just a dent, however, in education reform; reconstruction is still slow in coming. The real problem is that our preoccupation with the economy has constrained our thinking. The language ("delivery," "hard outcomes," "raising standards," for example), the procedures (measuring, goal setting, comparing, performance-related pay), and the values (materialism, competition, capitalism) have created accepted norms for the system. Few people inside the system now seem able, or willing, to think outside the box.

Therefore, there is huge resistance to contrary ideas. Radical proposals from brain scientists, sociologists, and education theorists—people who know about learning—are generally blown off. At the same time, the government's own initiatives haven't amounted to much. Potentially exciting possibilities have been suffocated by the blanket domination of goals and standards. The ultimate answer, of course, is to base policy on what we know about learning. Professor Robert Sylwester sums up the position: "The brain is a biological system, not a machine. Currently we are putting children with biologically shaped brains into machine-oriented schools. The two just don't mix. We bog the school down with a curriculum that is not biologically feasible" (1993–1994, 46).

> ### Learn More about Alternative Education
>
> The alternative education movement is buoyant, as is clear from *Creating Learning Communities* (Miller 2000), a stimulating collection of examples of grassroots innovation, summaries of underpinning ideas, and insights into key thinkers. Visit the website: www.CreatingLearningCommunities.org.

Return to the Forbidden Planet?

So this is the political and professional arena into which the theoretical and practical ideas in the *Toolkit* are pitched. But most ideas in this book are not that new after all. Many brain-friendly ideas simply confirm older notions. Much of humanistic psychology, with its optimistic view of human capacity, its mission to overcome barriers to personal growth, and its holistic agenda, has been affirmed by neuroscientists and neurolinguists. As a young teacher in 1985, I had the privilege of cowriting *A Guide to Student-Centred Learning* (Brandes and Ginnis 1986), and in 1992, *The Student-Centred School* (Brandes and Ginnis 1992), with Donna Brandes, the internationally acclaimed and exceedingly gifted educator and therapist. Inspired by Carl Rogers's client-centered work, many of the books' central themes, such as the need for emotional safety, the significance of self-esteem, and the power of personal responsibility, are now commonplace within the emergent new orthodoxy. The importance of mental and physical activity, clarified by our modern understanding of the neocortex and the role of kinesthetics in learning, is in direct line with "active learning" of the past. Developmental group work, flexible learning, and supported self-study all find reflections in the mirror of modern teaching and learning.

John Abbott, the determined and erudite commentator on educational futures, writing with Terry Ryan near the dawn of the new millennium, makes a similar point that would have John Dewey, the father of experiential learning, rejoicing in his grave: "The mass of evidence that is now emerging about learning and brain development is spawning a movement toward educational practice which confirms the earlier intuitive understanding abut learning through direct involvement with the activity" (1999b, 263). In other words, the only way to learn *how* to do something is by doing it!

The farther they traveled, the stronger the sense that their distant destination was strangely familiar.

So the basis of good practice may have shifted from psychology and philosophy to biology, and many new insights have been added, but in some key respects, ideas that disappeared underground with the rise of the reductionist thinking that has dominated political visions of education since the mid-1980s have now been given fresh impetus and value. This is encouraging for many established teachers who might otherwise feel resistant to "yet another set of newfangled ideas."

Head in the Clouds, Feet on the Ground

So far, I have attempted to paint a picture of the background to the practical ideas in this book. It is at once an exciting and a depressing sight. And it's easy to get carried away with the discussion, but let's keep things in perspective. *The Teacher's Toolkit* has its feet firmly on the ground; it is rooted in the here and now and suggests only strategies that can be tried today, tomorrow, or next week in regular classrooms in ordinary schools. However, it is not just a new collection of quick and easy classroom ideas. It is more than a random and aimless set of tips for teachers. Its core purposes are in line with the best of modern thinking, and these now need to be clarified. They say that a journey of a thousand miles starts with a single step—but that step has to be in the right direction. Fortunately, modern researchers and commentators have given us compass bearings and a map.

So let's now look at a modern agenda for learning in more detail. This will give us the specifications for the design of effective learning strategies, even within the limitations of the present system. From the wealth of insight available, I have selected certain key ideas on the basis that they translate directly into the construction of concrete classroom activities. The first two groups of points, dealing initially with similarities and then with differences between learners, draw largely on the brain sciences. But beware: This is nowhere near the full gamut of brain-compatible learning—just a few edited highlights. Keep an eye out for volume 2 of the *Toolkit,* and see the recommended resources (page 225) for books and websites with further information.

Similarities among Learners

Emerging from the latest neuroscientific research are several truths about the way that all brains seem to function. Four of the similarities are explained in this subsection, the ones that have particularly informed the preparation of the *Toolkit*'s practical ideas. In the next subsection, we look at key differences among learners. Before any of it will make sense, though, we need to familiarize ourselves with the brain's processing method: the biology of learning.

The Biology of Learning

Susan Greenfield likens the brain to the Amazonian Basin. She says that the number of neurons in the human brain is about equivalent to the number of trees and other plants in the 2.7-million-square-mile rainforest. The number of dendrites (the fibrous extensions from the neuron cell body that act as receptors) is more or less equivalent to the number of leaves on those plants and trees. In the jungle that is 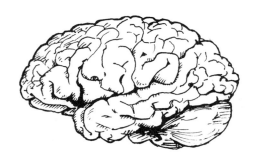 the brain, all these are busily and continuously connecting with each other. One cubic millimeter of brain tissue has more than a million neurons, which means that all the world's telecommunications systems could fit into an area of the human brain about the size of a pea.

The good news is that you have the same number of brain cells as Albert Einstein. Everyone does, unless one's brain is diseased or damaged. The even better news is that every student in your school has the same number of brain cells as you. There is, therefore, a biological basis for optimism. One hundred billion neurons per person, up to twenty thousand dendrites per neuron, all multiplied together means that the number of potential connections among brain cells in any brain is 10 to the 100 trillionth power, actually far greater than the number of particles in the known universe, according to Paul Churchland (1995), professor of philosophy. In fact, if you were to count the actual connections in an adult neocortex alone (that is, in the thin outer covering of the brain), at a rate of one per second, it would take you 32,000,000 years!

Neurons are responsible for processing information. Each neuron has one axon, a thin fiber that can be up to six or seven feet long (and operate your big toe, for example) but is more often a half-inch or so long. The axon is the transmitter, passing information on in the form of electrochemical stimulation. Its job is to connect with the dendrites of other neurons, thousands of them, which means it has to subdivide itself to create multiple terminals. Each neuron is in effect a tiny battery, powered by the difference in concentration between sodium and potassium ions across the cell membrane. An electrical charge, the *action potential*, is generated in the cell body of the neuron and travels down the axon at a rate of between 3 and 330 feet per second.

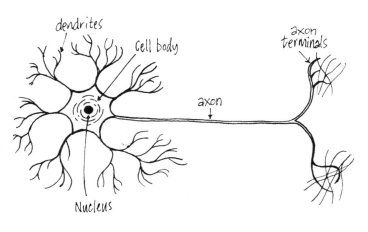

A SINGLE NEURON

Dendrites, meanwhile, are the branchlike extensions from the neuron cell body that act as receptors. The information flow between neurons is only one way: from the cell body, down the axon, and then via synaptic connections to the dendrites of other neurons, which carry the signal to their own cell bodies. The axon terminal never touches the dendrite. There is always a tiny gap—the *synaptic cleft*. The electrical pulse traveling down the axon reaches the terminal and activates neurotransmitters (chemical cocktails stored in vesicles in the tip of the axon) that carry the message across the synapse and stimulate (or inhibit) the electrical charge in the receiving dendrite.

A single neuron can simultaneously receive signals from thousands of other neurons, even as far as three feet away. The sum total of all the signals arriving from all the dendrites to the cell body determine whether the neuron will itself fire a charge. Because its axon can branch repeatedly, a firing neuron can send the signal on to thousands of other neurons.

So this is learning: New mental or motor experiences provide stimuli, which are converted to nerve impulses that travel to sorting stations, such as the thalamus (in the midbrain area). From here, signals are sent to specific areas of the brain. Repeated stimulation of a group of

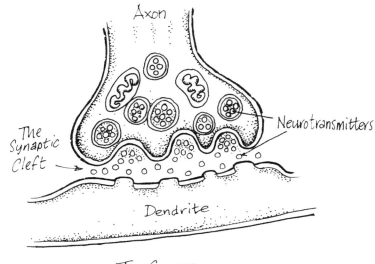

THE SYNAPSE

neurons causes them to develop more dendrites and therefore more connections, and so an entire forestlike network of neurons is established that creates a grasp, an understanding, a mastery. In time these neurons "learn" to depress "wrong" connections and to respond positively to weaker signals from other cells—in other words, to do the same mental or motor process with less "effort." Cells change their receptivity to messages based on previous stimulation.

From Biology to Classroom

The teacher's job is to support students in translating their brains' remarkable biological potential into actual performance. In pursuit of excellence in learning, then, it seems that the skilled educator faces three tasks.

1. Encourage new neural connections through appropriate challenges that create high levels of stimulation.
2. Consolidate existing connections. The more a neural pathway is used, the more efficient it becomes. Axons become insulated with a white fatty substance called *myelin,* which speeds up the electrical-chemical-electrical signaling process, and neurons respond with less effort to the original prompt. On the other hand, unused connections are eventually lost; they are pruned away.
3. Reconfigure existing webs of neural connections by seeking out and providing information that will straighten out a misunderstanding, refine a concept, complete an understanding, or hone a skill.

This last one sometimes feels like quite an effort. Eric Jensen sums up the job: "The key to getting smarter is growing more synaptic connections between brain cells and not losing existing connections. It's the connections that allow us to solve problems and figure things out" (1998, 15).

To achieve the best results, it's obviously important to work with the brain's natural processes, to teach in a way that is compatible with the student's natural learning methods. Some of these points, a selection of the similarities and differences among learners, will be discussed shortly. But, generally, learning should get off to a great start because it appears that everyone is born with several predispositions, including

- a desire to work cooperatively with others
- the inclination and ability to learn language
- the will and skill to make patterns
- a natural propensity to learn math

In support of this last point, Brian Butterworth, professor of cognitive neuropsychology, argues that math ability is natural. As the dustjacket of his book *The Mathematical Brain* summarizes "our genes contain a set of instructions for building a mathematical brain, and this is why, without benefit of teaching, human beings are born to count" (1999).

However, it's not all smooth sailing. Some of the factors that affect the translation of potential into performance are outside of the teacher's control, so let's get the depressing parts out of the way first. One obvious example is lifestyle during pregnancy. A developing fetus is very sensitive to stress and nutrition. The mother's emotional state, diet, and intake of substances affect the development of the brain, which is creating neurons at a rate of up to 15 million per hour between the fourth and seventh month of gestation (Ratey 2002).

A second example is nutrition. Mothers' breast milk appears to contain certain nutrients that stimulate the production of neurotransmitters, which are essential to the efficient firing of synapses. Also, fast foods and most cheaply produced packaged foods simply don't contain enough of the items that the brain needs for optimum performance: proteins, unsaturated fats, complex carbohydrates, sugars, and trace elements such as boron, selenium, vanadium, and potassium. The negative effects of many soft drinks and most food additives are well known.

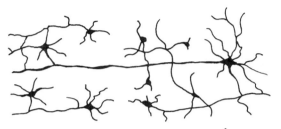

Few connections through lack of stimulation

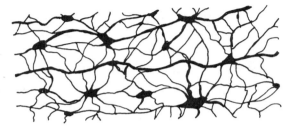

A young, stimulated brain rich in neural connections.

A third area is early-years stimulation. In middle-class homes, for example, parents say, on average, twice as many words per day to toddlers, compared with working-class homes. Such enrichment in early years is crucial to the construction of the brain's basic architecture. So is the amount of early-years laughter, touch, freedom, visual stimulation, tactile manipulation, music, motor stimulation, environmental variety, and cooperative play. The infant brain is utterly plastic and begins to customize itself from the moment a child is born. It configures itself to its environment and experiences. Over 50 trillion neural connections are already in place at birth, and millions more are added moment by moment; but unused connections begin to be cut away by the billion. Take emotional and social development. The evidence suggests that emotional intelligence develops early, perhaps even in the first year, and that the school years are only the last resort for nurturing emotional literacy (Hoff 2003).

Professor Philip Gammage, former de Lissa chair of early childhood, University of South Australia, is clear:

> At birth there are far more potential connections than the child can use, and by the age of three or so pruning has already started and systems of connection that are seldom or never used are being slowly eliminated. We are born, for instance, capable of learning phonemic combinations not native in our native language, but will lose that capability relatively soon. . . . By about five (or earlier) many predictive and causal social, as well as physical/locational attributions, have become quite settled. In a real way, the brain is then almost "cooked." (1999, 1)

It's a real case of "use it or lose it." Researchers are currently exploring the possibility that experience with foreign languages as adults may play a role in our ability to learn new languages (Kuhl 2004), but this research does not change the fact that even the first two years of life can decide between dramatically different possible futures. This is why Ernest Boyer, the late president of the Carnegie Foundation for the Advancement of Teaching, offers a sobering thought: "To blame schools for the rising tide of mediocrity is to confuse symptom with disease. Schools can rise no higher than the expectations of the communities that surround them" (quoted in Abbott and Ryan 2001).

A fourth example of a factor outside the teacher's control is sleep. Many children simply don't go to bed early enough, or, during puberty, they wake up too early. Modern thinking suggests that during deep sleep, the brain sorts and files the day's input. Consequently, learning is consolidated and memories are laid down.

Finally, we come to genetics. The extent to which intelligence is inherited is hotly debated. There are researchers who fiercely argue that it is, among them Professor Sandra Scarr, famous for her identical-twin studies, and Professor Robert Plomin, who claims to have virtually isolated the elusive gene for "general intelligence." (See, for example, Scarr 1992, 1993; and Plomin 1983.) One area is fairly clear: Susumu Tonegawa and Eric R. Kandel (with fellow researchers) have identified a specific gene that activates the critical memory function of neurons, and this may explain why some people have better memories than others do. Overall, it's now thought that 30 to 60 percent of the brain's wiring is due to heredity, and 40 to 70 percent is the result of the environment, depending on what type of behavior is being considered (Tsien et al. 1996; Malleret et al. 2001).

Now let's flip the coin over and see what's on the optimistic side. The good news is more powerful than the bad. Within the teacher's control are *expectations*. We have known since Robert Rosenthal and Leonore Jacobsen's *Pygmalion in the Classroom* (2003; originally published in 1968) that teachers' internalized views of students' capabilities have a direct impact on students' actual performance. In the studies, students were grouped randomly, but the teachers were told they differed in ability. Guess what? The results of the group that were mistakenly believed to be high flyers rose and the results of the "low achievers" went down. Rosenthal and Jacobsen identified six ways in which the teachers communicated high expectations:

1. The teacher expressed confidence in her ability to help the student.
2. The teacher expressed confidence in the student's ability.
3. The teacher's nonverbal signals—tone of voice, eye contact, level of energy—were consistent with what she said.
4. Feedback from the teacher was specific and ample and mentioned both good and bad.
5. The teacher gave detailed input to individual students.
6. The teacher encouraged individual improvement through challenge.

Teachers communicate expectations through the energy they bring into the classroom, through the words they say and the way they say them, through the effort they put into developing a good relationship with a class, and perhaps most powerfully, through the design of learning tasks. Together, these affect students' self-image and self-esteem (see page 208 for a detailed checklist of teacher attitudes that affect students). The resultant self-belief either drives or depresses motivation and perseverance.

Students receive expectations from other sources too—family, peers, the culture of a local community, the media—and in many cases, teachers have to work doubly hard to reverse negative messages. It is critical that we maintain high expectations even in the face of contrary evidence. Reading scores, baseline tests, predicted grades, and tiered test papers can easily limit our expectations of some students.

Also within the teacher's control is the culture of the classroom—the psychological and emotional environment for learning (section 3 is devoted to this). Likewise, we control the physical environment of learning. The brain needs a continual supply of oxygen (it uses one-fifth of the body's supply), cool temperature (open the windows), and preferably negatively ionized air (buy an ionizer unit for the classroom, or have a waterfall installed). The brain absorbs a surprising amount of information from peripheral material (have lots of displays). Colors, aromas, light, and furnishings (lay carpets, redecorate) have a profound effect on mood, and music can make a big difference. The brain turns music into electrical energy; music literally feeds the brain. Different types of music appear to have different effects (as explored in the Mozart debate). The type of lunch offered in the cafeteria is within the school's control, as is the provision of pure chilled water (have plenty of dispensers around the building). Every 24 hours, 198 gallons of blood pass through the brain. If the brain is insufficiently hydrated, its electrolytic balance is affected and mental performance suffers. Eight to ten glasses of water a day are required for optimum functioning. All in all, learners' states can be altered. Learners can be made more ready for learning (Jensen 2003).

Alistair Smith gives us a further reason to be cheerful: Children can become smarter through the teacher's *skilled intervention*. He explains how Robert J. Sternberg, Lev Vygotsky, Reuven Feuerstein, and Ya'acov Rand "pioneered work on cognitive modifiability through cognitive mediation and created a structure for developments such as 'thinking skills.' They showed that 'intelligence' could be modified and thus expended and developed" (1998, 57). Michael Howe, professor of psychology, who is on the "environmentalist" side of the debate about intelligence, also encourages us to believe that the conditions we create make a profound difference: "It is not true that a young person's intelligence cannot be changed. There is abundant evidence that the intelligence levels of children increase substantially when circumstances are favorable" (1997, 161).

So, overall, the prospects for raising achievement look good. Of course, there are major challenges, especially in difficult socioeconomic and sociocultural circumstances. Teachers can make a difference, however, and will do so if they follow some simple guidelines. At last we can begin to spell them out.

Here are the promised four *similarities* among learners:

1. We all need to figure things out for ourselves.
2. Experiences that are multisensory, dramatic, unusual, or emotionally strong are remembered far longer and in more detail than ordinary, routine experiences.
3. Everyone needs to feel emotionally secure and psychologically safe.
4. Learners are more motivated, engaged, and open when they have some control over their learning.

---

1. WE ALL NEED TO FIGURE THINGS OUT FOR OURSELVES.

Learning occurs through the brain making its own meaning, making its own sense of things. Many researchers distinguish between two types of meaning: *reference meaning* and *sense meaning* (Kosslyn and Koenig 1995), or *surface meaning* and *deeply felt meaning* (Caine and Caine 1997). Take, for example, knowing the Pythagorean theorem. Reference, or surface, meaning refers to the ability to name and reference an idea—you would know that the square of the hypotenuse is equal to the sum of the squares of the other two sides. You might even be able to use this formula to conduct simple calculations. You would certainly be able to quote the definition in a game of Trivial Pursuit.

Sense, or deeply felt, meaning is different. It involves understanding *why* the square on the hypotenuse is what it is. It's a conceptual grasp, probably the result of hearing the idea explained several times by different people, seeing it presented visually, happening to catch a TV program about its importance in architecture, "doing" it with pieces of cardboard, and reading about what prompted Pythagoras to make his discovery in the first place. These separate fragments weave together in your mind, and suddenly it all makes sense: The penny drops. You can now explain the theorem to someone else and use it in a range of contexts. This deeper meaning, or internalized understanding, is the kind of learning that concerns us here.

As long ago as 1983, Leslie Hart found that such pattern making is one of the innate characteristics of the neocortex. The neocortex, part of the cerebral cortex, is the convoluted outer covering of the brain (*cortex* is Latin for bark or rind). Only three millimeters thick, comprising six layers of neurons, with the total surface area of a closed newspaper, this "is what makes human beings what they are. Within the vast human cortex lies a critical part of the secret of human consciousness, our superb sensory capacities and sensitivities to the external world, our motor skills, our aptitudes for reasoning and imagining, and above all our unique language abilities" (Thompson 1985, 18). The cerebral cortex is home to rationality, logic, and conceptualization.

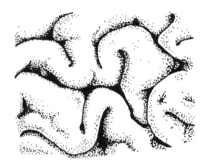

The convoluted surface of the neocortex

Students create personal concepts by recognizing gestalts, not by adding up pieces of information in a digital manner. The dictionary defines *gestalt* as a "perceived organized whole that is more than the sum of its parts." Biologically, these are physical interconnections of neurons, webs, neural fields, axon-synapse-dendrite networks created by existing neural groups suddenly connecting, like a series of light bulbs coming on together—in fact, we often use the light bulb image when people finally get an idea that we've been wanting them to grasp for some time.

Hart says, "It can be stated flatly . . . the human brain is not organized or designed for linear one-path thought" (1983, 95). This fits with modern scientists' view of the brain as dynamic and responsive, not computerlike. Gestalts form unpredictably when a number of realizations occur together, triggered by who knows what. So it's no use explaining first about squares, then about square numbers, then about triangles, then about the relationship between the three sides and expecting every student to be with you every step of the way. Rather, students form gestalts by deciphering clues, indexing pieces of information, and recognizing relationships across a range of sources. They don't grasp things just because you've explained them.

In fact, Hart goes as far as to say that "learning is the extraction of meaningful patterns from confusion," and "There is no concept, no fact in education, more directly important than this: the brain is, by nature's design, an amazingly subtle and sensitive pattern-detecting apparatus" (1983, 117). Concept formation depends on what students do, in their heads, not what the teacher does. The implications are obvious: Make learning mentally active and set up investigative, problem-solving types of activities that invite the brain to operate according to its natural inclination—to play detective. Section 2 is full of strategies designed to get students to think and come to conclusions for themselves.

Obviously, "pattern recognition depends heavily on what experience one brings to a situation," says Hart (112). This is why students grasp ideas at different times and learn at different rates. Back to our earlier discussion about the Pythagorean theorem: A student who was taught about square numbers in grade school or who plays a lot of games in which triangles matter, such as pool, or whose father is a math teacher and has pointed out lots of applications of geometry since the student was a toddler will get it faster than a student who has never had these experiences. How often do you, as a teacher, have to go back with a student repeatedly, scraping away conceptually until you find a firm foundation of understanding to build on? This makes the case for the differentiation and personalization of learning. (See volume 2 of the *Toolkit* for practical differentiation and personalization techniques.)

In *Descartes' Error: Emotion, Reason, and the Human Brain,* Antonio Damasio (1994), professor of neurology, explains further. As we are presented with new information, he says, the brain recalls past experience and references the new stuff to the base data from different locations simultaneously. The new material is integrated into existing neural networks, which are consequently changed, giving us an enriched template of experience. "Some circuits are remodeled over and over throughout the life span, according to the changes an organism undergoes," he writes. "Other circuits remain mostly stable and form the backbone of the notions we have constructed about the world outside" (1994, 112).

As the brain becomes more experienced, as it takes in more and more data, it clears up misconceptions, completes understanding of half-understood ideas, and ditches erroneous notions. This gives us more clues about how to teach effectively: Work from students' prior knowledge; accept their misunderstandings and half-baked ideas; start from where the students are, not from where you think they should be because of their age. Create both the climate and the opportunity for them to be honest about their confusions, frustrations, and struggles. Create time for reflection. Expect conceptual leaps to occur at different times for different students for different reasons.

One principle kept them sane; when in doubt, check a List.

This pattern-based explanation of the learning process is known as *constructivism,* further defined by Abbott and Ryan:

> Constructivism holds that learning is essentially active. A person learning something new brings to that experience all of their previous knowledge and present mental patterns. Each new fact or experience is assimilated into a living web of understanding that already exists in that person's mind. Constructivist learning is an intensely subjective, personal process and structure that each person constantly and actively modifies in light of new experiences . . . With a constructivist form of learning, each child structures his or her own knowledge of the world into a unique pattern, connecting each new fact, experience, or understanding in a subjective way that binds the child into rational and meaningful relationships to the wider world. (1999a, 66–67)

To support students' individual mental patterning, which is the key to concept formation and internalized understanding, I offer six guidelines.

(i) Encourage students to find things out, and figure things out, for themselves.

Make the implicit, natural function of the neocortex explicit. Capitalize on the student's innate curiosity and desire to make connections that stems from this part of the brain. At the simplest level, reverse the usual process and have students ask you the questions. Use "Question Generator" (page 119), or "Hot Seating" (page 95), for example. Make them work for information; don't hand it to them on a silver platter. Use "Double Take" (page 86) to strengthen research skills. Structure opportunities for them to figure things out, to come to conclusions by pulling together several threads of information and by deducing, reasoning, and intuiting. The best examples of how to structure these opportunities are "Assembly" (page 62), "Silent Sentences" (page 128), "Ranking" (page 126), and "Guess Who" (page 90).

(ii) Encourage students to articulate draft ideas.

Checking something out, talking something through, getting it off our chest, speaking off the top of our heads—these all play natural and key roles in the process of concept formation. We are social creatures. Our brains develop in a social environment, and we often make meaning through social intercourse. So discussion, peer teaching, draft writing, presentations to others, and "think-talk-respond" are classic ways of getting students to articulate their thinking and thereby speed up the process of sorting and connecting in their heads. In the process, language itself is clarified. Students are not using language just to "do the activity"; they are using the activity to develop language. "Back to Back" (page 64) is a crystal clear example of this.

What's more, William Glasser (1986) suggests that people retain 95 percent of what they teach to someone else. In many classrooms this means shifting the ratio of teacher talk to student talk. Alistair Smith suggests that we "adopt a policy of no more than 16 minutes an hour of direct instruction" (1998, 88). Section 2 of the *Toolkit* contains many ideas for structuring peer teaching and articulation. "Pairs to Fours" (page 112), "One to One" (page 110), "Corporate Identity" (page 76), "Discussion Carousel" (page 80), and "Center of the Universe" (page 72) are just some of the classic activities to try.

Articulating draft ideas doesn't have to be oral. It's possible to take "draft action," that is, to give it a try, even though you're not sure whether you can do it or how it will turn out. Encourage students to use trial and error as a deliberate learning strategy and encourage them to demonstrate what they have done so far, even though it may not be the finished product. The most structured version of this in the *Toolkit* is "Value Continuum" (page 139).

(iii) There is little point in giving students ready-made meaning.

By "ready-made meaning," I mean such things as printed notes, dictation, copying, predrawn Mind Maps, and fill-in-the-blank exercises. Such material might be filed neatly in students' folders and give everyone the comforting impression that work has been done, but little deep learning will have occurred. Instead, teach students different ways of arriving at and recording their own patterns of meaning. Use what are sometimes known as *graphic organizers*: keyword plans, Mind Maps from scratch (see Tony Buzan's extensive and much-copied work), flowcharts, sketches, diagrams, webs, bulleted lists, graphs, storyboards, and so on. Eric Jensen makes the point strongly: "Humans don't really understand or learn something (with the exception of motor or procedural learning as an infant) until they create a personal metaphor or model" (1995b, 20). See "Conversion" (page 74), "Distillation" (page 82), and "Hierarchies" (page 92) for more details.

(iv) Come at the same key concepts from different angles, in different ways.

Building a logical and linear series of steps toward a concept, and then moving on to the next, will not work for most students. They usually need to have lots of examples and applications, along with several explanations in different media if they are to get it (deep learning), rather than just rote learn it (shallow learning). Continually moving from the big idea to the details and back again, drawing it, miming it, speaking it, charting it, saying it, singing it, demonstrating it, modeling it, listing it, hot seating it (ever had a conversation with the water cycle?), dancing it, writing it—unusual combinations of these techniques presented in rapid succession help the left and right hemispheres of the brain to work together and encourage that penny to drop. The most efficient way for some students to "get" a concept is to see pictures and "do" the idea rather than listen to it or read about it.

(v) Provide interactive feedback that is specific and immediate.

Think about what happens in computer games: Students learn to progress through levels quickly because they get instant and precise feedback on the decisions they make. The brain is exquisitely geared for feedback—it decides what to do next based on what has happened before. It is self-referencing and self-rectifying; it readily builds feedback that's "hot," in other words, relevant and immediate, into its developing concepts and skills. Of course, it's not easy for the teacher to get around to everyone quickly enough (see "Dreadlines" on page 88), but there are ways of checking students' understanding collectively so that you can make appropriate interventions. Methods include "Calling Cards" (page 70), "Thumbometer" (page 137), "Beat the Teacher" (page 66), and "Spotlight" (page 133).

Apart from the teacher's feedback, the reactions of peers, verbal and nonverbal, are vital sources of information for the learner. These can be spontaneous, a by-product of the give and take of regular classroom activity, or planned, as in peer redrafting and peer-assessment activities such as "Pass the Buck" (page 114), "Stepping Stones" (page 135), and "Wheel of Fortune" (page 146). Feedback has maximum effect when it is controlled by the learners—they choose when to receive it and how much to receive. This builds another case for democratic and student-centered practice.

(vi) Punctuate the learning.

According to Jensen, there are three reasons to punctuate learning: "First, much of what we learn cannot be processed consciously; it happens too fast. We need time to process it. Second, in order to create new meaning, we need internal time. Meaning is always generated from within, not externally. Third, after each new learning experience, we need time for the learning to 'imprint'" (1998, 46).

The brain continues to process information long after we are aware that we're doing it. The catch is that further external input can get in the way. According to J. Allan Hobson (1994, 1998, 1999), association and consolidation processes can occur only during down time, when other external stimuli are shut out. In practical terms, this means having a few mini-breaks within a double lesson. Two to five minutes every ten to fifteen minutes is recommended for heavy, new material, and a couple of minutes every 20 for lighter, more familiar stuff. Teachers who relentlessly get through the curriculum often find that they have to reteach a lot of the content before the exam—now we know why.

On top of all this, didactic-transmission teaching is simply inefficient. When students are asked to be passive, they are using only a fraction of their brains' power. That's why there's a lot of doodling, daydreaming, and surreptitious chitchat during "boring" lessons—students are using spare capacity. By contrast, when a brain is asked to solve a problem, decipher a code, solve a mystery, unravel a puzzle, respond to a curiosity, or answer a creative request, it immediately bursts into life. Nancy Denney (1985), professor of psychology, considers problem-solving to be akin to aerobic exercise for the brain. The brain needs novel, complex, and challenging tasks for its health. Scans show that as soon as the brain is asked to work actively on problems, there's a virtual explosion of neural activity, causing synapses to form, neurotransmitters to activate, and blood flow to increase.

The neocortex of the human brain is designed to operate in this active, investigative way. It is irrepressible in its automatic search for the best answer to a question in which it is interested, and it continually scans to resolve unfinished business. It's like a nonstop search engine. This is why we sometimes wake up in the middle of the night with an unexpected solution to a worrisome issue. Working with the "grain of the brain"—using intriguing questions, challenges, conundrums, and creative activities—does everyone a favor. Students become more engaged and achieve deeper levels of understanding. Teachers therefore have to push less. Clearly, these insights support the current interest in thinking skills.

The catch to the guidelines in this section is that many teachers feel that they can't afford the time to teach like this because they have "a curriculum to get through." Yet many of the same teachers complain that the students don't remember what they've covered. The answer may lie with the principal of a high school who recently told his complaining science department to cut the mandated curriculum by 20 percent. His argument was that if you cut 20 percent of the content and give yourselves time to teach properly, then the 40 percent that the students currently learn by covering 100 percent of the syllabus will become 60 percent, even though they'll do only 80 percent of the total. Confused? More is less! How does that work?

2. EXPERIENCES THAT ARE MULTISENSORY, DRAMATIC, UNUSUAL, OR EMOTIONALLY STRONG ARE REMEMBERED FAR LONGER AND IN MORE DETAIL THAN ORDINARY, ROUTINE EXPERIENCES.

Certain types of experiences are memorable because of three aspects of brain function. First, the brain has an attentional bias for novelty. It is far more interested in what's new than in what's normal. Robert Sylwester and Joo-Yun Cho (1993) discovered that the brain has a built-in bias for certain types of stimuli. Since it can't give attention to *all* types of incoming data, it sifts out those bits that are less critical to our survival. Any stimulus introduced into our immediate environment that is either new (novel) or sufficiently different in emotional intensity (showing high contrast) immediately gets our attention. For example, when middle-school geography students saw house bricks and pieces of chalk, rubber, wood, and stone waiting for them on their desks, they started beaming and chattering with anticipation. During the lesson, on rates of erosion, everyone was focused and stayed on task pretty much the whole time. According to the final exam results, this was a far more memorable experience than the regular lessons of teacher talk, textbooks, and worksheets.

Clearly, the immediate minimum requirement is to ensure plenty of variety within a lesson and over a series of lessons. Mix it. A number of studies in the 1980s by Ilya Prigogine and Isabelle Stengers (1984), James Gleick (1987), and William E. Doll, Jr. (1989) found that students actually achieve a richer understanding of content in a climate of suspense, surprise, disequilibrium, uncertainty, and disorder. According to Prigogine and Stengers, the brain naturally responds to chaos by creating purpose and direction. Because the brain loves to sort things out for itself and loves variety, super-ordered behavioristic approaches are actually the least likely to produce desired results. Effective learning is either real-life learning or designed like real life.

Second, there is no single part of the brain used to store memories. It used to be said that we have two types of memory, short term and long term, but nowadays it's generally thought that we have at least five. *Working memory,* situated in the prefrontal and parietal cortices, is extremely short, only a few seconds long. *Implicit memory,* sometimes divided into *reflexive* and *procedural,* is stored in the cerebellum. This type of memory enables us to juggle or ride a bike after years of inactivity, or drive a car on autopilot. The remaining three are collectively known as *explicit,* or *declarative,* memory: *Remote memory,* spread around the neocortex, is the lifetime collection of data about a whole range of topics—ideal for Trivial Pursuit; *episodic memory,* the record of specific personal experiences (that is, locations, events, persons involved, circumstances), is stored in the hippocampus; *semantic memory,* created in the hippocampus and stored in the angular gyrus, retains the meaning of words and symbols from textbooks, people, videotapes, films, diagrams, computer programs, written stories, and so on; gives us our general knowledge about the workings of the world; and is the stuff of tests.

These different types of memory explain why some people are good at remembering what they did on vacation 10 years ago (episodic) but can't remember the name of someone they met two days ago (semantic). In addition, peptide molecules, which circulate throughout the body, also store and transfer information. Memory is hard to pin down.

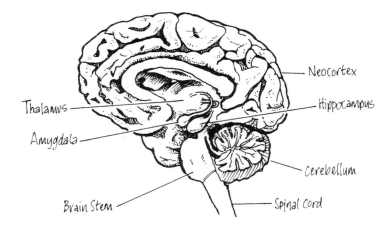

Inside the brain

How are memories made? Memories appear to be the result of a rapid alteration in the strength of synaptic connections, a process known as *long-term potentiation,* which is activated by specific genes and a protein molecule known as cyclic AMP-response element-binding protein (CREB). (See http://web.sfn.org/content/Publications/BrainBriefings/creb.html for further information about CREB.) The physical evidence of memory is stored as changes in neurons along specific pathways. Some researchers, such as William Calvin (1996), a neurobiologist, and Michael Gazzaniga (1996, 1998), director of the Center for Cognitive Neuroscience at Dartmouth, have explained the retrieval process: When enough of the right type of neurons are firing in the right way, dormant neurons are activated and successful retrieval occurs. The process is triggered by association. The word "birthday," for example, will activate not just one memory of one birthday but hundreds of neural fields connected with many experiences of your own and other people's birthdays and patterns abstracted from those experiences. Some studies have shown that we can retrieve almost everything we paid attention to in the first place, but only when we are in the right state and in the right context. We all know how a song we haven't heard for years will bring memories flooding back, usually with associated smells and feelings.

The strength of a memory, and therefore the ease with which it is retrieved, seems to depend on the strength and processing of the initial input. Now the importance of multisensory learning becomes clear. When several senses are simultaneously involved, the message is received through a number of different channels and stands a better chance of remaining prominent. There are also more ways to trigger the memory: location (where were we?); feelings (what was it like?); movements (what did we do?); the names and faces of other people (who else was there?); as opposed to just words (what did the teacher or textbook say?).

To maximize learning, make it active, make it episodic. When possible, design activities that involve students in *physical doing* as well as speaking, listening, reading, and looking. Create learning experiences that really are experiences. Episodic learning is effortless; it happens all the time quite naturally. By contrast, semantic recall requires huge amounts of internal motivation, is triggered by language alone, and is the weakest of our retrieval systems, because in the long haul of evolution, it is the most recently developed.

Beyond this, make learning experiences dramatic; give them an emotional edge. According to journalist Jill Neimark, "a memory associated with emotionally charged information gets seared into the brain" (1995, 49). Highly charged events, whether positive or negative, are remembered well because the chemicals released—such as adrenaline, norepinephrine, enkephalin, vasopressin, and adrenocorticotropic hormone (ACTH)—act as memory fixatives. They tell the brain to retain events that might be vital points of reference in the future. Ask the students to take risks, to take part and try things they haven't tried before. Tell strong stories, use analogies that excite the imagination, create tension and suspense.

The more the amygdala (the almond-shaped, "emotional" organ in the midbrain area) is aroused, the stronger the imprint will be. The pioneering studies of psychobiologist James McGaugh (1989, 2000) have led him to conclude that emotions and hormones are capable of improving retention and in fact do so. His research clearly shows that even relatively ordinary emotions improve memory, so we don't always have to put students through shocks, horrors, and life-threatening situations to get them to learn.

In fact, at Stanford University Medical School, Professor William Fry's research (1997) suggests that the body reacts biochemically to laughing. He says, "Having a laugh while you're studying is a good idea because it increases the brain's alertness" (1998). The chemical balance of the blood is altered, and this may boost the body's production of neurotransmitters. So it's OK to have fun. Some *Toolkit* ideas are designed to do just that. Check out "Games" (page 166), "Bingo" (page 68), "Verbal Football" (page 142), "Dicey Business" (page 78), "Quick on the Draw" (page 121), and "Verbal Tennis" (page 144).

The third aspect of brain function related to memorable experiences is movement. The old idea that mind and body are separate has recently gone out the window, for strong biological reasons. For example, various studies of the cerebellum, classically considered to be concerned only with motor function, have revealed that it is closely associated with spatial perception, language, attention, emotion, decision making, and memory. It's only 10 percent of the brain by volume, but it possesses over half of the brain's neurons. It sends signals to many parts of the cerebral cortex, not just to the motor cortex, as earlier thought. Susan Greenfield declares that there is no single movement center in our brain. Movement and learning are in a continual and complex interplay (Greenfield 1994).

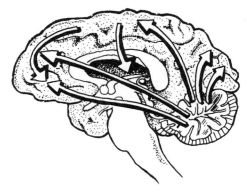

The relationship between movement and cognition

The implication is clear: Make sure that there is sufficient physical movement, even within an academic learning situation, which is the reverse of what most teachers have been brought up to believe. But will movement raise achievement? Yes! In a Canadian study of over 500 students reported by Carla Hannaford (1995), author of *Smart Moves: Why Learning Is Not All in Your Head,* those who spent an extra hour each day in a gym class far outperformed on tests those who didn't exercise.

Apart from anything else, physical activity increases blood flow to the brain. Sometimes it's helpful to ask students to do a quick bit of physical exercise in the middle of a lesson—for instance, jog on the spot for a minute, stretch, or do one or two cross-laterals—just to liven things up (Dennison and Dennison 1988). According to researcher Max Vercruyssen, simply having students stand up while you talk to them helps them take more in (cited in Jensen 2000a, 170). At the start of some lessons, play a physical game such as "Caterpillar" (page 168) or "Giants, Dwarfs, and Wizards" (page 167).

3. EVERYONE NEEDS TO FEEL EMOTIONALLY SECURE AND PSYCHOLOGICALLY SAFE.

We can thank Daniel Goleman and his concept of emotional intelligence for bringing this point to international prominence. The author of many books, Goleman for years covered the behavioral and brain sciences for the *New York Times* and was senior editor at *Psychology Today.* However, he wasn't the first to describe the significance of emotions. Joseph LeDoux, Candace Pert, Jerome Kagan, and Antonio and Hannah Damasio paved the way. Goleman, summarizing some of their key findings, explains that, in the Western world,

> We have gone too far in emphasizing the value and import of the purely rational—of what IQ measures—in human life. Intelligence can come to nothing when the emotions hold sway. . . . To better grasp the potent hold of the emotions on the thinking mind, consider how the brain evolved. . . . From the most primitive root, the brainstem, emerged the emotional centers. Millions of years later in evolution, from these emotional areas evolved the thinking brain or "neo-cortex." . . . Because so many of the brain's higher centers sprouted from or extended the scope of the limbic area, the emotional brain plays a crucial role in neural architecture. At the root from which the newer brain grew, the emotional areas are entwined via myriad connecting circuits to all parts of the neurocortex. This gives the emotional centers immense power to influence the functioning of the rest of the brain—including its centers for thought. (1996, 4–12)

Learn More about Movement and Learning

For a full account of the role of the body in the learning process, and how to make the most of it, consult Hannaford's *Smart Moves.* Similarly, Roy Anderson, in *First Steps to a Physical Basis of Concentration* (1999), suggests that many behavioral and apparent learning difficulties can be resolved by attending to the physical origins of inattention and by deploying a range of specific physical exercises, stimuli, and postures.

For further practical insights into educational kinesiology, see *Brain Gym,* by the Dennisons (www.braingym.com), *Every Body Can Learn* (1997), by Marilyn Nikimaa Patterson, and *Learning with the Body in Mind* (2000c), by Eric Jensen.

Our clever neocortex might enable us to *think* about our feelings and to choose from a range of subtle responses, but, when the emotional chips are down, the thinking brain tends to defer to a reflexive response. Emotion is stronger than thought. We all know how hard it is to concentrate on a difficult letter we're trying to write when we've just received some tragic news or had an argument. Emotions are different from feelings. Emotions include joy, fear, surprise, disgust, anger, and sadness—these are universal phenomena, entirely biological, traveling the brain's superhighways. Feelings are culturally and environmentally developed responses to circumstances and take a slower, more circuitous route around the body.

In extreme cases, when we feel seriously at risk, for example, pure instinct takes over and the desire to survive dominates. For example, if someone shouted "Fire!" right now, you wouldn't carry on reading this fascinating section—you'd throw the book down and bolt for the nearest exit. The brain is designed primarily for survival, not for learning.

If the brain even *suspects* that an input signals danger—the footsteps behind us *may* mean that we are being followed, the sound of breaking glass in the middle of the night *could* mean that a burglar has broken into the house—it immediately sends the information downward. The amygdala, which is at the center of all fear and threat responses, is called into action. It activates the entire sympathetic system, releasing adrenaline, vasopressin, and the peptide cortisol, which collectively change the way we think, feel, and act. Our blood pressure rises, our large muscles tense, and our immune system becomes depressed. This instinctive reaction results in running to get away or hiding under the sheets. This is our *reflexive* response, our *first* response, just in case. But as Robert Sylwester (1998) has pointed out, our brain's response system is complex. It is capable of parallel processing which allows simultaneous thoughtful evaluation for a reflective response.

If further sensory input does not confirm our fears (the footsteps become more distant, the house remains silent), we might, in a reflective mode, rationalize and investigate. The thalamus sends signals to the cortex for more thoughtful, considered responses. Then we discover that the predator was actually an innocent pedestrian who turned off down a side street. And the glass? Well, it was only the cat, who'd knocked over a vase.

If our reflexive response is not overridden, heart rate and blood pressure increase, maximizing the supply to the base of the brain, and blood is drained from the neocortex, debilitating higher-order thought processes. Consequently, survival behaviors take over: walking away from the problem; burying your head in the sand; being defensive; counterattacking; ganging up; playing dead; lashing out. In other words, fight or flight. The tendency is to do what's worked before in similar situations: All attention becomes focused on the source of the threat; peripheral vision and rationality go out the window. Lateral thinking? No chance. At this point, the brain is closed to hearing or trying anything new. Learning is impossible.

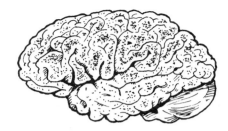

Blood distribution under normal Conditions

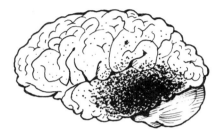

Under threat : blood Concentrated in the ancient parts of the brain

The kinds of threats that trigger this sort of behavior may be physical, such as the possibility of being bullied, or of not being able to get from room to room because there are no ramps. They may be psychological and emotional—the fear of being ignored, of being the last one picked, of being shown up in class, of being called names, exposed, belittled, ridiculed, caught in a mistake, told off, excluded. Here at home, for example, my son, Steven, declared that he didn't intend to get higher than C grades in his practice mandated tests because he'd be in for so much teasing from his friends if he did really well. Whenever my younger daughter, Helen, is asked what kind of a day she's had at school, she doesn't talk about lessons but about how she's getting along with her friends, whether she's "in" or "out" with this person, that group, or that teacher. For both Steven and Helen, acceptance is the bigger issue.

Threat can also come from the prospect of failure. A task that is perceived to be too difficult, or for which the resources are inadequate or inaccessible, is likely to be refused. The threat of punishment can actually exaggerate the behavior it's designed to eradicate: inattentiveness, for example. Even rewards can be anxiety provoking and threatening: Will I have done enough to deserve it? With every reward there is the implied lack of reward, which is a covert punishment. Whatever the source of threat, the reaction is always the same: Play it safe. Recent research suggests that, in stressful environments, levels of serotonin (the ultimate modulator of our emotions) are reduced. This often results in increased violence. Continued stress leads to a depressed immune system and the increased risk of some illnesses. In *Accelerated Learning in Practice*, Alistair Smith quotes an interesting finding: "A recent Medical Research Council study reported that only 10 percent of low serotonin amongst depressives is caused by genes . . . it is the social environment which is crucial" (John Oliver quoted in Smith 1998, 45).

That said, human emotions don't have only a negative relationship with the learning process. Take motivation. People want more of what they experienced as pleasurable, and less of what is boring or painful. The brain has an internal reward system, producing opiates that attach a sense of pleasure to a satisfying behavior. Students who succeed feel good. Often, at the end of a particularly enjoyable lesson, students will say, "Can we do that again?" and will frequently turn up next time full of anticipation, asking excitedly, "What are we doing today?" Beyond this, the joint and separate studies of John O'Keefe and Lynn Nadel (O'Keefe and Nadel 1978; Nadel 1990; Nadel, Wilmer, and Kurz 1984) have shown that we make better conceptual maps when we feel positive. The happier we are, the faster and more accurately we sort and connect incoming data. Who said learning shouldn't be fun?

Learn More about Fear in Schools

Roland Meighan has clear and sharply worded insights into the fear that pervades schools. In particular, read "How Many Peers Make Five?" and "In Place of Fear," available with his other columns for the UK journal *Natural Parent* on the Roland Meighan pages of www.gn.apc.org/edheretics and in book form: *Natural Learning and the National Curriculum* (2001).

Compared with the central nervous system, in which axon-synapse-dendrite connections travel only along fixed pathways, chemicals are much more pervasive. We now know that the chemicals that create emotions are produced and distributed throughout the body. Peptide messenger molecules *(ligands)* are released into the bloodstream and have access to all areas: Every cell has countless receptor sites for ligands, creating feelings or moods throughout the entire body. We might get a gut feeling because the peptides that are released in the brain are simultaneously released into the intestines. Miles Herkenham of the National Institute of Mental Health suggested that 98 percent of all communication within the body may be through peptide messengers (cited in Jensen 2001). This has led some to regard the bloodstream as the body's second nervous system. The effect is that emotions create distinct mind-body states that strongly influence behavior. Richard Bergland, a neurosurgeon, goes so far as to say that "thought is not caged in the brain, but is scattered all over the body" (quoted in Restak 1993, 29). The brain operates more like a gland than like a computer. It produces hormones, is bathed in them, and is run by them: In other words, emotions rule. What we know about the dominance of emotions leads us to examine three aspects of practice.

(i) Classroom rules

Learning occurs most efficiently when the learner is *not at all* fearful of being bullied, mocked, ridiculed, ignored, left out, called names, belittled, or shown up. Firm classroom ground rules, made *with* students, can secure positive behavioral norms based on listening and the elimination of put-downs. The idea of creating this kind of harmonious, civilized community connects strongly with citizenship education and the drive for inclusion. It is so fundamental that the whole of section 3 is devoted to it. Beyond your own classroom, start to work on whole school behavior and ethos.

The ship would often make its extensive range of feelings known.

(ii) Our own demeanor and manner

This means the way we come across to students. Researcher R. C. Mills (1987) discovered that learners pick up on the emotional state of the teacher, which affects their cognition. Teachers who use humor, smile warmly, have a joyful demeanor, and take genuine pleasure in their work will have learners who outperform those students whose teachers do not demonstrate these qualities. Encouragement, positive feedback, and acknowledgment all seem to release serotonin—an essential neurotransmitter that aids neural interconnection.

Much communication is nonverbal, so the way we look, how we speak, and what we do, combined with what we actually say, make the total impact. The effect of "the way the teacher is" on students is twofold—first, directly on their own feelings of well-being, and second, on their perceptions of what's acceptable. We model norms to them; they take their lead from us. So if we are sarcastic, for example, students are likely to feel nervous *and* are likely to use sarcasm themselves. It's easy to see how the teacher can affect the state of the learner, as NLP and accelerated learning would describe it. Of course, this calls for teachers to be self-aware and skilled, in other words, to be emotionally intelligent themselves.

Here's an example. Soon after our book on student-centered learning was published in 1986, Donna Brandes and I received a remarkable essay from a science teacher. He wrote about his commitment to developing a student-centered approach and recognized the need to attend to his own attitudes and skills first: "I can identify strongly with the essential beliefs and attitudes which underscore student-centered learning. At the same time I am aware of my own limitations in terms of being able to translate and communicate through behavior, my attitudes and beliefs. My immediate goal is to develop my own interpersonal skills in such a way that I am able to provide the facilitative conditions for personal growth in a student-centered classroom" (White 1989).

Again we see that the pursuit of excellence to which the *Toolkit* is committed takes us beyond the superficial level of classroom techniques and into the more personal territory of teachers' language and skills, and further into the domain of their attitudes, beliefs, and values—and ultimately their own self-esteem.

The Harwich School takes these matters seriously. When candidates are considered for the post of learning-support assistant, they are observed at work with students and assessed on a five-point scale.

	1 2 3 4 5	
Offers success	|———————————————|	denies success
Is enthusiastic	|———————————————|	is reserved
Asks questions	|———————————————|	lectures
Praises	|———————————————|	is critical
Is patient	|———————————————|	is impatient
Is optimistic	|———————————————|	is pessimistic
Is supportive	|———————————————|	is alienating
Puts at ease	|———————————————|	discomforts
Is accepting	|———————————————|	is hostile
Has sense of humor	|———————————————|	is overly serious

Adapted from original by Harwich School

(iii) Teaching emotional intelligence

Apart from students and teachers behaving well toward one another, which has been the essence of our discussion so far, there's the prospect of students being able to identify, name, and describe feelings. Their ability to manage their own, and respond to other people's, emotions appropriately is a crucial skill. Also important is the development of desirable qualities such as impulse control, perseverance, and social deftness, as well as desirable values such as honesty and a commitment to justice. Underpinning these is the acceptance of personal responsibility: the willingness to see life as a series of moment-by-moment choices, and the willingness to change behaviors, feelings, and beliefs based on an awareness of personal potential and self-imposed limitations. Remarkably, all this can be taught.

Using a slightly different term, but defining the same territory, Stephen Bowkett says, "Self-intelligence is about equipping children with an emotional toolkit, and giving them the skills to pick the right tool for the job. Emotional resourcefulness . . . is the capacity to know and understand yourself and make best use of that understanding" (1999, 7). Many resources in this growing field, such as *Teaching Emotional Intelligence,* by Adina Bloom Lewkowicz (1999), take their structure from Goleman's five emotional competencies:

- self-awareness
- managing emotions
- self-control/self-motivation
- empathy
- handling relationships/social skills

Mike Brearley, in his book *Emotional Intelligence in the Classroom* (2001, v) defines emotional intelligence as "the ability to control and use our emotions to enhance our success in all aspects of our lives" and offers a suite of structured classroom activities to develop what he calls the "five emotions of success": self-awareness, ambition, optimism, empathy, and integrity.

All this material resonates strongly with the life skills and health education programs and the active learning initiatives of the past. A lesson learned then was that teaching such issues only through separate dedicated lessons, no matter how well designed and delivered, always fails. To stand a chance, these concepts, beliefs, and skills have to be part of the fabric of school life at every level.

Developing emotional intelligence is an intention of the *Toolkit* and surfaces most strongly in activities such as "Discussion Carousel" (page 80), "Silent Sentences" (page 128), and "Value Continuum" (page 139). The subject gets explicit attention in section 3, where self-discipline and relating skills are tackled through "Murder Mystery" (page 152), "Framed" (page 156), "Observer Server" (page 159), and "Learning Listening" (page 161). Personal responsibility is tackled in "Sabotage" (page 164) and to a great extent in volume 2 of the *Toolkit*.

Some years ago Nathaniel Branden (1994), a practicing clinician, related what we now call emotional intelligence to self-esteem. He suggested that self-esteem can be defined as "the disposition to experience oneself as competent to cope with the basic challenges of life and as worthy of happiness" (27) and is fed by six characteristics of living:

- living consciously
- self-acceptance
- self-responsibility
- self-assertiveness
- living purposefully
- personal integrity

These behaviors are in a relationship of "reciprocal causation" with self-esteem, he argues. In other words they are both the *products* of healthy self-esteem and the *creators* of healthy self-esteem. After well over 30 years of work in this field, Branden concludes: "It is cruel and misleading to tell people that all they need do to have self-esteem is decide to love themselves. Self-esteem is built by practices, not by emotions" (2001). To find out more about self-esteem, and to check your impact on students, see page 205.

4. LEARNERS ARE MORE MOTIVATED, ENGAGED, AND OPEN WHEN THEY HAVE SOME CONTROL OVER THEIR LEARNING

Attention and engagement are driven by a complex interplay of neurological activities that involve a number of brain areas, processes, and chemicals. They are connected to an individual's deep-seated values, basic interests, and aspirations, to the brain's internal reward system and, it seems, to the fundamental human drive for self-determination. People pay attention to whatever seems to meet their needs.

Think of attending a school training session. As long as you are fascinated by the presenter's information, you don't notice the noise of traffic outside, the clanking in the school kitchen, the fluttering curtains, or the changing weather conditions through the window. If the trainer talks for too long, however, you start to lose interest and pay attention instead to these peripheral stimuli. Your mind then turns to more pressing matters, such as what you're going to cook for dinner and all the chores you have to do that evening. If, however, you believe that the content of the training will help you to fulfill your ambition of becoming a principal, then you will probably continue paying attention, despite the odds. Attention depends on what *we* perceive to be meeting *our* needs or to be relevant to *our* purposes at any moment.

There are times when very basic needs take over. This is why hungry and thirsty children on a long road trip, excited at the thought of where they are going and wanting to get there quickly, will start spotting restaurants and minimarts. Their attention will turn from their personal CD or game, or from the interesting new scenery, to persuading you to stop at the very next food outlet. Their attention has shifted in response to increasing hunger signals. The more basic the need, the greater the priority given to it by the brain.

Then there are needs that we create for ourselves by making a decision or creating a "want." Imagine going out to buy a new car. You look around the showrooms, and after much uncertainty, you see it. "This is the car for me: a Mustang GT. Yes!" For the next few days, you drive around in your old vehicle while the new one is being prepared, and the road is suddenly full of Mustang GTs! Yet you can't remember ever seeing one before. Previously, they were of no interest to you, so you never noticed them. Now, they are connected to a personal desire, to your internalized goal, and they are everywhere.

In fact, choices are inherently motivating. According to researcher Robert Ornstein (1991), the chemistry of our brains changes when we encounter a choice. Feelings of control over a new learning activity trigger the release of endorphins, which enhance our confidence in our abilities to be successful in the given task, a confidence that is empowering and motivating.

Finally, it suits us to pay attention to whatever is novel or surprising, which serves the brain's innate drives for survival and development. We immediately notice that our child looks pale, that the car isn't running as smoothly as normal, that summers aren't like they used to be. We are so tuned in to novelty, that we automatically spot relatively trivial changes: A house along our route to work has just been put up for sale; a colleague had her hair done during the weekend; the newspaper delivery is late today. Our attention is drawn to any change to our routine or environment, in fact anything that might alter the status quo. We have a natural curiosity for new phenomena, and at a base level we are glad for relief from monotony and boredom. Even the turning of the classroom door handle in the middle of the teacher's long lecture will draw everyone's immediate attention. There are at least five implications for this for teaching and learning.

First, provide novelty and variety to sustain attention, both within and between lessons. This has already become a recurring theme.

Second, understand that the brain will give first priority to basic needs—if students are hungry, thirsty, cold, or desperate to go to the restroom, they are not going to pay attention to the Pythagorean theorem, no matter how important we tell them it is.

Third, take time to unfold the big picture and to "sell the benefits" (as Alistair Smith puts it; 2003) the big picture. If students understand the purpose of the lesson or unit, what it contains, how it fits in with what they've already learned, what it will lead to later, and why it's necessary for some future assessment, they are more likely to pay attention. If students accept that this purpose is personally important—in other words, they want it— they take ownership of it.

One by one, they mastered the natural laws of their new world.

Fourth, help students set personal goals. In most schools, goal setting with students is done badly. There's not enough time given to the diagnostic discussion; there's no real relationship between the teacher and student in the first place; the goals end up being general (such as "I will improve my writing") or trivial (such as "I will bring a pen to class"); there's no flexibility in the system to allow students to concentrate on more meaningful learning goals anyway (they still have to go through the rigid lesson regime, with all lesson content and processes sewn up by the teacher); and it all feels like a ritual.

Deeply internalized personal goals, however, are a different matter. These are the result of people identifying an ambition and developing a sense of what it will be like to achieve the ambition. The process takes time: It involves recognizing wants and needs, weighing pros and cons, sifting options, and making genuine priorities. The result is an internalized goal, a clarified personal purpose. This degree of personal desire results in self-motivation, self-sufficiency, and perseverance. For this to work fully, schools would need a substantial overhaul; teachers would need to be more like counselors and coaches; relationships between teachers and students would need to be authentic; the prescribed curriculum would have to go; and learning resources, including time and space, would need to be used much more flexibly to enable students to follow personal pathways.

As things stand, most teachers do all the planning *for* learners, then wonder why students are not attentive or motivated. Which brings us to . . .

Fifth, plan *with* learners. This is the route to ownership and self-motivation and is possible even within the prescriptions of federal legislation and state standards. If you're ready to try a new system with your students, see volume 2 of this book, in which I explore a range of options from giving students some control over pace and depth to open negotiation with learners about every aspect of the learning process.

As Eric Jensen maintains "the easiest way to reach all of your learners is simple—provide both variety and choice" (1995b, 31). Many studies confirm the importance of students having some control over their learning. Edward Deci, Richard Ryan, and other researchers (Deci and Ryan 1985, 2002a, 2002b; Ryan and Deci 2000; Ryan and La Guardia 1999; Deci, Vallerand, Pelletier, and Ryan 1991; Deci, Hodges, Pierson, and Tomassone 1992) conclude that motivation and standards decrease in situations where learners have no choice. Their research led Deci and Ryan to formulate self-determination theory (SDT), which argues that human motivation is fundamentally determined by the degree to which people are able to "endorse their actions at the highest level of reflection and engage in the actions with a full sense of choice" (SDT 2004).

Learn More about Self-Determination Theory
For further information about SDT, along with access to publications, discussions, and questionnaires, visit www.psych.rochester.edu/SDT.

What's more, deciding personal goals and accepting responsibility for negotiating, or at least choosing, learning strategies is the essence of lifelong learning. The earlier people get used to it, the better. Finally, the connections with good citizenship are clear. Choice, negotiation, collective decision making, and personal responsibility are at the heart of democracy. These attitudes and skills can be acquired only experientially.

Differences among Learners

People are different. People react differently to the same circumstances; they have different likes and dislikes; they have different default behaviors; they perceive and process experience differently. Biologically, each person's brain is as individual as her fingerprint, the result of a fantastic process of neural interconnection running at a rate of between 300 and 500 million new synapses per second in the earliest phase of life. During this period the basic architecture of the brain is established, and, not surprisingly, preferred learning styles are determined. Faced with the diversity of student learning preferences, a teacher can easily feel overwhelmed, and this is where learning-style models come in. They simplify the complexity and enable us to manage the territory.

Whenever a problem arose, there were always six different ways of tackling it.

Learning Style

According to Rita Dunn, Jeffrey S. Beaudry, and Angela Klavas (1989), "Learning style is the way in which each learner begins to concentrate on, process and retain new and difficult information." It can be seen as a "set of personal characteristics that make the same teaching method effective for some students and ineffective for others" (50). J. W. Keefe (1979) describes it as one's consistent and personal approach to handling information.

Rita and Ken Dunn (Dunn, Dunn, and Price 1996) created a learning-styles framework that brings several of these approaches together. They propose five strands, or stimuli, comprising 21 elements. Learning style is a combination of these elements from all five strands.

- Environmental: sound, light, temperature, design
- Emotional: motivation, persistence, responsibility, structure
- Sociological: self, pair, peers, team, adult, varied
- Physical: perceptual, intake, time, mobility
- Psychological: global/analytic, hemisphericity, impulsive/reflective

Building on Dunn's work, Barbara Prashnig (1998) offers a helpful pyramidal model that again combines different sets of variables. Her Learning Styles Analysis (LSA), which has been thoroughly researched and tested in a range of contexts, assesses a total of 49 elements in six basic areas. The six areas are set out as layers of a pyramid, with the bottom four being biologically or genetically determined, she argues, and the top two being conditioned or learned.

The six areas, from the bottom up, are social groupings, environment, physical needs, sensory modalities, and left/right brain dominance.

Some suggest that the factors determining a person's learning style are hierarchical. The most fundamental influence, they say, is personality type—these characteristics are least likely to change. The next strongest influence is sensory preference (the way you take information in), then information processing style (the way your mind works on that incoming data), then social interaction style (ways of involving others, or not, in your learning process), then instructional preference (preferences for certain types of content, or the drive for information acquisition compared with the drive for good grades), then learning environment (your response to physical and emotional conditions).

Even though people develop their dominant style early in their lives, or may indeed be born with it as part of their prewritten "life script," some researchers (Torrance and Ball 1984, for example) suggest that these natural styles can be changed as a result of intense experience. For some people, making changes is desirable—their future success may depend on it. Anthony Gregorc found that most successful professionals learn, somewhere along the way, to use various styles (2000–2001). He argues, however, that the changes are superficial. People never change their dominant Mind Style™, as he calls it, or the shape of their Mind Field (see page 38), only their behavior. Such superficial changes might be the result of "a phase they are going through" (most evident in childhood), external demands (the requirements of a job, for instance), internal ambitions, or simply the consequence of trying to survive in an incompatible environment.

Given the way that schools and the big wide world operate, student success and life chances are clearly at stake. Students and employees cannot afford always to follow their own path—it usually leads to trouble of one sort or another. Learning and working institutions are not sufficiently person-centered and are not likely to begin accommodating diverse individuality in the current political and economic climate. Getting the balance right between supporting and challenging students' modes of learning is therefore crucial. If students are allowed always to work within their preferred style, they will remain narrow and ill equipped. On the other hand, if they are forced too early or too often to work against their preferences in uncomfortable ways, they are bound to underachieve and may well become alienated. The solution to this is twofold.

First, ensure that each learner experiences sufficient success to create a platform of personal confidence. This requires us to be sensitive to each student's personal style. Study after study in the heyday of learning-style research found that whenever learners are taught in their own style, their motivation, initiative, and results improve (Carbo 1980; Carbo, Dunn, and Dunn 1986; De Bello 1985; Della Valle 1984; Hodges 1985; Shea 1983; Shipman and Shipman 1983; Virostko 1983; White 1980). The issue of learning styles is, at its root, an equal-opportunities issue.

> **Learn More about Learning-Style Studies**
>
> For many more up-to-date studies on the relationship between learning styles and attainment, visit www.learningstyles.net/bib.html.

Second, students who have been sufficiently successful, and therefore believe themselves to be capable learners, are likely to rise to and master the challenge of working in unfamiliar ways. Encourage them to do so. Provide opportunities for students to work in new ways. Provide training—show them how to do it. Provide information—explain why it's a good idea. Do it with sensitivity, self-awareness, and a firm intention to inflict no harm.

Before looking at three learning-style models in more detail, let's register the practical implications so far.

1. RECOGNIZE THAT YOUR OWN PREFERRED STYLE CAN GET IN THE WAY OF EFFECTIVE LEARNING.

Over the years researchers have consistently found that teachers' own dominant learning styles tend to determine the plans they make for children: the way they structure a topic; the selection of teaching methods and resources; the design of tasks; the allocation of time; and the type of evidence of learning to be produced by students—the assessment method. More than this, teachers' underlying mindsets determine the way they organize the learning environment; the value they place on homework, tests, grades, and pecking orders; their reaction to misbehavior; their creation of unwritten classroom norms; their subtle nonverbal communication; as well as their explicit delivery of information and instructions.

Therefore, the first base for the concerned teacher to get to, clearly, is increased self-knowledge. Bruno Bettelheim, the psychologist, said, "There are . . . utterly destructive consequences of acting without knowing what one is doing" (quoted in Gregorc 2005). Beyond this, aim for second base: the will to accommodate students' individuality.

To learn how to encourage individuality, they regularly practiced on visitors from Planet Uno.

Learn More about Your Style

To recognize your own style, I recommend Gregorc's excellent book *An Adult's Guide to Style* (1982 [2001]) and his Gregorc Style Delineator instrument. Both are available from Gregorc Associates at www.gregorc.com. These tap into your mindset, not just your preferred learning or teaching strategies, so that they provide information about deep rather than surface style issues. It's important to get feedback from lots of sources, so surf the Internet and find ways of figuring out your intelligence profile and your sensory dominance. Reflect on the Honey and Mumford learning styles categories at www.campaign-for-learning.org.uk/ aboutyourlearning/whatlearning.htm, or pay to try the full questionnaire at www.peterhoney.com/LS80. See the recommended resources section on page 225 for more options.

All of the tools recommended in the box at left build personal awareness and will help you to recognize the relationship between your own learning style and your natural teaching instincts.

They may well reveal the difference between your natural teaching style—the one you would use if left to your own devices—and your role-based teaching styles, in other words the ones you use because of some constraint or forced expectation. Where there is strong dissonance between the two, frustration and distress build up, as many of you know. Above all, discovering your own Mind Style, or learning style, gives you the wherewithal to resist the temptation to operate automatically from habit, but instead to stop, to think empathetically, and to begin to break out of your own mold.

2. UNDERSTAND LEARNERS' PREFERRED STYLES, BUT DON'T PIGEONHOLE.

Don't get hung up on just one learning-style model: None of them is an adequate description of reality; each is only a simplified projection of its creator's view of reality. Familiarize yourself with several. Be aware that not every model will suit every teacher. Gregorc makes the point: "My experience says that anyone can gain topical information about any model. But, each fully practiced model will make further specific mental demands on the implementor. As a result, some people, because of the natural strengths and limitations of their Mind Styles, will not be able to fully utilize certain models with ease and integrity" (2001, 23).

Therefore, choose a model that passes three tests of "rightness" for you: "First, is it a coherent system which addresses your needs? Second, does the theory and practice of the model work in the crucible of the everyday world and help to improve it? And third, do your mind and Self accept the model so that the theory and practice become silent guides to harmless behaviors?" (Gregorc 2001, 25). For four practical ways of spotting students' styles, see "Check Your Students' Learning Styles" on page 195.

Please remember that everyone uses more than one style. "Since people are multi-faceted, each person has more than one way of learning. But most of us have predominant clusters, preferred channels, and secondary, subordinate approaches," says Priscilla Vail (1992, 3). Therefore, aim to sensitize yourself to differences rather than to categorize students.

3. ACCOMMODATE DIFFERENT STYLES, BUT DON'T TRY TO BE TOO PRECISE.

Beyond increased self-knowledge, a will to accommodate individuality and an understanding of students' style types enables the delivery of diversity. The key to this is to have lots of practical teaching techniques at your fingertips. Not all teachers feel that they have. The answer is to read books such as this one, or James Bellanca's *The Active Learning Handbook for the Multiple Intelligences Classroom* (1994). Or plan with colleagues with whom you don't normally work, as an experienced physics department head did by planning a series of lessons on renewable energy with a young art teacher. Afterward he said, "This has been the most productive meeting I have been to in my whole career." It resulted in exciting and workable classroom ideas that he confessed he would never have thought of himself. Too often we meet with the same old colleagues, usually in our department. Mix it. Arrange to brainstorm and plan with colleagues who teach quite different subjects and who probably have different learning styles from your own.

Use a learning-style construct to audit and then stimulate your practice. Many people these days like the simplicity of VAK, though Gregorc is more penetrating. Work with two or three so that your thinking doesn't get too narrow and exacting. Run your chosen models past your existing lesson plans; this will expose any style gaps in methodology. Check out your assumptions. I recently worked with science department staff who told me, "We do lots of variety." On closer inspection, their lesson plans were full of nothing but Abstract Sequential (AS) and Concrete Sequential (CS) lessons (see page 38 for further information on these learning styles). Of course, the science teachers were all strongly AS and CS, so they couldn't see this bias. They were shocked to learn how narrowly they had been focusing their lessons and quickly began identifying lessons that could be rewritten in more random modes. When they taught these lessons, they reported higher levels of achievement among "mischievous students." Learning style constructs help to pull thinking and planning in unfamiliar directions.

Planning became a wild and dangerously productive business.

Armed with loads of practical and diverse ways of helping students achieve the learning objectives, you then decide how to present these strategies to students. Sequencing learning activities so that different styles are accommodated *over time* is the simplest, and for many teachers the most comfortable, way of going about things. This approach is the minimum professional response to the challenge of learning-style research, to guarantee all learners a regular dose of their preferred modus operandi. Beyond it are more sophisticated ways of delivering personal styles: by building them into differentiated routes, through structured choices and open negotiation. Volume 2 of the *Toolkit* presents specific ideas for each of these methods.

4. BEGIN TO ADDRESS THE BIGGER ISSUES.

Most schools are geared for certain types of learners. Bernice McCarthy's research (1980, 53) led her to ask, "If 70 percent of our students learn most comfortably in ways not generally attended to in our schools, how should we proceed?" In training sessions, teachers often say to me, "The exams require students to demonstrate abstract and sequential learning; therefore we must teach in this way." Of course, this logic is flawed, but the continued dominance of narrow forms of assessment does create enormous injustice, and signals to teachers and students alike the value placed by the nation on certain learning styles compared to others. Then there is the issue of resources. Textbooks, worksheets, and exercise books still dominate the "deskscape" of most classrooms. In fact, the rooms themselves are a problem. Often there's just enough space for students to sit cramped behind desks for lesson after lesson. The boxlike nature of most school buildings resonates with the gridlike nature of the timetable. Times are fixed, subjects are fixed, teachers are fixed, even movement is fixed. Life is compartmentalized; everything feels tight and contained. No wonder student behavior problems continue to increase.

Three Popular Learning-Style Models

Three well-used learning-style models are worth understanding in more detail: sensory preferences, cognitive predilections, and intelligence profiles.

1. SENSORY PREFERENCES: VISUAL, AUDITORY, KINESTHETIC

The basic idea of this construct is that everyone has a dominant sense. Everyone prefers to use one sense to let in and deal with new information—some will prefer to look at, others will prefer to listen to, others will prefer to engage physically with new data. The dominant sense creates the preferred channel for receiving and processing material and consequently the most efficient and default way of learning.

Naturally, for everyone all three senses continually work together, with information from one being supplemented and complemented by information from another. Also, different combinations of senses are required in different situations. Therefore, no one is entirely visual or auditory or kinesthetic (physical). However, the research suggests that everyone *does* have a dominant and preferred sense, to one degree or another, and that the opportunity to use this preference when learning has a significant effect on a person's level of achievement and feelings of competence.

Some students with a visual preference respond to the visual impact of *words*, and others are attentive to graphics shown on an overhead projector, a traditional or computer slide show, a videotape, a poster, a field trip, or to a diagram, photograph, or drawing in a textbook. They engage most readily with visual material and learn most efficiently through this channel.

Those with an auditory preference engage with, and learn most easily from, sound—the sound of the teacher's voice, fellow students in discussion, peer presentations, or commentary on a videotape or CD, or from a guest speaker.

Those with a kinesthetic inclination need to "do" the learning. Some are happy with tactile activity—making models, sorting cards, folding, cutting, sticking, arranging, handling artifacts. Others need to be up and doing. They are "with it" only when they are physically active, demonstrating a process, role-playing, preparing a still image, standing on a value continuum line, miming, moving between resources, going on a field trip. These students tend to give us the most grief if their needs are not met; they easily become restless. These are the ones most at risk of underachievement and exclusion, largely because most middle and high school teachers have not been trained to teach them effectively. According to Mike Hughes, "Kinesthetic learners are the students who are most disadvantaged in secondary schools, simply because so many learning activities are based upon reading, writing and listening. This is partly because most teachers, who themselves have been successful in the reading, writing, listening world of formal schooling, are visual or auditory learners and predominantly teach in their preferred style. . . . Kinesthetic learners generally find that opportunities to work in their preferred style significantly decrease as they get older" (1999, 41)

Rita and Ken Dunn suggest that everyone has a dominant sense and a secondary sense (cited in Dryden and Voss 1999). If the teacher is not catering to their dominant sense, most students compensate by using their fallback position. Although there are many students whose sensory modalities are sufficiently balanced for them to adapt and take in information however it's presented, there are some who have such a strong single dominance that they will absorb information only if it is presented in their favored style. Unless their learning-style needs are sufficiently met, these students quickly become frustrated, bored, alienated, and mischievous. They then generally end up in groups of "low ability" students. Many people still confuse ability, behavior, and learning style.

The implications for teachers are clear. The obvious minimum requirement is to check that all lessons have sufficient elements of all three modalities. Naturally, some topics appear to lend themselves to one or two senses and not the third. For example, how do you present quadratic equations kinesthetically? The key is to think laterally and imaginatively, to consider rather than dismiss wacky ideas, to look at the lesson through the eyes of a student whose learning style is different than your own, and to start with the assumption that there are multisensory ways of doing everything and that you have to be convinced otherwise—each topic in every subject is innocent until proven guilty. Check out ideas such as "Assembly" (page 62), "Now You See It . . ." (page 106), "Quick on the Draw" (page 121), and "Value Continuum" (page 139) to stimulate your thinking about tactile and whole-body kinesthetic possibilities.

Skilled as they were at juggling priorities, sensory preferences proved to be a bit more of a handful.

Beyond this balancing act, consider offering structured choices to students. Ask them individually to choose between a visual, an auditory, and a kinesthetic way of reaching the learning outcome. If you feel confident enough, go even further and negotiate learning with students. Take into account what they say about their preferred style and see if it can be built into the program. (Volume 2 of the *Toolkit* provides practical, specific guidance in building this type of program.) There are various ways of detecting students' sensory preferences. Consult "Check Your Students' Learning Styles" on page 195.

2. COGNITIVE PREDILECTIONS: GREGORC'S ANALYSIS

For Anthony Gregorc, learning involves the dual processes of perceiving and ordering information. He distances himself from the brain-based learning crowd, believing mind and brain to be separate: "The mind is the instrument by which and through which we interact with the world. It is the primary medium for the learning/teaching process" (2004) The mind arises from the individual's psyche, like a tree growing from a seed. All minds are *similar* in that they are made of the same "stuff": various qualities such as abstractness, concreteness, sequentialness, and randomness. "On the other hand," Gregorc points out, "each mind is also inherently different because of a natural variance in the amount of 'stuff' that is at our disposal. Some of us have more of the Concrete Sequential qualities. Others have more Abstract Sequential, etc. These quantitative differences account for our specialized abilities and our inability, beyond the basics, to understand and relate to all others equally well" (2001, 13).

He explains that "style is the outward product of the mind and psyche," and goes on, "The human mind has channels through which it receives and expresses information most efficiently and effectively. The power, capacity, and dexterity to utilize these channels are collectively termed 'mediation abilities.' The outward appearance of an individual's mediation abilities is what is popularly termed 'style'" (2001, 1).

The brain, meanwhile, "is a physical organ which serves as a vessel for concentrating much of the mind substances. Along with the spinal cord, nerves and individual cells, it comprises the 'machinery of the mind' for receiving and transmitting data to various parts of the body. It is part of the essential hardware that permits the software of our spiritual forces to work through it and become operative in the world" (1982, 5).

After almost three decades of phenomenological research, Gregorc confidently proposes that there are differences in the way people both *perceive* (let in, grasp) and *order* (organize, store, and reference) data. These differences in mental operation are the result of possessing common mental qualities to different degrees. Take perception first: The differences can be plotted on a continuum from *concrete* to *abstract*.

Concrete └──┘ Abstract

PERCEPTION

Extremely *concrete* people are focused on physical reality. They are sensate. They concentrate on what they can see, feel, hear, smell, and touch. They have little patience with offbeat ideas and fluff. They are down-to-earth and live in the here and now. They have a strong tendency to be objective. When it comes to learning, the experience has to be physical. If the learning can't be seen, touched, and "done," nothing goes in. Extremely *abstract* students, on the other hand, quickly and naturally turn experience into abstract thought. They live in their heads: they think; they feel; they look for patterns, make connections, seek generalities, want ideas, and love theories and big principles. They "see" the invisible. They tend to be subjective. Remember, this is a continuum, with most people occupying positions somewhere between the two ends.

Ordering refers to the way in which people organize and store data in their heads. Again, there are big natural differences, from *sequential* to *random*.

Sequential └────────────────────────────────────┘ Random

ORDERING

Strongly *sequential* people store ideas and facts systematically. They seem to have filing cabinets in their heads; they are logical and precise. To get from A to E mentally, they first go from A to B, then B to C, then C to D, and finally arrive at E—and they can describe all the steps clearly. They are linear, structured, step-by-step thinkers who will pursue only one idea or line of thought at a time. They are telescopic rather than kaleidoscopic. By contrast, strongly *random* people seem mentally chaotic. They appear to store things all over the place, without rhyme or reason, yet can make intuitive connections and creative leaps that sequential people never do. They can go from A to E in one shot but have no idea how they got there. They store information in categories that make sense to them but to no one else. They tend to deal in big chunks, make connections this time that aren't the same as last time, see the whole rather than the parts, and weave many strands together simultaneously. They are kaleidoscopic rather than telescopic. Again, these are extreme positions, and most people are somewhere in between.

Gregorc (1982) combines these mental qualities to form four distinctive styles and designates them Concrete Sequential (CS); Abstract Sequential (AS); Concrete Random (CR); and Abstract Random (AR).

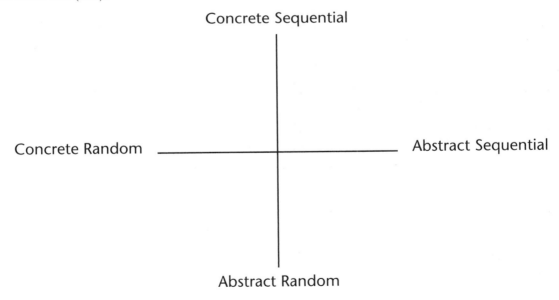

He stresses that everyone has all four of these styles, but usually in different proportions. Some people might be fairly well rounded and have more or less equal facility in all four modes, but most have a natural inclination to one or two. Some people strongly favor one style. If you imagine plotting your personal position on each of the four points in the figure above, and then joining the dots with straight lines to form a kite or diamond shape, the area enclosed by the lines is your Mind Field. This territory is deeply rooted in your psyche; it is to be honored and nurtured; it is not changeable; it is *you*. It could be said to be your comfort zone.

Gregorc's extensive research across the two genders and across all age ranges, abilities, socio-economic backgrounds, and ethnicities suggest that *any* class you teach will comprise students of all kinds. Some will have a strong disposition; others, a mild disposition; and a few (Gregorc's initial studies indicated about 5 percent) will have no significant disposition at all (1982, 1998, 2001). This model and the consistency of findings over the years provide us with an excellent way of planning for diversity.

Students with a dominant CS style learn best through structured practical activities. They relish hands-on learning with step-by-step instructions, such as following a computer program, playing a game with clear rules, making a model from a set of instructions, completing a list of short tasks, following a prescribed route, painting by numbers, observing and imitating an expert, and working through a manual.

Students with a dominant AS style learn best through structured academic research. They like to be guided to see the connection between ideas, the reasons for such-and-such being the case, the theory behind a concept. Preferring to work alone, they welcome structured worksheets, books, and exercises in logic and detail such as "find the missing link," "extract the core concepts," "present the key words," "compare *x* with *y*." They take pride in carrying out instructions thoroughly. They like to think things through.

Students with a dominant AR style learn best through unstructured group work. They love to talk, brainstorm, reflect, imagine, explore ideas, go off on tangents, and make personal connections. The freedom to use images, sounds, and movement; to be dramatic; and to use a range of resources is important to AR learners. Tasks that value feelings, impressions, and whole ideas are particularly suitable; for example, "Together, find a way of presenting the main idea of joint stock companies and how they affect all our lives."

Students with a dominant CR style thrive on open-ended practical work. They tend to resist prescriptions, deadlines, and guidelines. Typically, they want to work out their own method and timescale. They usually want to explore alternatives and to experiment to find things out: "See if you can work out a way of . . ."; "Come up with the best design for . . ."; "Can you find the answer to such and such? Off you go . . ."; "Prepare some teaching resources to get this across to eight-year-olds . . ." are the best kinds of tasks. CR learners like to have finished, tangible outcomes to show for their efforts.

Insightfully, Diane Gregorc, Anthony's wife, captures the essential qualities of the four Mind Styles by suggesting correlations with the four elements of the ancient world (Gregorc 1997, 70 ff):

CS = **earth**
AS = **air**
AR = **water**
CR = **fire**

There are two levels at which we do well to respond to these differences. The first is to incorporate these Mind Styles into our lesson plans. The simplest way of doing this is to check that over a series of, say, four lessons, all four styles have been accommodated. Alternatively, different learning strategies can be prepared and offered to students as a menu of options. Or learning strategies can be negotiated with students so that their natural preferences are built directly into democratically created learning plans. See volume 2 of the *Toolkit* for details and practical applications.

To help you consider the teaching and learning characteristics of each style, my attempt at a summary is in the chart below.

Abstract Sequential		Concrete Sequential	
reading	analysis	hands-on learning	maps
other people's ideas	evaluation	concrete examples	diagrams
reasoning	sitting down and	doing things	short explanations
theorizing	working	clear-cut objectives	lists
debating	lectures	structured learning	following rules and
notetaking	libraries	step-by-step	conventions
content	academic work	approaches	tried and tested
logic	research	data and figures	methods
knowledge	intellectual work	checklists	specific answers
quiet thinking	essays	clear instructions	tangible outcomes
individual study	quiet	attention to detail	methodical learning
tests	comprehension	computers	honesty
structured learning	philosophy	charts	field trips
mental exercises	documentation	outlines	consistency
hypothesizing	objectivity	deadlines	plans
vicarious experiences	comparisons	manuals	
		real experiences	
Concrete Random		**Abstract Random**	
problem solving	creating models	group work	intuition
investigation	own timetable	humor	self-expression
ingenuity	up and doing	games	own timetable
finished products	practical work	movies	imagination
choice	broad guidelines	nonlinear thinking	peer teaching
independence	tangible outcomes	relationships	open-ended questions
experiential learning	real world connections	own ideas	and tasks
risks	experiments	belonging	art
exploration	creativity	music	discussion
open-ended questions	trial and error	human angle	drama
and tasks	options	emotions	media
big picture, not details	challenge	color	creativity
curiosity	games	spontaneity	fantasy
originality	flexibility	flexibility	personalized work
exploration	lots of resources	stories	poetry
invention		cooperation	time for reflection
few restrictions		visualization	subjectivity
		movement	

The second level of response is to take into account Mind Style differences in our interventions with individual students. Consider, for example, a student who is off task. If the student is dominantly AS, she will probably respond to knowing why the work needs to be finished, what it's leading to, how it connects conceptually with what's been done already, and what will be done later. A strongly CS student is likely to benefit from having the task broken into small steps, each with a clear deadline; but a dominantly AR learner might learn best by teaming up with one or more like-minded students and letting off some steam for a few minutes about how boring it all is, and then tackling it together. Try asking the strongly CR learner to find his own way of finishing the learning by the start of the next lesson; he can change the task as long as he achieves the learning outcomes in time.

However, it's not necessarily as easy as it sounds, as Gregorc pointed out to me in private correspondence: "Please note that the individual Mind Styles of teachers can prevent them from understanding and reaching all children equally well. As a matter of fact, some teachers can't fully connect with some students no matter how hard they try. This is a point where I differ from most other style model developers."

If you genuinely want the best for all students and are excited about the insights provided by learning-styles research, it is tempting to believe that you can be trained to reach all students. The risk, though, is that you end up feeling anxious and guilty because you *should* be able to meet the needs of all learners but find that the limitations of your own Mind Style genuinely prevent it. This is no excuse for not trying!

Some crew members struggled to fit the new regime - many began to wonder if the machine itself was faulty.

Gregorc's work more than anyone else's, I believe, sheds light on some uncomfortable management and policy issues. Most school administrators remain unaware of Mind Style differences and make demands on their colleagues that reflect their own way of doing things. For example, a principal with a dominantly CS style might insist on a uniform way of writing units and lesson plans, or instigate a uniform approach to discipline; she might value punctuality at meetings above ideas and cut short a creative discussion because it's time to move on to the next item; she might make a big fuss about the tidiness of classrooms, the neatness of displays, and the orderliness of movement around the building. Conversely, a strongly CR principal might have a million ideas a minute and expect everyone to live in a state of continual experimentation, when what they really want is some stability and continuity for a while. I know of many battles that have been fought between principals and teachers, and of colleagues who have left the profession over issues that were really matters of style—neither side could let the other just be.

In terms of educational policy and practice, we have been in the grip of CS thinking for many years. The imposition of a rigid one-size-fits-all curriculum with a standard linear notion of progression is one product. The idea of a standard "good" lesson that always begins by explaining learning objectives in advance and the insistence on neat and tidy documentation and neat and tidy classrooms are further manifestations. The sidelining of the arts in education, the introduction of rigid lesson structures for numeracy and literacy, the deconstruction of teaching into a series of checklist competencies, the increase in prescriptions for this and guidelines for that—all are hallmarks of the CS mindset. And we wonder why we cannot persuade people to enter or, more significantly, remain in the profession!

3. INTELLIGENCE PROFILES: HOWARD GARDNER

We have come long way in our thinking about intelligence since the days of Francis Galton, Alfred Binet, William Stern, Lewis Terman, and Robert Mearns Yerkes, who were collectively responsible for the creation of intelligence tests purporting to measure the intelligence quotient. For a start, intelligence is no longer regarded as fixed at birth: It can be enhanced by every person. In fact, the process of improving intelligence can be taught—read, for example, Harvard professor of education David Perkins's *Outsmarting IQ* (1995). What's more, intelligence now comes in different shapes and sizes. For example, Jerome Bruner, former professor of psychology, proposes two types of intelligence, cognitive and narrative (see Bruner 1996); Charles Handy (1996) suggests logical, spatial, musical, practical, physical, intrapersonal, and interpersonal; David Perkins defines neural, experiential, and reflective types; Denis Postle, a psychotherapist and counselor, offers emotional, intuitive, physical, and intellectual (1989). Robert Sternberg (1994), professor of psychology and education, has a *triarchic theory* with *componential intelligence* (the kind of linguistic, logical, and mathematical abilities typically valued most in schools), *contextual* (the source of creative insight), and *experiential* (street-smart intelligence).

Peter Salovey and John Mayer (1990) were the first to formulate the idea of emotional intelligence, a concept expanded and popularized by Daniel Goleman (1996). On a different tack, Arthur Costa (1995), co-director of the Institute for Intelligent Behavior, proposes the notion of *intelligent behavior,* in other words, intelligent thought transposed into action. He argues that some apparently bright students don't have a sufficient repertoire of skills with which to apply their intelligence, but that these skills can, and must, be taught in order for a person to be actively intelligent. While we're at it, let's not forget Robert Coles's moral intelligence (1997) and Danah Zohar and Ian Marshall's spiritual intelligence (2001).

The best-known thinker about multiple intelligences is Howard Gardner, who first coined the phrase "multiple intelligences" in his multiple intelligences (MI) theory. As early as 1983, in *Frames of Mind,* he proposed what was then a radical break with tradition: "There is persuasive evidence for the existence of several relatively autonomous human intellectual competencies or 'frames of mind.' The exact nature of each intellectual frame has not so far been satisfactorily established, nor has the precise number been fixed. But the conviction is that there exist at least some intelligences, and that these are relatively independent of one another" (1983, 8).

He went on to define seven distinct types of intelligence, each, he claimed, traceable to a separate area of the human brain. Many of these had previously been called gifts, talents, skills, capacities, abilities, or human faculties, but never *intelligences*. In making this well-researched and deliberate linguistic switch, Gardner seriously expanded the world's thinking and broke the shackles imposed by the psychometricians. Many years, several books, and numerous articles later, he now proposes that all humans have eight types of intelligence:

- verbal-linguistic
- logical-mathematical
- musical-rhythmic
- visual-spatial
- interpersonal
- intrapersonal
- bodily-kinesthetic
- naturalist

Gardner has strict criteria for defining intelligence. In 1983 he called it "the ability to solve problems or to create products that are valued within one or more cultural settings" (1983, 33). In *Intelligence Reframed,* he offers a more refined definition. "I now conceptualize an intelligence as a biopsychological potential to process information that can be activated in a cultural setting to solve problems or create products that are of value in a culture. . . . Intelligences are not things that can be seen or counted. Instead they are potentials—presumably, neural ones—that will or will not be activated, depending upon the values of a particular culture, the opportunities available in that culture and the personal decisions made by individuals and/or their families, school teachers and others" (1999, 34).

Not all academics agree with Gardner. The questions of inherited intelligence, the definition of intelligence, the measurability of intelligence, and the relationship between intelligence and social class continue to be fiercely debated. In the meantime, in classrooms around the country, students' achievements and self-esteem are being raised by the optimistic and positive message that everyone is intelligent, but in different ways.

A friend and colleague of mine, Tony Salmon, told Howard Gardner during a seminar: "The strength we get from your work is that you do use the word 'intelligence,' because the kids have been told so often—not explicitly, but they have picked up the message—that they are not intelligent" (Craft 1997, 19). Tony was expressing just one of the benefits of Gardner's work, the flattening of the ancient hierarchy of educational values. The upgrading of everyday abilities to the status of "intelligence" suddenly gives everyone a place in the world. Nobodies become somebodies overnight. Self-images and self-expectations are transformed. What's more, the fact that this idea has a credible, internationally renowned, academic, weighty source makes it easier to persuade teachers to bring their habits into line with the new order, on three counts: their *thinking* (they can't write off anyone anymore); their *language* (they drop the limiting language of ability); and their *classroom techniques* (they broaden learning and assessment strategies). These three thrusts characterize the high-aspiration strategies adopted by raising achievement initiatives all over the country. Moms and dads are also benefiting from briefings on the theory and its practical parenting implications.

Apart from MI theory's power to convince adults, it can be used directly with students. Its upbeat message is appealing and easy to communicate, and the differing characteristics of the various intelligences can be used to help students with self-study. Once they have the idea that they have their own individual intelligence profiles, that all of them is capable in their own way, students can start to select appropriate learning methods. This is particularly applicable to home study, where the teacher's imposed methodology doesn't apply. Many modern self-study courses and study guides offer notetaking, organizing, and memorizing techniques across the full range of intelligences. Students are encouraged to sample various methods and then settle on the ones that work best for their personal dispositions. Many schools claim improvements in test results after encouraging students to base their preparation on MI theory. The chart opposite could give students, parents, and even teachers a basic guide to the eight intelligences. Remember, everyone has all eight, but to varying degrees.

Type of intelligence	With this intelligence you . . .
Verbal-linguistic intelligence	• think in words • like to read and write • like stories • like to play word games • have a good memory for names, places, dates, poetry, lyrics, and trivia • spell well • have a well-developed vocabulary
Logical-mathematical intelligence	• see patterns easily • like abstract ideas • like strategy games and logical puzzles • figure out sums easily in your head • ask big questions, such as "where does the universe end?" • use computers with ease • devise experiments to test things you don't understand • think in categories and see relationships between ideas
Visual-spatial intelligence	• think in images and pictures • easily remember where things are • like drawing, designing, building, daydreaming • easily read maps and diagrams • easily do jigsaw puzzles • are fascinated by machines • reproduce images accurately
Musical-rhythmic intelligence	• often sing, hum, or whistle to yourself • remember melodies • have a good sense of rhythm • play an instrument • are sensitive to sounds in the environment • need music on when studying
Bodily-kinesthetic intelligence	• remember through bodily sensations • find it difficult to sit still for long • have gut feelings about exam answers • are good at sports, dance, acting, or mime • have excellent coordination • communicate well through gestures • learn best through physical activity, simulation, and role play • easily mimic people
Interpersonal intelligence	• understand people well • learn best by interacting and cooperating with others • are good at leading and organizing • pick up on other people's feelings • mediate between people • enjoy playing social games • listen well
Intrapersonal intelligence	• like to work alone • motivate yourself • are intuitive • are independent • are strong-willed and have strong personal opinions • set your own goals • are self-confident • are reflective • are aware of your strengths and weaknesses
Naturalist intelligence	• recognize flora and fauna • make distinctions and notice patterns in the natural world • use common and distinguishing features to categorize and group phenomena • use criteria consistently • use this ability productively, for example, farming, pet keeping, conservation

---

> ### Learn More about MI and Lesson Planning
>
> The final benefit of multiple intelligence theory is its usefulness as a lesson-planning tool. A huge amount of secondary literature has grown up around the idea. Numerous books offer practical strategies to suit different intelligences; see the bibliography on page 229 for titles by David Lazear, Sally Berman, James Bellanca, Bonita DeAmicis, Carolyn Chapman, Ellen Arnold, and others.

The cataloging and categorizing of techniques may wear thin after a while, but the principle is sound: Use MI as another way of thinking about differences among students; use it to increase your empathetic understanding of students; and, if the notion feels comfortable, use it to help you plan your lessons alongside, or instead of, the models described above. Ensure that over a series of lessons you have required students to use the full range of intelligences. As with VAK and Mind Styles, encourage students to operate within their comfortable range initially, but then challenge them over time to push the boat out and begin to strengthen intelligences that are weak. To support you, the activities in section 2 cover different intelligences in different combinations.

Other Learning Agendas

Current thinking about learning is affected by the desire to address a number of pressing social and economic concerns and the firm belief in certain values. This creates a combination of pragmatism and ideology. Take citizenship, for example, where belief in democracy meets a concern about the state of today's youth. Inclusion is the marriage of social justice with a drive to stop wasting our economically valuable talent. Learning to learn combines the ideal that all learners should make the best of their lives with the need for commercial competitiveness.

Learning to Learn

We are being swept toward a universal acceptance of the need to learn how to learn. The accelerating pace of technological change and increasingly fragmented work and career patterns create a need for people to possess skills that will enable them to retrain professionally and make the most of their lives personally. These learning skills, along with underpinning attitudes such as perseverance and the will to defer gratification, can be acquired only over time, with lots and lots of practice. As things stand in schools at the moment, this doesn't seem to happen—at least not consistently. Take a look at "Check Your Delivery of Independent Learning Skills" (page 213) and see whether you think I'm right.

Mike Roberts, a high school vice-principal, published an interesting study over a decade ago (1994). He noticed that most of the school's students were not coping well with autonomous, or self-managed, learning. After two years of detailed investigation, he concluded that two skill sets are required:

Information processing skills	Underlying core skills
1. planning	1. time management
2. gathering	2. social
3. processing	3. reflective
4. presenting	4. self-appraisal
	5. seeking help

In fact, he found that "autonomous learning was a novel experience for most learners which demanded skills they did not possess" (56). Why? Because "the scale, breadth, depth and complexity of skills demanded for autonomous project management were neither understood nor appreciated by teachers" (55). Most high school and college educators that I meet tell me that they face a similar situation. But it doesn't have to be this way. Frequently using strategies such as "Dreadlines" (page 88), "Step On It" (page 175), "One to One" (page 110), and "Double Take" (page 86) would start students on the path to independence.

Under continual pressure to get good test results above all, most schools don't have the courage or the energy to take independent learning seriously. However, two current trends support the cause. First, liberating technology: Students can obtain most of the information and many of the skills they need for exam success through online or media-based resources. They can study at least as well at home or in the cyber café as they can in school. They can follow personalized learning pathways and take diagnostic assessments when they are ready. Teachers are increasingly putting lesson and homework materials onto school websites or intranets for students to follow. E-tutoring and virtual schooling are catching on. Learning, even formal learning, is no longer teacher dependent. Given sufficient hardware resources, teachers can now become managers and facilitators, counselors and coaches. At the high-tech School of the Future in Alameda, California, teachers don't even have to organize: they are simply "on hand."

The second supportive trend is the prevailing interest in thinking skills. To be fully independent, students need to be able to think in a variety of ways. So what are these thinking skills? Bowring-Carr and West-Burnham offer a helpful definition (1997, 94–95). They say that "cognitive skills, and thus the basis for the thinking curriculum" can be summarized as follows:

- problem solving
- critical thinking
- reasoning
- creative thinking

They go on to say that more specific strategies might include

- recognition and clarification of a problem
- mapping and ordering relevant information
- generating alternative solutions
- applying logical criteria
- implementing a solution
- monitoring
- communicating
- evaluating outcomes
- generating conclusions
- transferring to other situations

With a little imagination, anyone can design learning activities that efficiently cover the curriculum and thinking skills at the same time. Examples in the *Toolkit* to get your creative thinking going include "Assembly" (page 62), "Calling Cards" (page 70), "Guess Who" (page 90), and "Ranking" (page 126).

Another useful tool for the design of thinking tasks is Benjamin Bloom's classic *Taxonomy of Educational Objectives* (1956). As you move from bottom to top of the taxonomy, you demand increasingly sophisticated skills of your students.

Evaluation	assess, judge, weigh, rate, determine, rank, assay, decide, arbitrate, grade, appraise, classify
Synthesis	combine, build, originate, regroup, conceive, blend, develop, mix, compound, structure, make, generate, join
Analysis	break down, examine, dissect, scrutinize, inspect, sort, analyze, separate, investigate, compartmentalize, classify, take apart
Application	apply, adapt, transfer, adopt, transcribe, solve, use, transform, employ, manipulate, use, transplant, relate
Comprehension	reword, convert, outline, explain, define, interpret, reconstruct, paraphrase, transpose, understand, conceive, calculate
Knowledge	determine what, who, when, and where; recall; locate; repeat; name; recite; list; find; identify; label

As always, the temptation is for us to focus mainly on logical thinking involving the processes of analysis and deduction. Creative thinking, lateral thinking, intuitive thinking, random thinking, and spiritual thinking all have a vital place in the complete life and in the complete society. In our rational and empirical world, we don't value them half enough. Just look at the status of drama, dance, music, and visual art in the school curriculum.

Of course, beyond just thinking, there's *metacognition,* which is the sophisticated business of thinking about thinking, involving ongoing debriefing and reflection. According to Robin Fogarty in *How to Teach for Metacognitive Reflection* (1994, viii), "metacognition is awareness and control over your own thinking behavior." This involves making implicit skills explicit, learning new ones, and making choices. Arthur Costa (1995) defines metacognition as the uniquely human awareness of our thinking while thinking, being aware of our problem-solving process while solving a problem, a process that resides in the cerebral cortex of the brain. He points out that good problem solvers use metacognition when they plan before acting, scrutinize and adjust the plan during the process of acting, and evaluate the plan and their actions after they have finished the task.

But why bother with metacognition? Because it supports the independent learning process.

Back to patterning and constructivism: "Constructivists view learning as the process individuals experience as they take in new information and make sense of that new information. By making meaning, they are acquiring knowledge. However, individuals who construct knowledge and are aware of the gaps in their understanding of that knowledge are actively using both their cognitive and their metacognitive strategies. In their awareness of what they know and what they don't know, they take the first step in remedying the deficit areas" (Fogarty 1994, xvii). Or, as

Jean Piaget, the Swiss psychologist known for his pioneering work on intelligence, said, intelligent behavior is knowing what to do when you don't know what to do (Piaget 2001).

This connects with David Perkins's (1995) view that there are three types of intelligence: neural (genetically inherited—there's nothing we can do about it); experiential (the result of our experiences as we attempt to navigate our world); and reflective. This last can be developed—it is within our control. It amounts to the ability to make better use of our minds. We can *learn* better strategies for dealing with problems and better ways of remembering details, for example. Metacognition is the process by which we become more intelligent in the reflective sense.

Cooperation, Democracy, and Citizenship

Why should citizenship be an integral part of high school curricula? The increase in juvenile crime and political apathy among young voters are two excellent reasons, and at a deep level, what John Dewey (writing in 1916!) said is true: "We have taken democracy for granted; we have thought and acted as if our forefathers had founded it once for all. We have forgotten that it has to be enacted anew in every generation, in every year and day in the living relations of person to person in all social forms and institutions."

I am a great supporter of citizenship education, but I find it difficult to see how this high aim can be realized, for several reasons. For starters, there are strong contradictory messages in the educational system. Fiona Clarke (2000) says, "I think in terms of experiential learning and wonder how [students] are expected to grasp the ideas of democracy and citizenship when they have been trapped in a totalitarian educational system which does not recognize their right to choose what they learn or how they learn it. Isn't the whole of their schooling a lesson in living under a dictatorship?"

What we need are "citizenship schools," as Titus Alexander (2000) calls them.

Even without these schools, however, we should do what we can to develop the habits of democracy. We might follow England's example in this respect, where students in the equivalent of U.S. grades 5 through 8 are expected to

- think about topical political, spiritual, moral, social and cultural issues, problems and events by analyzing information and its sources
- justify orally and in writing a personal opinion about such issues, problems or events
- contribute to group and exploratory class discussions, and take part in debates
- negotiate, decide and take part responsibly . . .
- reflect on the process of participating

(QCA 2005)

Many of the *Toolkit* techniques in section 2 contribute to these outcomes in various combinations. Take "Value Continuum" (page 139) and "Corporate Identity" (page 76), for example. What's more, the whole of section 3 is devoted to the creation of a civilized, participatory, self-regulating minisociety. In addition, the tone of this entire book supports the more general points about the type of teaching methods required for effective "active citizenship" education. Clearly, citizenship learning has to be experiential. Underpinning a flourishing democracy are interdependent, mutual behaviors. Procedures and constitutions are required to keep everything in place in large democratic groups, but they can become cold, combative, and abused. A democratic *will*, which shows itself through cooperative attitudes and skills, brings life to the dead hand of procedure. Neuroscientists say that people are born with such a will, a "social brain," and that "there are critical periods of development for the social brain just as there are for other brain functions" (Ratey 2002, 300).

In middle and high schools, we can do our best to regenerate the will to be cooperative and to provide training in democratic skills. Even when the institution itself is undemocratic and the attitude of government toward education is dictatorial, we can still

CITIZENSHIP? EDUCATION?

use lots of collaborative group work and interdependent learning activities in our own classrooms. Over the years the research of Robert Slavin (2003); the Johnson brothers, David and Roger (2005); and the classic work of Spencer Kagan (2004) have defined the practice and the benefits of cooperation. As long ago as 1984, David R. Johnson, Roger T. Johnson, and Edythe Johnson Holubec's extensive studies led them to conclude: "The results indicate that cooperative group learning experiences tend to promote higher achievement than do competitive and individualistic learning experiences. The results hold good for all age levels, for all subject areas, and for tasks involving concept attainment, verbal problem solving, categorization, spatial problem solving, retention and memory, motor performance, guessing, judging and predicting" (104).

We can go further, if we have the courage, and create relative democracy in our classrooms. Lesley Browne did. She asked her 12th-grade sociology class to choose one of four different ways of studying the course:

- teacher directed
- consultative model
- democratic learning cooperative
- individual study programs

They chose the democratic learning cooperative (DLC), immediately spent time thrashing out a set of 13 principles and procedures, and then proceeded to organize and monitor their own learning. They called on the teacher as a resource for subject knowledge, exam requirements, and advice about the learning process. In the end they did well on their exams, but looking back, one of the students, James Baldaro, says: "The relative success of the group in external examinations, despite seeming to mean 'everything' at the time, is actually secondary. The real success of the democratic learning cooperative lies in how it instilled key notions of cooperation, mutual support and tolerance in a group of 16–18 year olds. . . . Coupled with the confidence developed through the DLC's reliance on continued public speech and teaching and discussion with others, I believe our experiences equipped us with essential transferable skills" (1995, 2).

Browne herself implies that there are two further, automatic benefits to teaching democratically—students learn how to learn and develop cognitive and metacognitive skills: "Possibly one of the most important practices in democratic learning environments is that of dialogue between students and teachers, questioning and discussing together how they might improve their practice. If democracy in the classroom is about anything, it is the free exchange of ideas. Without this open continuous debate, power-sharing is pointless" (1995, 71).

We can begin to see how it all fits together. Some types of classroom practice actually deliver most current agendas simultaneously and naturally. Key aspects of citizenship can be delivered through academic lessons by choosing the right methods. Traditional teacher-dictated learning simply cannot do the job. It can only tinker with thinking skills, learning how to learn, citizenship, and inclusion, because the method is incongruent with the purposes.

Inclusion and Differentiation

The concern for inclusion has a moral basis. It is a matter of social justice and equal opportunity. Too many students are still excluded from real success for a range of complex reasons. Apart from the most obvious—some form of disability or learning impairment that separates them—there is the mismatch between students' language, behavior, or cultural norms and those of the institution; low self-esteem and anger about failures of the past; poor basic skills; and so on. In *Understanding Barriers to Learning* (1999), Peter Maxted helpfully categorizes the problems into cultural, structural, and personal issues. Although summarizing 10 years of research into why people don't continue their learning beyond school, the analysis and main messages are entirely pertinent to K–12 education.

Inclusion and the subsequent differentiation of the curriculum quickly become resource issues. Providing the right courses, necessary facilities and personnel, and appropriate materials and equipment all require money. Even so, they get us only to first base. Resources create the *possibility* that learning will occur. For example, hearing aids make it possible to hear, large print makes text easier to see, ramps make it possible to get into a school and a classroom, specialist teachers and learning assistants make it possible for individual needs to be met. Beyond first base is the challenge of translating possibility into solid achievement.

INCLUSION?

At a minimum, this requires the teacher to create an acceptant learning community within which each and every student, no matter what, is guaranteed freedom from ridicule and belittlement. As we have already discussed, students' full participation in learning is dependent on such conditions. Section 3 spells out the steps that need to be taken. In addition to this minimum, the teacher will need to follow the "natural laws of learning" proposed earlier (see page ix). Otherwise, students who are physically present in the classroom will still be effectively excluded from the achievements of which they are capable.

One of these natural laws is, of course, the accommodation of different learning styles. Thomas Armstrong, in his provocative book *In Their Own Way* (1987), positions learning styles as the solution to most "special needs":

> Six years ago I quit my job as a learning disabilities specialist. I had to. I no longer believed in learning disabilities. . . . It was then that I turned to the concept of learning differences as an alternative to learning disabilities. I realized that the millions of children being referred to learning disabled classes weren't handicapped, but instead had unique learning styles that the schools didn't clearly understand. Furthermore, it seemed to me that the reason so many millions of additional children were underachieving, experiencing school phobias, or just plain bored in the classroom was because no one had recognized and used what they really had to offer in the learning place—their special talents and abilities. (ix–x)

Though not in itself the answer to inclusion, the accommodation of diverse learning styles is an example of the lengths that teachers need to go to. Using the principles of differentiation and offering students choices of strategy, consulting them about their needs, negotiating deadlines and assessments, and actively raising self-esteem through the careful use of language all contribute to the possibility of success for all. For specific differentiation strategies, see the work of Carol Ann Tomlinson (such as 1999, 2001, 2003, and 2004), Gayle Gregory and Carolyn Chapman (2002), and Martha Kaufeldt (2005).

The Recipe

The size of the issues discussed in this opening section invites us to rethink our practice and structures on a huge scale. However, *The Teacher's Toolkit* does not set out to redesign the education system, desirable as that may be. It does not even attempt to revolutionize classroom practice. Rather, it simply puts into the hands of teachers the means by which they might begin, or continue, to move in the right direction. When all the brain research and the socioeconomic, political, and philosophical considerations have been put through the mill of critical thought, there emerges, remarkably, a set of consistent conclusions about the way to go.

We can have confidence in the practical ideas in this book because they serve a number of converging purposes. In sum, they are designed to do the best for students of all learning styles, backgrounds, and previous attainment in an age when qualifications appear to matter most. They are designed to support students in becoming socially skilled, independent thinkers and self-sufficient learners with a strong sense of personal and collective responsibility. Consequently they are designed to equip individuals and society with the means of creating a fruitful and morally sound future.

The learning principles behind these high ambitions—the theoretical ideas discussed earlier in this section—shake down into a handful of planning purposes. These have guided the design of the learning activities. By *planning purposes* I mean the reasons for approaching learning in a particular way, the intentions behind the activity, the goals that the activity is meant to achieve. There are seven.

1. thinking: actively processing data creatively, logically, laterally, imaginatively, deductively, and so on
2. emotional intelligence: learning to manage emotions and relate to others skillfully; developing positive personal qualities, such as self-control, and values such as justice
3. independence: acquiring the attitudes and skills that enable students to initiate and sustain learning without a teacher
4. interdependence: engaging in mutuality, which is the essence of cooperation and the basis of democracy
5. multisensation: experiencing through a number of senses simultaneously—in effect seeing, hearing, and doing
6. fun: enjoying the activity and therefore enjoying learning
7. articulation: speaking, writing and or doing, often in draft form, as an essential part of the process of creating personal understanding

Just a quick word about number six. Not all learning can be fun, nor should we try to make it so. Nor does learning always have to be heavy. Students' days in secondary schools are filled with huge doses of sitting, listening, reading, and writing. For concentration and interest to be sustained over a day, never mind a week, the human mind requires variety and contrast. It requires learning experiences to be variously serious and light, active and passive, individual and collective, controlled and loose, noisy and silent. Kept in perspective, fun is a serious business.

These seven planning purposes are effectively the ingredients of the recipe of *The Teacher's Toolkit*. In section 2 they are presented alongside each activity as a quick guide to its intended benefits. By being made explicit, they enable you to go on to create your own strategies—simply mix the same underpinning ideas and mentally bake. In addition, each activity includes a list of its key features, which describe its character: individual work, group work, moving, speaking, listening, reading, writing, looking, and choice. This allows you to see, at a glance, what you are taking on. See the matrix on pages 54 and 55 for a quick guide to the purposes and features of each activity in section 2.

The body of research also suggests that there are four additional factors to take into account. These create the environment for optimum learning. The techniques described in sections 2 and 3 will be truly successful only if these contextual characteristics are in place and refreshed day by day:

1. The communication of optimism and high expectations: achieved by exuding energy, using positive language, and designing challenging tasks.
2. The creation of a physical environment conducive to learning: achieved by paying attention to the basics of oxygen, ionization, temperature, hydration, access, aesthetics, aroma, sounds, furnishings, and peripherals.
3. The accommodation of diverse learning styles: achieved by providing variety (the minimum requirement), by offering choices, and by negotiating learning strategies with students.
4. The preservation and enhancement of students' self-esteem: achieved by establishing ground rules, by using affirming language, by turning mistakes into positive learning, and by following all the other guidelines in "Check Your Impact on Students' Self-Esteem" in section 4.

Activity Purposes and Features Matrix

ACTIVITY	Thinking	Emotional Intelligence	Inde-pendence	Inter-dependence	Multi-sensation	Fun	Artic-ulation
Assembly (page 62)	★ ★ ★ ★ ★	★	★ ★ ★	★ ★ ★ (variable)	★ ★	★ ★	★ ★ ★
Back to Back (page 64)	★ ★ ★ ★ ★	★ ★	★ ★	★ ★ ★ ★ ★	★ ★	★ ★ ★	★ ★ ★ ★ ★
Beat the Teacher (page 66)	★ ★ ★ ★ ★	★	★ ★	★ ★ ★ (variable)	★	★ ★ ★ ★	★ ★
Bingo (page 68)	★ ★ ★ ★ ★		★ ★	★ ★ ★ (variable)		★ ★ ★ ★	★ (variable)
Calling Cards (page 70)	★ ★ ★ ★ ★	★	★ ★ ★ ★		★	★ ★	★ ★
Center of the Universe (page 72)	★ ★ ★ ★	★ ★	★ ★ ★ ★	★	★ ★ ★	★ ★ ★	★ ★
Conversion (page 74)	★ ★ ★ ★ ★	★	★ ★ ★ ★		★	★	★ ★ ★ ★
Corporate Identity (page 76)	★ ★ ★	★ ★	★ ★ ★	★ ★ ★ ★ ★		★	★ ★ ★
Dicey Business (page 78)	★ ★ ★ ★	★ ★	★ ★	★	★	★ ★ ★ ★	★ ★ ★
Discussion Carousel (page 80)	★ ★ ★ ★	★ ★	★ ★	★ ★ ★	★ ★	★ ★ ★	★ ★ ★ ★
Distillation (page 82)	★ ★ ★ ★		★ ★ ★ ★	★ ★		★	★ ★ ★
Dominoes (page 84)	★ ★ ★ ★	★	★	★ ★	★	★ ★ ★	★
Double Take (page 86)	★ ★ ★	★	★ ★ ★ ★ ★	★	★ ★ (variable)		
Dreadlines (page 88)	★ ★	★ ★ ★	★ ★ ★ ★ ★				
Guess Who (page 90)	★ ★ ★ ★ ★	★	★ ★	★ ★ ★ ★	★ (variable)	★ ★ ★	★ ★ ★ ★
Hierarchies (page 92)	★ ★ ★ ★ ★		★ ★ ★ ★			★	★ ★ ★ ★
Hot Seating (page 95)	★ ★ ★ ★	★ ★	★ ★ ★ ★	★ ★	★ ★	★ ★	★ ★ ★
Inspiration (page 98)	★ ★ ★ ★	★ ★ ★	★ ★ ★ ★ ★	★	★	★	★ ★
Mantle of the Expert (page 100)	★ ★ ★ ★	★ ★	★ ★ ★ ★ (expert)	★ ★ (audience)		★ ★	★ ★ ★ (expert)
Masterminds (page 102)	★ ★ ★ ★	★	★ ★ ★ ★	★ ★ ★ ★	★	★ ★ ★	★ ★
Memory Board (page 104)	★ ★ ★ ★		★ ★ ★ ★	(variable)		★ ★	★ ★ ★ ★
Now You See It . . . (page 106)	★ ★ ★ ★ ★		★ ★ ★ ★		★	★ ★ ★	★ ★ ★ ★
On Tour (page 108)	★ ★ ★ ★ ★	★	★ ★ ★	★ ★ ★ ★		★	★ ★ ★ ★ ★
One to One (page 110)	★ ★ ★ ★	★	★ ★ ★	★ ★ ★ ★		★	★ ★ ★ ★
Pairs to Fours (page 112)	★ ★ ★ ★ ★	★ ★	★ ★ ★	★ ★ ★ ★		★ ★	★ ★ ★ ★ ★
Pass the Buck (page 114)	★ ★ ★ ★ ★	★	★ ★ ★	★ ★ ★		★ ★	★ ★ ★ ★ ★
Prediction (page 116)	★ ★ ★ ★ ★	★ ★	★ ★ ★ ★	★ ★ ★	★	★	★ ★ ★ ★
Question Generator (page 119)	★ ★ ★ ★	★	★ ★ ★ (variable)	★ ★ ★ (variable)		★	★ ★ ★
Quick on the Draw (page 121)	★ ★ ★ ★	★	★ ★ ★ ★	★ ★ ★	★ ★	★ ★ ★ ★	★ ★
Randomizer (page 124)	★ ★ ★ ★	★ ★	★ ★ ★ ★	★ ★ ★		★	★ ★ ★
Ranking (page 126)	★ ★ ★ ★ ★	★	★ ★ ★	★ ★	★ ★	★	★ ★ ★ ★
Silent Sentences (page 128)	★ ★ ★ ★ ★	★ ★ ★		★ ★ ★ ★ ★	★ ★	★ ★ ★	
Sorting Circles (page 130)	★ ★ ★ ★ ★	★	★ ★ ★	★ ★ ★ ★	★	★	★ ★ ★ ★
Spolight (page 133)	★ ★ ★ ★ ★		★			★ ★	★ ★ ★ (volunteer) ★ (class)
Stepping Stones (page 135)	★ ★ ★ ★ ★	★	★	★ ★	★ ★ ★	★ ★ ★	★ ★ ★ (volunteer)
Thumbometer (page 137)	★ ★ ★ ★	★ ★	★ ★ ★		★	★ ★	★ ★
Value Continuum (page 139)	★ ★ ★ ★ ★	★ ★ ★ ★	★ ★ ★	★ ★	★ ★	★	★ ★ ★ ★ ★
Verbal Football (page 142)	★ ★ ★ ★	★	★ ★ ★	★ ★ ★ ★	★	★ ★ ★ ★ ★	★ ★ ★
Verbal Tennis (page 144)	★ ★ ★ ★ ★		★	★	★	★ ★ ★ ★	★ ★ ★ ★
Wheel of Fortune (page 146)	★ ★ ★ ★		★	★ ★	★ ★	★ ★ ★	★ ★ ★ ★

Activity Purposes and Features Matrix

FEATURES

Individual Work	Group Work	Moving	Speaking	Listening	Reading	Writing	Looking	Choice
* * * *	* * * (variable)	*	* * * (variable)	* * * * (variable)	* * * * (variable)		* * * *	
* *	* * * *		* * * * *	* * * * *			* * * * *	
* * *	* * *		*	* * * *		*	* * * * (variable)	
* * * *	* * (variable)		*	* * * *	* *	* *	* * *	*
* * * * *				* * * *			* *	
* *	* * * *	* * *	*	* * * *			* * *	* * *
* * * * *				*	* * * *	* * *	* *	*
* * * *	* * * *		* *	* *	* *	* *	*	*
* *	* * * *		* * *	* * * *	*		*	
*	* * * *	* *	* * * *	* * * * *				
* *	* * *	*	* * *	* * *	* * * *	* * *	* *	*
* *	* * *			* * *	* * * *	* *	*	
* * * * *		*		* * * *	* * *		* * (variable)	* * *
* * * * *			*	*				* * (variable)
*	* * * *	* * * * * (variable)	* * *	* * * *	*		* (variable)	*
* * * * *				*	* * * *	* * *	*	
* * *	* * * (variable)		* * *	* * * * *		* * * (variable)	* * *	* *
* * *	*		* *	* * * *	*	*	* * * *	*
* * * * * (expert)	* * (audience)		* * * * (expert)	* * * * (audience)			* * (audience)	* * *
* *	* * * *		* * *	* * *	* * * *	* *	* * (variable)	* *
* * * *	(variable)				* * *	* * * *	* * *	
* * * *					* *	*	* * *	
	* * * *	* * * * *	* * *	* *	* * *	* * * *	*	* * *
* * *	* * *	*	* * *	* * *	* * * *	* * * *	* *	
*	* * * *	*	* * * * *	* * * * *	* *			
	* * * *		* * *	* * *	* * *	* * * * *		
*	* * * *	*	* * * *	* * * *	* (variable)	* *	* (variable)	
* * * (variable)	* * * * (variable)		* * *	* * *	*	* *		* * *
*	* * * * *	* * *	* * *	* *	* * * *	* * *	* *	
* * * *	* * (variable)		* * *	* * * * *			* *	
	* * * *		* * * * *	* * * *	* *		* (variable)	
	* * * * *				* * * *		* * * * *	
*	* * * *	* (variable)	* * * *	* * * *	* * (variable)		* * * (variable)	
* * * * *		*	* * * (volunteer)	* * * * (class)		*		
* * * * (volunteer)	* * * * (variable)	* *	* * * * * (volunteer)	* * * * (class)			* * *	* *
* * * * *				* * *			*	* * * *
* * *	* *	* * *	* * *	* * * * *			* * * *	* * * *
* *	* * * *	*	* * * *	* * * *	* * * *	*	*	* *
*	* * *		* * * * *	* * * * *				
* * * (variable)	* * * (variable)	* *	* * * *	* * *	*		*	

The seven planning purposes and four contextual characteristics combine to create a simple model for the design and delivery of effective learning experiences:

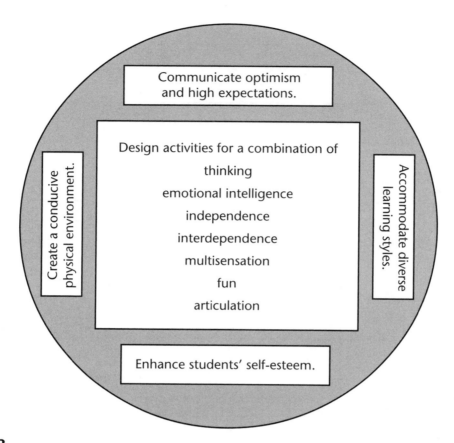

Why Not?

This section began with the question "why?" We have surveyed a number of answers and are left with the question "why not?" Simply, if we don't begin to make fundamental changes to our educational practices, we're in trouble. Nationally, our education policies are not going in the right direction—research from neuroscience, sociology, anthropology, philosophy, and psychology tells us so. But what can *you* do? Begin by checking your own methodology against the evidence. Be willing to make whatever adjustments are needed to bring your teaching more and more in line with natural features of the learning process and students' and society's future needs, as far as the school and the system allow.

Yes, But . . .

Sometimes a teacher will take a *Toolkit* technique and come back with, "I tried that and it didn't work." Why not? Clearly there are lots of requirements for the successful implementation of the ideas in this book. A reasonably sized classroom that allows furniture to be reconfigured, enough large paper and felt-tip pens, colored posterboard and construction paper, scissors, and a generous photocopying budget are needed for a start. Some of these physical prerequisites cannot be conjured up by the individual teacher—they depend on the allocation of resources to, and within, schools.

Decisions about grouping students, the school's discipline policy, whether students are allowed to go to the school library during class, whether they're allowed in at recess—all these procedures and policies create the culture of a school, which affects student attitudes. For instance, it's hard to create an inclusive classroom in a school that locks students out, segregates by social class (under the guise of "ability"), and favors those with 100 percent attendance by giving them a day trip to a theme park. Equally, it is hard to establish the habits of independence when students are blatantly bribed to behave and have all the real decisions (except, perhaps, whether they are going take drama or drafting as an elective) made for them.

However, this book takes the optimistic view that even in a hostile climate, the individual teacher can go a long way to create a dignified oasis of success. Two qualities are required: skill and will. Organizing the furniture beforehand and putting it back afterward simply means making a little extra effort. In the hands of skillful and willing teachers, or at least those who are willing to become skillful, the techniques in this book can be remarkably successful, even against the apparent odds.

So, if you're up for it, read on.

SECTION 2

Tools for
Teaching and
Learning

Introduction

The learning activities presented here cover a wide variety of styles and purposes. Variety is important in itself. It's the spice of life; we all need it to keep our concentration and motivation alive—students and teachers alike.

Beyond this, the activities are deliberately designed to accommodate a mixture of learning styles. The natural instinct of teachers is to do the best for each and every student, but because every human brain is as unique as a fingerprint, the task can feel overwhelming. Learning-style constructs help us to make sense of this diversity and give us the means of planning our lessons.

There are many learning-style models available these days. Take your pick. The three that have informed the preparation of this section are discussed in section 1:

- Visual, auditory, kinesthetic: the sensory-preferences model.
- Anthony Gregorc's Mind Styles: an information-processing model similar to Kolb's, Honey and Mumford's, and McCarthy's, and the basis of Kathleen Butler's RAPID system (1986).
- Multiple intelligences theory: the acclaimed creation of Howard Gardner.

Consequently, in this collection you will find group work and individual work, academic and practical, up-and-doing and sitting still, open-ended investigation and structured research, drama, analysis of text, competition, cooperation, fun, careful concentration, debate, peer teaching, construction, deconstruction, and more.

But there's more. Other agendas need to be addressed. For a range of sound social and moral reasons, we want to create genuine inclusion, promote citizenship, and develop thinking skills. In fact, the major goals of the broad-based approach to education suggested by the *Toolkit* are

- to help people become skilled, self-aware, and independent learners
- to help people become skilled, socially aware, inclusive, and democratic citizens

Of course such learning can occur only experientially. These goals are achieved only if they regularly determine the character of learning experiences. The good news is that it's possible to address several of these learning agendas simultaneously. Through cleverly designed activities, you can cover the content of your curriculum efficiently and develop students' thinking skills and citizenship at the same time.

Four further points:

1. Not all of these activities will work with all classes. Different exercises require different levels of social and study skills. Use your judgment. If a technique seems too ambitious, identify the enhancements needed and work on these with your class for a while. For example, develop listening skills through "Discussion Carousel" (page 80) to enhance students' success in "Pairs to Fours" (page 112), or use "One to One" (page 110) to give students peer-teaching practice before they try it in the more advanced "Corporate Identity" (page 76). It should be possible to mix and match the activities in this section to tailor a program to your group.

2. Many readers will recognize a number of these activities. Some have been in circulation for years, having been invented in the mists of time when experiential learning, discovery learning, active learning, and student-centered learning were in their prime. It's

been fascinating in recent years to see how the new thinking about the brain has validated such older strategies. I've drawn on this heritage, tested techniques in hundreds of classrooms, rejected ideas that didn't work, adapted others, and invented new ones. This is a collection of my current favorites.

3. Many teachers complain that interactive teaching techniques need many resources that take lots of time to prepare. Sometimes this is true, but not always. Flip through the resource lists for the activities. You'll see that many don't require students to have anything, or require just a pen and paper.

4. These activities are only for starters. I am presenting them to show how modern learning theory can be turned into classroom practice. The activities make certain principles concrete. But they are only examples. Sophisticated teachers will get under the surface of the techniques, identify the principles upon which they are based, and create their own practice. This is the ultimate intention of the *Toolkit,* not to provide teaching by numbers, but to indicate directions, offer examples and reasons, and then set you on your own way.

Just a final word about the panels in the margin of each activity. These summarize

- the purposes of the activity (related to the theories in section 1—see "The Recipe" on page 52)
- the key features of the activity (such as reading, writing, speaking, working independently or in groups, and so forth)
- the room layout (whether a specific layout is required)

Learn More about Drama and Learning

To find out more about the dramatic techniques described—in "Hot Seating," for example—and to discover other ways in which drama can be a powerful learning medium, consult the work of Jonothan Neelands (1984; 1990; 1992).

Assembly

Everyone loves assembly. No, not the early-morning gathering in the auditorium, but the human instinct to put things together, to make a finished product from bits and pieces.

Purposes	
Thinking	★★★★★
Emotional intelligence	★
Independence	★★★
Interdependence	★★★ (variable)
Multisensation	★★
Fun	★★
Articulation	★★★

Skills Used	
Individual work	★★★★
Group work	★★★ (variable)
Moving	★
Speaking	★★★ (variable)
Listening	★★★★ (variable)
Reading	★★★★ (variable)
Writing	
Looking	★★★★
Choice	

Specific Room Layout?	
Yes	(No)

How?

1. Students work on their own or in pairs to assemble logically coherent material that has been cut up into separate parts. Choose the material and the divisions carefully.

2. The simplest form of assembly is sequencing. There must be enough clues in each separate piece for it to be possible to connect the pieces in a logical sequence. The sequence could be provided by chronology (a timeline, for example); the correct order of steps in an experiment or technological process; the order of events in a story; the logic of a mathematical calculation; or the rationality of a cumulative argument. (See "Applications" for more ideas.)

3. The material to be assembled might be text, pictures, symbols, or a combination.

Applications

*   The big picture: "Assembly" is an excellent way to help students get their heads around the big picture of the curriculum. Rewrite the curriculum in students' language, retaining as much of the official terminology as possible. Cut it up into logical sections, being careful to separate elements that go together, for example, category headings and their subdivisions, quotations and their sources. Students, working in pairs, match and sequence the pieces of paper to resemble the original document as closely as possible. Once the original and the students' attempts have been compared and adjustments

made, ask each pair to mount the pieces on poster paper in a way that makes sense to them, using colored lines or yarn to make connections. This visual representation can then be displayed on the classroom wall or stored for easy reference.

- Foreign languages and ESL: Students sequence the jumbled text of a story or put together text and pictures—these activities force reading and comprehension. Another idea is to have students position cut-out items based on comprehension of a text or spoken description in the target language: For example, students could position furniture on a room plan, people in a scene, buildings on a street plan, or settlements on a map.
- Geometry: Students construct five equally sized squares from an apparent jumble of shapes.
- Physical education and health: Using stick-figure drawings, students place the precise movements of a warm-up or skill in the correct order before doing it.
- Industrial arts, home economics, and science: Students predict, or record, the steps of a process or experiment, the events in a chain reaction, or the sequence of atomic changes in a chemical reaction. Students select and position cut-out drawings of scientific apparatus for an experiment before trying it, various tools before attempting a project, or pattern pieces before sewing.
- Any subject: Students correctly insert labels that have been cut out from diagrams; show the connections between causes and effects by physically placing cards with keywords on them in relation to each other (to study wars, crises, and revolutions in history or fictional characters and their actions in a novel or play); show relationships using distance (the distance between the cards symbolizes the strength of the relationship between them—the farther apart, the weaker the relationship); or physically map out an action plan with main tasks, small steps, dates, and resources on separate cards.

Why Do It?

- Students practice key thinking skills such as sequencing, categorizing, selecting, and matching.
- The exercise feeds off natural human curiosity and the brain's desire to make connections, to see how things fit together.
- Many students benefit from the tactile nature of the exercise. They remain more motivated and focused when pushing pieces of paper around the desk than when staring at a blank page, pen in hand.

Variations

- Inject an element of competition—race against each other or the clock.
- Students could work in threes for some jobs. For complex tasks where there could be differences of opinion, use "Pairs to Fours" (page 112) to compare results and discuss a final solution.
- Give students an assembled piece in which there are mistakes and challenge students to find them. At a high level, there could be just one tiny mistake, forcing close attention to detail.

Back to Back

This is an easily applied and fun activity that promotes verbal skill, listening, observation, comprehension, and cooperation. What more could you want?

Purposes	
Thinking	★★★★★
Emotional intelligence	★★
Independence	★★
Interdependence	★★★★★
Multisensation	★★
Fun	★★★
Articulation	★★★★★

Skills Used	
Individual work	★★
Group work	★★★★
Moving	
Speaking	★★★★★
Listening	★★★★★
Reading	
Writing	
Looking	★★★★★
Choice	

Specific Room Layout?	
Yes	(No)

How?

1. Students sit in pairs back to back—the chair backs should touch so that the students are close enough to hear each other above the noise that will follow. They decide who is A and who is B.
2. A is given visual material, which he holds close to his chest (so that prying eyes around the room can't see it). B is given a piece of plain paper and a pencil.
3. A describes the visual to B, while B draws it, trying to make a perfect replica that is exact in size, shape, and detail, complete with labeling. No peeking! Describers are not allowed to draw in the air with their fingers.
4. This is a cooperative exercise. B may ask as many questions as she likes and A's job is to be as helpful as possible.
5. When the time is up, partners compare the original with the attempted copy.
6. Partners swap roles and try it again, using different material, with B describing and A drawing.

Applications

- Geography: Students describe and re-create diagrams of different types of volcanoes.
- Geometry and trigonometry: Students give and try to re-create precise details of angles, lengths of lines, and diameters.
- Science: Students describe and re-create scientific apparatus, circuit diagrams, sketches of equipment, or what one can see under a microscope.

- Foreign languages and ESL: Students use the language they are studying to describe and re-create a cross-section of a house showing the positions of different rooms, routes on a map, the items on different shelves of a refrigerator, furniture in a room, or descriptions of people.
- Designs in home economics and industrial arts: Use to draw attention to features of different designs—watch faces or quilt patterns, for example—prior to a design task.
- Any subject: This activity works with almost any visual material, such as photographs of landscapes, settlements, historical monuments, works of art, maps, fashion garments, religious buildings, flowcharts, maps, and plans.

Why Do It?

- Lasting learning occurs through the focused attention to detail and the struggle to use appropriate language.
- Listening and questioning skills are deliberately developed—these are two of the essential ingredients of effective independent learning.
- Visual and interpersonal intelligences are required. By removing the need to read and write, this exercise gives nonacademic-oriented students a chance of success and satisfaction. It is inclusive.
- Those with a strongly visual learning style are satisfied.
- It's an exercise in cooperation—each student depends on the other for success. This is an ideal opportunity to get students working in unusual combinations across typical friendship and gender boundaries.

Variations

- Try it with graph paper, inviting students to use coordinates in the desire for accuracy.
- Have students try it face to face rather than back to back, with papers hidden behind boards or books. In this case they benefit from eye contact but are not allowed to use gestures or trace shapes in the air. The describer should not be able to see the drawer's work during the process.
- After a while, stop the process and discuss with the class the technical terminology demanded by the exercise, for example, *apex, equilateral, isosceles.* Make a list on the board of terms and their meanings—this creates a word bank, which supports language learning and application. The students then get back to the activity and are expected to make greater use of the technical language. Wander around and make sure they do!
- Use the activity for three-dimensional modeling—for example, to re-create circuit boards, clay models, wire sculptures, and so forth.
- Use an overhead or data projector to present the image. One partner faces the screen, the other has her back to it.

Beat the Teacher

Go on, class, fulfill your fantasy!

Purposes	
Thinking	★★★★★
Emotional intelligence	★
Independence	★★
Interdependence	★★★ (variable)
Multisensation	★
Fun	★★★★
Articulation	★★

Skills Used	
Individual work	★★★
Group work	★★★
Moving	
Speaking	★
Listening	★★★★
Reading	
Writing	★
Looking	★★★★ (variable)
Choice	

Specific Room Layout?	
Yes	(No)

How?

1. Explain that you are going to describe a procedure, read a text, write a passage on the board, demonstrate a practical activity, explain a concept, work through a calculation, draw a diagram on the overhead projector, or whatever activity is relevant to a particular lesson. Tell students that you are likely to make some mistakes.
2. The students' job, working individually, is to spot and take note of the mistakes.
3. At the end of your presentation, students pair up, compare results, and come up with a joint list of mistakes.
4. Ask each pair to offer a mistake. Discuss to clarify the points.
5. To conclude, everyone writes up the corrections.

Applications

- Foreign languages and ESL: Read a passage in the target language, give dictation, or provide a listening test. Mistakes can include mispronunciation, incorrect syntax, mixed tenses, and so forth.
- Technical vocabulary: Students have to spot where you could have used a technical word but didn't in science, technology, art, math, geography, or physical education and health.
- Science: Conduct an experiment without sufficient attention to health and safety details.

- English, history, and drama: Play a role from a book, history, or play, speaking in character and making deliberate mistakes in fact or in characterization. (Could use in combination with "Hot Seating," on page 95—in other words, you respond to students' questions.)
- Any subject: This activity will work with any demonstrable process, complicated drawing or calculation, or substantive explanation or description.

Why Do It?

- All students are alert and thinking.
- The activity confirms understanding in students' minds as they automatically compare what they think they know with what they see and hear.
- The novelty value of students pitting their wits against the teacher is usually motivating.
- The process can create a softer relationship between class and teacher.

Variations

- Initially, students could work in pairs. Then, after your presentation, pairs join up to make groups of four. They discuss and decide on a definitive list.
- Students could use "Calling Cards" (page 70) or "Thumbometer" (page 137) to signal your mistakes during the presentation.
- Students could beat the teacher in a different sense by having to do something faster than you, for example, conduct an experiment, do a calculation, come up with a design, write a model answer, translate a passage, take notes on a passage. Students might work in pairs to give them an advantage.
- Reverse the process. Students in pairs could devise a presentation that contains deliberate mistakes. If you don't spot them all, they have beaten you.
- After an initial period of individual research, students could pair up and devise questions to take their knowledge further. They put these to you, and you score a point for each question you can answer off the top of your head. The pair gets a point for every answer you don't know.

Bingo

Call eyes down for a novel and light-hearted way to reinforce key concepts and vocabulary.

Purposes	🔧
Thinking	★★★★★
Emotional intelligence	
Independence	★★
Interdependence	★★★ (variable)
Multisensation	
Fun	★★★★
Articulation	★ (variable)

Skills Used	🖌
Individual work	★★★★
Group work	★★ (variable)
Moving	
Speaking	★
Listening	★★★★
Reading	★★
Writing	★★
Looking	★★★
Choice	★

Specific Room Layout?	🛶
Yes	(No)

How?

1. Before class, choose 12 key terms from the current topic and write the definitions on small cards. Put the cards in a bag to draw from, or keep them together as a pack.
2. During class, have everyone draw, quickly and freehand, a blank nine-square bingo grid.
3. On the board, write the 12 key terms.
4. Ask students to fill in their nine squares, putting their choice of 9 of the 12 key terms in any order, making a personalized bingo card. If they're wise, they'll choose the ones they know best.
5. Call "eyes down." Read out the definitions of the 12 terms, one at a time, in random order. Shuffle the pack or shake the bag so that everyone can see the order is random, as in real bingo.
6. Students cross off the terms on their cards if and when they match the definitions. When someone calls a line (horizontal, vertical, or diagonal), he reads back the key terms and their meanings.
7. Then proceed to a full house. Again, the winner (the first person to fill the entire card) reads back the terms and meanings. The rest of the class are asked to agree or disagree with the student's answers.

Applications

- To revise a topic just covered.
- To assess prior knowledge of a topic before it is tackled.
- As a novel way to give a test.
- An ideal end to a lesson that has introduced a number of technical terms.

Why Do It?

- It's engaging, it's novel, and it's painless.
- It tells you and the students a great deal about levels of understanding and retention. The diagnosis can then inform your choice of reinforcement and extension activities.
- It encourages students to realize that learning can be fun, as well as giving them a review technique to use at home.

Variations

- Try a 16-square grid with 25 terms.
- Students could work in mixed-performance pairs instead of individually.
- Instead of reading definitions, you could devise more demanding questions with answers that will fit on the bingo card.
- Use the grid to review spelling. Students learn 12 words, then choose the nine that they are most confident about and write them in the boxes—from memory. You then spell out the 12 words one at a time in random order. The students may only cross them off if they have spelled them correctly.

Calling Cards

Calling out is rude. In the polite social circles of your classroom, calling cards are much more civilized.

Purposes	
Thinking	★★★★★
Emotional intelligence	★
Independence	★★★★
Interdependence	
Multisensation	★
Fun	★★
Articulation	★★

Skills Used	
Individual work	★★★★★
Group work	
Moving	
Speaking	
Listening	★★★★
Reading	
Writing	
Looking	★★
Choice	

Specific Room Layout?	
Yes	No

How?

1. This simple idea allows students to signal a response by holding up, or placing on their desks, a card. Make cards for each student, using index cards with different colors or symbols on each card. For most purposes, it's useful for students to have three cards each: red, green, yellow, or checkmark, X, and question mark.
2. Distribute the cards to each student and explain how to use them. For example, students can use the cards to indicate responses to questions: "I know I know the answer" (checkmark or green), "I know I don't know" (X or red), or "I'm not sure whether I know" (question mark or yellow). Because everyone is required to show a card, this is more challenging and participatory than asking students to put their hands up.
3. The only rule is to be honest.

Applications

- The cards can be used to signal confusion: Students hold up the yellow or question mark card when they're beginning to lose the thread of what you're saying; hold up the red or X card when they've completely lost it. A good example is in a foreign language or English as a second language course, when you are giving instructions or explaining a concept in the target language, or when reading a comprehension piece. It is an excellent diagnostic tool, enabling you to fix students' problems precisely.

- They can be used to signal that a student wants to ask a question, wants clarification, or wants to make a statement—more grown up than putting a hand up. This is good for discussions and debates and is a more interactive way of listening to guest speakers.
- They can be used to spot check understanding—at any point, you can stop and ask for a show of cards: completely understand everything so far (green or checkmark); half understand (yellow or question mark); don't have a clue (red or X).
- Ideal for student council meetings, and even for department or staff meetings, as a quick way of gathering opinions and making decisions.

Why Do It?

- The technique encourages participation. The cards create the expectation that everyone will take an active part in proceedings. They beg to be used.
- *Everyone* having them levels out the playing field. The strategy has an inclusive feel to it, especially because it removes the barriers of speaking, reading, and writing.
- The cards suggest that it's OK not to understand everything, that we are here to learn, not just go through the motions of learning. They signal that learning involves confusion, misunderstanding, and mental struggle, that this is natural, and that we learn most efficiently if we are honest and up front about our state of mind.
- Above all, the cards demand that students think: They have to listen, absorb, synthesize, connect, and check. The device supports the natural process of pattern making, which is the route to internalized understanding.
- Consequently, the cards strengthen the idea of personal responsibility in learning.
- This is a democratic procedure and therefore contributes to citizenship education.

Variations

Have students use three different hand signals or three different facial expressions.

Center of the Universe

Create the center of the universe in the comfort of your own classroom.

How?

1. Clear the desks to the side and create a circle of chairs.
2. Provide a round cardboard bull's-eye or a rope circle, about two feet in diameter, on which students can stand. Place this in the center of the circle; it represents the center of the universe.
3. The first volunteer student stands at the center of the universe and makes a statement about the topic at hand. All the other students respond. The more they agree with the statement, the closer to the middle they stand. If they totally disagree, they remain seated. Those who agree completely with the statement stand shoulder to shoulder at the center of the universe. Then they all sit down.
4. Another student takes over, stands in the middle, and makes a fresh statement. The process continues with volunteer students taking turns to have their say.

Purposes	
Thinking	★★★★
Emotional intelligence	★★
Independence	★★★★
Interdependence	★
Multisensation	★★★
Fun	★★★
Articulation	★★

Skills Used	
Individual work	★★
Group work	★★★★
Moving	★★★
Speaking	★
Listening	★★★★
Reading	
Writing	
Looking	★★★
Choice	★★★

Specific Room Layout?	

Yes   No

Applications

- Review any topic. Students at the center state facts, or better still explain concepts or give judgments; for example, "Overall, Franklin Delano Roosevelt did more for the United States than any president before or after him because . . ."
- Explore prior knowledge at the beginning of a new topic: "What do we already know, or think we know, about . . . ?"

- Initiate a class discussion, for example, "Sole proprietorship is the most efficient type of business"; "We will never know the truth about how the world began"; or "The world's climate is changing because of global warming."
- Evaluate learning, for example, "How could we improve the experiment we just carried out?"; "Next time we do group work, what should we do differently?"
- Gather whole-class opinions quickly on sensitive issues such as bullying, or to make decisions about where to go for a class field trip; this is an ideal way for student council representatives to consult the class.

Why Do It?

- It maximizes participation—everyone is part of the process all the time.
- There's no hiding place; there are no passengers. Everyone is asked to think and respond. There's always the prospect that you will spot and challenge those who are just following the crowd.
- The physical aspect of the exercise is appealing to many students, and can come as a welcome relief to everyone.

Variations

- As students stand in response to a statement, you or other students could challenge them to justify their position. This keeps students from just going through the motions.
- The exercise could be used to start a formal debate.
- Quick sketches could be made or digital photographs taken to create a record of each statement.
- You could join in too, as a respondent or to make a statement of you own, especially if you feel that some crucial point has been overlooked.

Conversion

To maximize learning, convert your students to the idea that any material can be converted.

Purposes	
Thinking	★★★★★
Emotional intelligence	★
Independence	★★★★
Interdependence	
Multisensation	★
Fun	★
Articulation	★★★★

Skills Used	
Individual work	★★★★★
Group work	
Moving	
Speaking	
Listening	★
Reading	★★★★
Writing	★★★
Looking	★★
Choice	★

Specific Room Layout?	
Yes	(No)

How?

1. Ask students to convert material that is presented in one format into a different format. Typical examples:

   - Turn text into a Mind Map.
   - Turn text into a flow chart.
   - Turn text into a storyboard.
   - Turn text into a table.
   - Turn text into a keyword plan.
   - Turn text into overlapping circles.
   - Turn text into a graph.
   - Turn text into a bulleted list.
   - Turn text into a ranked numbered list.
   - Turn Mind Maps, flow charts, storyboards, tables, graphs, and bulleted lists into straight text.
   - Turn the teacher's explanation, or a videotape, into any of the above.

2. Other formats to convert material into include freeze frame or tableaux, drawings, models, arrangements of objects on the desk to represent component parts of an idea or process. Mix and match the combinations to suit the topic.

Applications

The applications are endless. For example:

- Foreign languages and ESL: Have students turn a story in the target language into a storyboard or vice versa.
- Physical education and health: Have students turn a complex movement or skill into a series of still images.
- Math: Have students turn a mathematical process or convention into a written description.
- History: Have students turn a narrative into a time line or description of cause and effect into a flowchart.
- English: Students could turn the theme of evil in *Macbeth* into a line graph, tracing the highs and lows of evil through each scene; turn relationships between characters into overlapping circles; or turn plot into a flow chart and character studies into Mind Maps.
- Geography: Students could turn climate graphs into a diary of the weather experienced by a resident throughout the year.
- Business studies: Students could turn a job description into a storyboard or advertisement.
- Science: Have students turn processes and reactions into working models using every-day items on the desktop.
- Home economics and industrial arts: Students could turn the your verbal instructions into a flowchart.

Why Do It?

- Material can be converted only if it is understood. This technique ensures that deep learning takes place.
- If students are struggling with the conversion, it reveals where their misconceptions and difficulties lie. In this sense, the exercise provides diagnostic assessment, and personal tutoring from you will be required.
- It equips students with a core independent learning and review skill. This will give them an advantage as they approach exams.
- The types of conversion suit different learning styles and intelligence profiles. The strategy encourages students to see that they can be successful with academic material whatever their style or profile, if only they adopt the right approach.

Variations

- Encourage students to take any material presented in lessons and convert it at home, even when you don't require it. This will deepen learning and make review much easier.
- Give students a choice of formats. Over time, demonstrate them all, teach them all, get the class to practice them all. Students will then be in a position to choose independently the ones that suit their strongest learning style or type of intelligence.
- Students could do conversions in pairs rather than on their own.

Corporate Identity

In this high-tech age of competition, here's a low-tech way of achieving cooperation.

Purposes	
Thinking	★★★
Emotional intelligence	★★
Independence	★★★
Interdependence	★★★★★
Multisensation	
Fun	★
Articulation	★★★

Skills Used	
Individual work	★★★★
Group work	★★★★
Moving	
Speaking	★★
Listening	★★
Reading	★★
Writing	★★
Looking	★
Choice	★

Specific Room Layout?	

(Yes)　　　　　No

How?

1. Organize the class into mixed-performance groups of, say, six. Select carefully so that each group comprises students with different levels of performance in your subject.
2. Within each group, members should sit so that they can all easily see and hear each other.
3. Work continues as normal, but members of the group are expected to support each other so that everyone understands all the material they are learning. The responsibility is shared. Those who are having difficulty with a particular instruction or concept are expected to ask for help from those who aren't. Those who do understand are expected to check that others also understand, and if not, to offer help. If everyone's stuck, they ask you.
4. Drop in on any member of the group at any time to question his knowledge and understanding of material that has been covered. If his answers are inaccurate or even half accurate, then *the group* has not fulfilled its duty. The whole group must stop work and explain the material to him.

5. This does not mean that everyone has to work at the same pace or even on the same material within the group. Faster workers can get ahead. The idea is to have groups large enough so that it's not always the same person being called on for help.

Applications

"Corporate Identity" works for any subject and is most effective when students are following a sustained piece of individual work—a series of structured worksheets, a booklet, or a project, for example.

Why Do It?

- Students often learn more efficiently from each other than from a teacher because they understand each other's confusion and use more relevant language and examples.
- It builds both personal responsibility and interdependence, and demonstrates a model of good citizenship and inclusion.
- It frees you to give substantial attention to those who need it most.

Variations

- The method is most successful when sustained for several lessons. This gives students a chance to get into the routine.
- Although it detracts from the cooperative nature of the exercise, you could award points to groups for members successfully passing your spontaneous "tests."

Dicey Business

Learning shouldn't be a lottery. Nor should it be dull and predictable. Just add a little spice with the dice.

Purposes	
Thinking	★★★★
Emotional intelligence	★★
Independence	★★
Interdependence	★
Multisensation	★
Fun	★★★★
Articulation	★★★

Skills Used	
Individual work	★★
Group work	★★★★
Moving	
Speaking	★★★
Listening	★★★★
Reading	★
Writing	
Looking	★
Choice	

Specific Room Layout?	
(Yes) No	

How?

1. Prepare a set of connected prompts or questions to which the students should respond, using index cards or something similar. Put them in logical order, lettered A, B, C, D, and so forth on the back, and make enough packs of the same cards so that each group of six gets one pack. Gather enough dice to give each group a die.

2. Each group of six sits at a table with its pack of cards in the middle, face down, with card A on top. The group also has a die. Each person has a number, one through six.

3. The group decides who goes first. The first player rolls the die, and the person with the number shown picks up the first card and responds to the prompt or question.

4. The second player throws the die. The person with the number shown picks up card B and responds, and so on around the circle as often as it takes to get through the cards. Because the prompts or questions are connected, and because no one knows whose number will be next, everyone has to pay full attention all the time.

Applications

- Foreign languages and ESL: Ideal for prompting a spoken story, sentence by sentence. Each card has a word or phrase that must be included in the next sentence. Or use pictures instead of words. At a higher level the prompts could indicate which tenses, parts of speech, or structures must be used.
- English: Ideal for prompting a piece of creative writing. Each card has an image or part of speech or new character that must be woven into a story or poem. The group's collective oral version models the idea for students' individual written efforts later.
- Home economics and industrial arts: Use to establish the design-and-make sequence—what has to be done at each stage of this new project?
- Science: Use to explain the elements, substances, reactions, and equations in a chemical process.
- Math: Use to explain steps in a complex calculation or to provide several examples of the same mathematical technique, such as calculating angles.
- History or political science: Students discuss an issue or argue a point from various angles. Each card has a different character or outlook—for example, a democrat, a republican, a human rights activist, a principal, and so forth.
- Any subject: Create a series of review questions on any topic in any subject.

Why Do It?

- As a piece of structured group work, it trains students in taking turns, listening, and collective responsibility.
- The randomizing effect of the die is fun and usually motivating.

Variations

- The pack of cards in the middle are unconnected questions. The game becomes a competition. When a person's number comes up, she picks up the next card and answers the question. The rest of the group decides whether the answer is right or wrong and, if necessary, you acts as arbiter. If the answer was correct, the player keeps the card, rolls the die, and the game continues. The player with the most cards at the end of the game wins. Great for assessing prior knowledge and for consolidating or reviewing a topic.
- If numbers don't allow groups of six, have smaller groups with void numbers on the die (for example, in a group of four, if number five or six comes up, everyone breathes a sigh of relief, and the player rolls again).
- Could be done as a whole-class activity, with everyone sitting in a circle and a pack of large cards in the middle. A die on a tray is passed around. When a student throws a six, she's next. For best results, the person who last threw the six should have to keep talking to the prompt or question until the next six is thrown.

Discussion Carousel

Try this device for getting everyone to take part in productive, if not circular, discussion.

Purposes	🔧
Thinking	★★★★
Emotional intelligence	★★
Independence	★★
Interdependence	★★★
Multisensation	★★
Fun	★★★
Articulation	★★★★

Skills Used	🥄
Individual work	★
Group work	★★★★
Moving	★★
Speaking	★★★★
Listening	★★★★★
Reading	
Writing	
Looking	
Choice	

Specific Room Layout?	✏️
(Yes) No	

How?

1. Move the desks and place chairs in two concentric circles, an outer and an inner circle, of equal numbers. The inner circle faces outward and the outer circle faces inward. In other words, everyone is facing a partner.
2. The facing pairs are given a prompt and have a conversation for, say, three minutes. They are asked to make sure that each has a chance to speak. Let them know when half the time is up.
3. When the whole time is up, the outer circle stands and moves to the left until you say stop. Students now sit down, facing a new random partner.
4. Before the new pair launches into conversation, developing the subject further, each has to summarize to the other her previous partner's contribution. Listening skills are crucial.
5. Once again, when time is up, the outer circle "spins," and new pairs are formed. Students have to summarize both their first and second partners' contributions before conducting their third conversation.
6. This may be repeated as many times as is useful.

Applications

- Useful for any type of discussion. The discussion could be very academic: an exam question; formulating a precise definition of a technical term or phenomenon; constructing a model paragraph answer to a reading comprehension question; or planning a method to test a hypothesis.
- Use it to review a topic or to find out what people already know before beginning a new topic.
- Use it to evaluate products (in technology, for example), or to evaluate the learning process itself.
- It is a way of broadening the mind whenever matters of opinion are to be discussed (in English, political science, health, and history, for example). It prepares students for argumentative writing.
- Use it to help students formulate their own opinions with a degree of privacy. It helps them gain confidence before taking part in an open whole-class discussion or formal debate.
- It can be used to air class opinion about a matter of common concern, such as what to do about bullying.
- "Discussion Carousel" can be conducted in a foreign language.

Why Do It?

- The activity creates maximum participation—half the class is talking at any one moment.
- It enables each student to hear a range of opinions quickly.
- Students practice listening skills.
- The process encourages empathy.
- It gets students used to working with others at random, which is likely to make group work easier in the future.
- It deepens individual students' thinking by making them test it on others.

Variations

- If the students are nervous and have poorly developed listening skills, you could allow them to take notes on what their partners say. This is a stage for them to grow out of quite quickly, though.
- To give everyone a chance to move, at changeover times, have both circles spinning, but in opposite directions.
- If it's not possible or desirable to move the furniture, have shuffling lines or slinking snakes around the classroom. The principal intention is to randomize pairings.

Distillation

Now this is how you create a good spirit in the classroom. At least you get the pure meaning across.

Purposes	
Thinking	★★★★
Emotional intelligence	
Independence	★★★★
Interdependence	★★
Multisensation	
Fun	★
Articulation	★★★

Skills Used	
Individual work	★★
Group work	★★★
Moving	★
Speaking	★★★
Listening	★★★
Reading	★★★★
Writing	★★★
Looking	★★
Choice	★

Specific Room Layout?	
Yes	No

How?

1. To completely mix scientific metaphors, distill the essential meaning of a text by using a filtration process. Begin by drawing a large filter funnel and beaker on the board.

2. Students work on a given text in pairs. Challenge them to find the five (or ten, or whatever number is appropriate, given the length and density of the text) most important words. Some discussion of what is meant by "most important" might be needed.

3. As soon as a pair is ready, one of the two comes to the board and writes their proposed five words in the filter funnel.

4. Other pairs follow and may add only words that are not already in the funnel.

5. As soon as every pair has contributed, lead a debate with the class about which five (or ten, or whatever) words to let through the filter funnel into the beaker. These should be *the* essential words that capture or trigger the meaning of the whole passage.

6. The agreed-on filtered words become the basis for notes, which everyone then writes individually.

Applications

- Any subject: In any technical text—in science, technology, business studies, geography—the filtered words are likely to be technical terms. This activity will work with any factual resource (in sociology, political science, health, and so forth) in which selected words capture key pieces of information.

- English: The criteria for "most important" words might change: for example, the five adjectives that are key to the author's description of the scene or character; the words most typical of this author's style; or the most persuasive, evocative, loaded, unexpected words in the passage. This activity is also useful to reduce a narrative to its key plot points.
- History: Have students reduce a historical narrative to its key moments in chronological order.
- Drama: Have students reduce dialogue to keywords to help actors memorize their lines.
- Foreign languages and ESL: Use with a text that has to be thoroughly understood for the keywords to be identified.

Why Do It?

- Distillation is the basis of all good notetaking. This exercise helps students gain the confidence to separate important from peripheral material.
- It demonstrates that time invested in selecting keywords is repaid in reducing the volume of written material and in aiding memorization.
- By showing how key pieces of information can be recorded quickly and lightly, this process encourages students to use a number of resources rather than get bogged down in one.
- In all these ways it supports the skills of independent research, which are crucial to coursework and individual assignments.

Variations

- Instead of writing words on the board, students could write them on cards and pin them to a bulletin board. Then you, or students, can physically move words around during the debate and final filtration.
- Reverse the image. Instead of a filter funnel, draw a cauldron. All the words are thrown in; then as the heat is turned up, words evaporate, eventually leaving a residue of essential items.
- Instead of distilling or boiling images, allow students a number of inches. They underline words and phrases in the text up to the maximum length total.
- Instead of the most important words from the text, students could choose words that summarize the meaning of the text from their own extensive vocabularies.
- The notes that students consequently make could be in various formats. Ask students to experiment with bulleted lists, keyword plans, Mind Maps, webs, flowcharts, and so forth.
- As exams approach, encourage students to take notes on their notes. Use "Distillation" to reduce existing notes so that final review is done with minimum materials. Show them how to use keywords as memory prompts.
- Use exactly the same process with videotapes, DVDs, audiocassettes, or your exposition instead of text and watch how quickly students sharpen their listening skills.

Dominoes

No matter what your learning or teaching style, there's always room for some serious fun.

Purposes	
Thinking	★★★★
Emotional intelligence	★
Independence	★
Interdependence	★★
Multisensation	★
Fun	★★★
Articulation	★

Skills Used	
Individual work	★★
Group work	★★★
Moving	
Speaking	★★★
Listening	★★★★
Reading	★★
Writing	
Looking	★
Choice	

Specific Room Layout?	
Yes	(No)

How?

1. Prepare a set of large index cards, each divided in half by a line, like a domino tile. On one half of each card is a question, on the other half an answer. The question and answer on any card do not match.

2. Shuffle the cards and give them out, one per person.

3. Anyone can begin by reading his question aloud. Someone in the room has the answer—she reads it aloud and everyone else has to indicate whether they think it is right or wrong by sticking their thumbs up or down. If no one offers an answer, ask for those who think they might have the right answer to respond; consequently, several people offer answers and the class debates which one is correct.

4. Whoever had the right answer asks the question on his card, and so on. When students have "played" their domino cards, they remain involved by judging whether other people's answers are right or wrong.

Applications

- Ideal for review of a topic just covered.
- It can be used at the start of a topic to find out what students already know.
- It can be used partway through a topic to consolidate basic ideas and diagnostically assess the learning so far.

Why Do It?

- It's novel and fun; therefore, students are more likely to remember the material.
- It requires students to think: to recall, predict, calculate, guess, and so on.
- The exercise requires everyone to be involved. It helps shy students to contribute publicly.
- At a more advanced level, questions can have particular angles and answers can have subtle differences, reinforcing the need to read the question properly and answer the question precisely. This is essential exam technique.

Variations

- To maximize participation, give everyone two or three cards each.
- Instead of making the cards yourself, have students work in groups to produce a set of dominoes. Different sets are used with the class at different times to review the same topic. This reinforces the idea that material has to be revisited time and time again if it is to stick.
- Allow students to look for the answers in their notes or in textbooks—use it to stimulate research and, again, to underline the idea of having to go back over work if it is to stick.
- "Dominoes" can be played in small groups rather than with the whole class. If groups have produced their own cards, they swap sets with each other.
- You could use pictorial questions and answers; for example, naming parts of apparatus, labeling diagrams, identifying the correct equipment to use for a particular purpose, choosing between right and wrong movements or procedures, connecting adverbs or adjectives with drawings (in foreign language or ESL classes, for instance).
- If students are at an advanced level, you could make the questions and answers less obvious. Use subtle nuances, angles, and details to test the students' ability to distinguish among the finer points of the material.

Double Take

Good news for the busy teacher: You can be in two places at once! Double your presence, double your impact, double your time—without increasing your stress.

Purposes	
Thinking	★★★
Emotional intelligence	★
Independence	★★★★★
Interdependence	★
Multisensation	★★ (variable)
Fun	
Articulation	

Skills Used	
Individual work	★★★★★
Group work	
Moving	★
Speaking	
Listening	★★★★
Reading	★★★
Writing	
Looking	★★ (variable)
Choice	★★★

Specific Room Layout?	
Yes	(No)

How?

1. Record key teaching points on audiocassettes, on videotapes, as computer slide shows, or as MP3, MIDI, or WAV files. If possible, post them on the school's intranet or website.

2. During normal classroom activity, students who need an exposition or explanation again don't have to bother the busy teacher—they can get access to the independent resource. It's like having two teachers in the room.

3. Students may need training to use the hardware and may take some time to develop the habits of independent learning.

4. If you use videos or computer slide show software, have the TV or monitor facing into a corner of the room so that other students are not distracted. Play audiocassettes on personal stereos or at listening centers with multiple headphones. Students can listen to mp3 or wav files through personal headphones attached to a PC or through portable Mp3 players.

Applications

- Art: Try a computer slide show presentation on an artist, such as Roy Lichtenstein and his work. Or prepare three five-minute video programs with your demonstrations and commentary on mixing watercolor paint; applying paint to paper; creating three-dimensional effects; and so forth.
- Math: Explain concepts and demonstrate procedures.
- Business studies: Define briefly different types of business, various business concepts, procedures, and roles each on an audiocassette. Number them and catalog them on a shelf.
- Foreign languages and ESL: Introduce and model new language structures and vocabulary on video—more or less the same as the live performance done with the class at the beginning of the topic.
- Home economics and industrial arts: Use to cover the safe use of equipment and standard measuring, cutting, forming, joining, and finishing techniques.
- Science: Use for demonstrations and instructions for conducting an experiment.
- Any subject: Use to cover any key concepts and facts.

Why Do It?

- Students often have to wait some time for the teacher's attention. This is frustrating for students and teacher alike. "Double Take" means more students get more help more often.
- It facilitates differentiation—those who need more support can get it. No one is held back by "slower learners."
- It promotes the attitudes and skills of independent learning—vital for students' future success.

Variations

- Students could make the resources themselves as a legitimate part of their learning process. These can be reproduced, stored, and used with future generations.
- Resources could be placed in the school library or learning center with added benefits: less distraction in the classroom and building the habit of using the central resources.
- If high-tech resources are not available, make low-tech versions: help sheets. These are large (at least 11 x 17) sheets of paper with information, techniques, explanations, instructions, and procedures in written and visual forms. Stored in a large folder, help sheets can be consulted by students whenever they get the urge.

Dreadlines

Just about everyone dreads deadlines. They create pressure, instill panic, and usually have terrible consequences attached. But they're good for us.

Purposes	
Thinking	★★
Emotional intelligence	★★★
Independence	★★★★★
Interdependence	
Multisensation	
Fun	
Articulation	

Skills Used	
Individual work	★★★★★
Group work	
Moving	
Speaking	★
Listening	★
Reading	
Writing	
Looking	
Choice	★★ (variable)

Specific Room Layout?	
Yes	(No)

How?

1. This is the simplest way to increase the pace of learning: Set challenging, just-achievable deadlines. Make sure there's a clock in the room!

2. Equip yourself with a list of students' names on a clipboard. Move around the class looking at students' work and talking with them about progress. As you move from student to student, agree with each of them on a deadline by which the next stage of the task will be completed. Explain that you will return at that time. You make a note of the deadline on your list, and the student makes a note in the margin of her notebook.

3. Sometimes it will be important to allow students to decide the deadline, perhaps because you want them to learn about time and task management, or because they are self-motivated and can be trusted. Sometimes you might need to impose a deadline to increase a student's sense of urgency, while at other times a negotiated deadline will be best. Remain flexible in your approach.

4. Return to each student at the stated time. If you're not there when you said you would be, they'll think you don't mean business. Look at what they've done and offer congratulations, challenge, support, or rebuke as appropriate. Then set a new deadline for the next stage of learning.

5. Time frames for deadlines will vary. Some students will need short steps and frequent visits, perhaps because they are not self-motivated, because they are struggling with this particular material, or because they have a strongly Concrete Sequential learning style. Others will need to see you less often.

6. To begin with, go to those students who are likely to need the most help or most prodding. Deal with them first. Once they are under way with the task, visit the students who are more self-sufficient.

Applications

- Any subject: Use this technique when students are working individually, for example, on worksheets, workbooks, extended research tasks, or extended writing assignments.
- Math: Use with students who are working through examples and exercises.
- English: Use for silent reading, to speed up the time it takes to get through text.
- Home economics, industrial arts, science, and art: Use for the steps of any hands-on work, as well as individual work on computers.
- Physical education: Use when students are practicing individual skills.

Why Do It?

- It keeps up the pace of tedious work.
- It provides external motivation for those who don't have much internal.
- It generally demonstrates to students that they are more capable than they thought. They can often work faster and learn faster than they normally do. It communicates high expectations, which strengthen self-belief, which in turn translates into improved performance.
- It allows for different learning styles. Those with Concrete Sequential or pragmatist tendencies can have short step-by-step instructions; those who are more abstract or activist can work for longer stretches without interference.

Variations

- The same procedures apply to paired or small group work as to individual work.
- You could set deadlines not for a certain amount of work to be done, but for certain learning points to be mastered. For example, "At 2:35 p.m., I'd like you to explain to me/show me how you /describe /be able to . . . ."
- Instead of setting deadlines for individual students, try setting them for the whole class. Write or draw the lesson sequence on the board, with clear steps to be completed by certain times . . . or else!
- Use "Dreadlines" to speed up reading time. Challenge individuals to read the information sheet, or section of the textbook, or a chapter in two-thirds of the time it would usually take. Test them on it afterward to prove that they can do it quickly and remember what they read. Challenge the whole class to halve their normal reading time. Teach them speed-reading techniques. Encourage them to skim and scan rather than decode every word. This usually boosts confidence and shows that reading doesn't have to be time consuming and laborious.

Guess Who

Even the most basic detective work requires interrogation skills, lateral thinking, wit, perseverance, and speed of thought. No wonder this simple strategy has universal appeal.

Purposes	
Thinking	★★★★★
Emotional intelligence	★
Independence	★★
Interdependence	★★★★
Multisensation	★ (variable)
Fun	★★★
Articulation	★★★★

Skills Used	
Individual work	★
Group work	★★★★
Moving	★★★★★ (variable)
Speaking	★★★
Listening	★★★★
Reading	★
Writing	
Looking	★ (variable)
Choice	★

Specific Room Layout?	
Yes No	

How?

1. Create a pack of cards for each group of four students. The cards should depict items that should have been learned, for example, people or events (in history), equipment (science apparatus), places (in geography), processes (in home economics and industrial arts), definitions (any subject)—using pictures and/or words.

2. In groups of four, students sit so that group members can easily see and hear each other. Give each group a pack of cards, shuffled and placed face down in the middle of the table.

3. Group members agree to take turns, or to have numbers and use a die to determine who goes next. The player whose turn it is picks the top card and looks at it, taking care not to let anyone else see.

4. The rest of the group asks questions. The player holding the card may answer only yes or no. You may wish to limit the number of questions or the time.

5. Once the item has been successfully identified by the group, the turn passes to the next player.

Applications

- Perfect for review in any subject. For example: characters in novels and events in plays in English; technical terms in business studies, physical education and health, geography, home economics, and industrial arts; elements, compounds, and mixtures in science; techniques in physical education; or random numbers in math.
- Conduct the entire exercise in a foreign language.

Why Do It?

- This is a classic lateral- and deductive-thinking exercise.
- It provides training in group work: taking turns, listening, and thinking before speaking.
- Students practice the art of asking the right questions, a vital ingredient in independent learning.
- Students will remember items because they have figured them out in their heads.

Variations

Two major variations:

1. Try it as a whole-class exercise. For example, studying famous designers in art and design or home economics:

   - Affix to the board pictures of items designed by, and items that inspired, various designers.
   - A volunteer sits at the front of the class and is given a prompt card, which supplies the designer's name, dates of birth and death, nationality, what he is famous for designing, and what inspired the design.
   - The class has to find out this information by using the visual clues and asking questions, to which the volunteer may answer only yes or no.
   - Limit either the number of questions or the amount of time.
   - After the first designer has been identified, a new volunteer continues the process with a different designer.

2. Try the party game version.

   - Each member of the class wears a sticker on her back or forehead giving the name of the person or object to be identified; the wearer doesn't know what it says.
   - Class members mill around asking questions of each other, each student trying to find out what her own sticker says.
   - Answers may be only yes, no, or I don't know.
   - Only one question may be asked of each student.
   - The goal is for students to figure out their own stickers before they run out of people to ask.
   - Once a student guesses who, or what, is on the sticker, she stays in the game, continuing to answer other people's questions.

Hierarchies

Nonfiction text is usually made up of hierarchies. Students who spot them and use them will soon rise to the top.

Purposes	🔧
Thinking	★★★★★
Emotional intelligence	
Independence	★★★★
Interdependence	
Multisensation	
Fun	★
Articulation	★★★★

Skills Used	🖌
Individual work	★★★★★
Group work	
Moving	
Speaking	
Listening	★
Reading	★★★★
Writing	★★★
Looking	★
Choice	

Specific Room Layout?	✏
Yes	(No)

How?

1. Each student draws a page-sized pyramid.

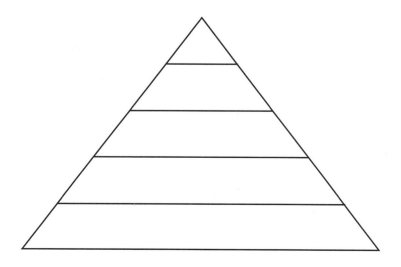

2. Explain that most nonfiction text is made up of hierarchies of information and that finding the hierarchies provides the structure for good notes. Show how newspapers make hierarchies explicit through the use of headlines, bold paragraphs, subheadings, and different type sizes. Well-written textbooks present information in a similar way. But not all texts are so helpful, and it's up to students to detect the status of information in order to separate major from minor points.

3. Give out a nonfiction text appropriate to the topic at hand and to the reading levels of the students. While students learn the "Hierarchies" technique, the vocabulary and syntax should not be too difficult.

4. Ask students to find the big idea in the text: the headline. They write this in the apex of the pyramid.

5. Students then figure out the next level of information—the main points—and note them in the next layer down.

6. Finally, students write the details within the base levels of the pyramid. The shape encourages students to recognize that there is usually one big idea, two or three main points, and lots of detail.

7. Ask students to memorize the material by covering up different layers, attempting to recall what they contain, then looking to check. In time, they should be able to work just from the higher layers, which prompt the recall of detail.

Applications

- Use with almost any nonfiction material.
- With fiction, use "Hierarchies" for character studies, interpretations, critiques, and summaries.

Why Do It?

- Passive reading is inefficient—the brain takes little in. For text to be understood, the material needs to be attacked with an active and purposeful mind. Deep learning occurs through understanding, not by rote. Exercises such as this force understanding.
- The brain's neocortex is designed to figure things out for itself, so this exercise goes with the grain of the brain. Although taxing, the exercise should feel natural, especially if presented as a mystery to be understood or a challenge to be met.
- Much independent learning rests on the student's ability to deconstruct text and make useful, efficient notes. This exercise, if done often enough in different guises, helps to break the habit of copying or condensing text and to establish the habit of discernment in notetaking.
- Exam success depends on effective review. Material has to be visited and revisited several times. This is much less daunting if notes are already in handy, review-friendly formats.
- "Hierarchies" provides a way of focusing attention and sharpening the challenge in what might otherwise be flat tasks.

Variations

- Experiment with different shapes. For example, target notes:

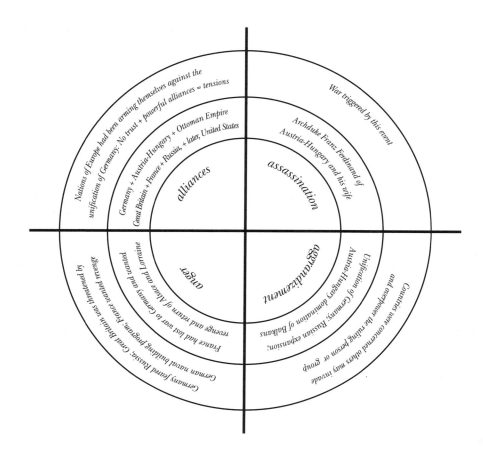

Take the causes of World War One, for example. There are generally thought to be four causes: alliances, assassination, aggrandizement, and anger. Each of these four headline words goes in a quarter of the bull's-eye. In the next layer out go key points: Alliances were between Germany and Austria-Hungary, later joined by the Ottoman Empire; on the other side, Great Britain, France, and Russia, later joined by the United States. In the outer layer go the details of how these alliances contributed to the heightening of tension. For other topics, adjust the number of sectors as appropriate.

- Instead of (or even as well as) shapes, use different colors for different levels of information.
- Instead of using text, ask students to figure out the hierarchies of information within an audiocassette, a videotape, an exposition by you, a presentation by their peers, or even a diagram in a book.
- This is an ideal listening exercise in foreign language and ESL classes.

Hot Seating

A nondidactic way for you to give information to the class, without giving up the spotlight!

Purposes	
Thinking	★★★★
Emotional intelligence	★★
Independence	★★★★
Interdependence	★★
Multisensation	★★
Fun	★★
Articulation	★★★
Skills Used	
Individual work	★★★
Group work	★★★ (variable)
Moving	
Speaking	★★★
Listening	★★★★★
Reading	
Writing	★★★ (variable)
Looking	★★★
Choice	★★
Specific Room Layout?	
Yes	(No)

How?

Best done with the desks cleared and the class sitting in a horseshoe around a chair (the hot seat), but can be done with a conventional classroom layout.

1. Decide on a character relevant to the topic at hand to portray for the class, such as a historical figure or a character from a novel. A small piece of a costume, such as a scarf, hat, or bag, helps everyone to tell when you are in and out of the role.

2. Announce that you will play a character and will answer the class's questions. Explain the reason for portraying the character: "I'll be Chaucer so that we can understand more about *Canterbury Tales* and its background."

3. Give the students time to understand the precise learning objectives—write them up for all to see: "For the exam, you need to know about Chaucer's background, when he wrote *Canterbury Tales,* why he wrote it, the social and political conditions in which it was written, and the language used." If you feel it's necessary, give the students time to frame a few quick questions so that the process gets off to a good start. Then spontaneity should take over.

4. Establish ground rules: no comments of any kind on either the students' questions or your answers, except by asking another question.

5. Sit on the hot seat (in the mouth of the horseshoe or in front of the class), or wander around theatrically, and answer the questions in character, providing answers that, at best, invite further questions. If you ham up the role too much, though, silliness can creep in and the power of the experience is lost.

6. It is crucial that you stay in character, behaving and answering consistently. If belief in the character is broken, the strategy will quickly fall apart. Therefore, if you wish to speak to the class *as the teacher* (to deal with discipline, for instance), then you should get off the hot seat and remove the symbolic costuming to signal the change. You can always go back into character after resolving the issue.

Applications

- Math: Be a ship's captain (to study coordinates), Pythagoras, or an accountant.
- Science: Be Marie Curie, Louis Pasteur, a physical therapist, a nuclear physicist, Albert Einstein, Thomas Edison, or a product designer.
- Art: Be Vincent van Gogh, Pablo Picasso, Claes Oldenburg, Piet Mondrian, an art critic, an art dealer, or an art teacher.
- Business studies: Be Bill Gates, Ben Cohen or Jerry Greenfield of Ben and Jerry's Ice Cream, or play different roles within an organization.
- English: Be a character in a play, novel, or poem; an author; or a book or theater critic.
- Geography: Be a migrant worker; a founding member of Greenpeace; a politician facing a potential natural disaster; a relief worker; a chair of the local city planning committee.
- Foreign languages and ESL: Students can prepare questions beforehand and record answers to translate later.
- History: Be any historical character, a fictional observer, or messenger characters who are reporting and interpreting events.
- Home economics and industrial arts: Be a famous fashion designer, chef, engineer, or an expert in a particular process, such as a consultant or technician.

Why Do It?

- Once under way, the process can be quite gripping, even moving.
- It gives everyone access to information, irrespective of reading ability.
- The exercise particularly suits learners with an Abstract Random, or reflective, learning style, but because of its soap opera feel, it actually appeals to most students.
- As the students determine what questions to formulate based on information they receive, they are practicing the management of their own learning in general, and the framing of good questions in particular.
- The information is usually well remembered because of the dramatic and relatively unusual (seeing the teacher acting) nature of the experience.

Variations

- Students could undertake research and prepare more sophisticated questions beforehand.
- Students could write up the answers afterward as a set of notes or a report. In order to record adequate information as they go along, students operate in pairs: one asking the questions, the other taking the notes. Periodically they switch. Alternatively, you can ban all notetaking and force the students to rely on their memories—this tends to sharpen those listening skills!

- Students could be assigned research tasks as a result of the *first* hot seat interview and be asked to bring the results to a *second* interview, when more detailed and complex questions are expected.
- Individual students could take the hot seat, especially after a period of research (done as homework, perhaps).
- Group hot seat: Students could work in small groups to prepare the character. The group puts forward one student as the spokesperson, with the others sitting behind as alter egos or brain cells ready to be consulted on what to say.
- Try hot seating objects instead of human characters—especially effective for science (an atom in a chemical reaction) or geography (a water droplet in the water cycle).
- Instead of genuine hot seating in which the questions are one way, try "In Conversation with. . . ." The subject (played by you or a knowledgeable student) could be "A Bunsen Burner" or "Mona Lisa" for example. The conversation is two way. The subject can invite questions from particular students, raise issues and ask for comments, or ask open-ended questions.

Inspiration

Prepare for take-off. Get your students going with a blast from the past.

Purposes	
Thinking	★★★★
Emotional intelligence	★★★
Independence	★★★★★
Interdependence	★
Multisensation	★
Fun	★
Articulation	★★

Skills Used	
Individual work	★★★
Group work	★
Moving	
Speaking	★★
Listening	★★★★
Reading	★
Writing	★
Looking	★★★★
Choice	★

Specific Room Layout?	
Yes	(No)

How?

1. Before tackling a new piece of learning, ask students to get excited about the outcomes they aim to achieve.

2. Ask the class to see, or hear, what previous students have done as a result of this learning. It is important to make this as concrete as possible. Show some of the best examples of other students' achievements. If possible, show the work of older students and explain that the goal is to do better than these, even though your students are younger. (See the examples in the applications section below.) Naturally, it is important to make sure that these pieces of work and demonstrations are not impossibly out of reach for your students.

3. Spend some time discussing these examples. What were the key features? With the class, turn these into a learning agenda.

4. While the learning is being carried out, ask students to return to the exemplars from time to time for further inspiration. This process keeps students' sights high and encourages them to check their progress, to congratulate themselves, and to set mini-targets for immediate action.

5. When the learning is over and it is time to demonstrate the new knowledge and skills, ask the students to compare their achievements to the originals.

Applications

- Foreign languages and ESL: Make an audio recording of older students holding the conversation that these younger students will soon be capable of themselves, or have a couple of older students come into class and perform a short role-play.
- Art: Show older students' pieces of work and keep them displayed for the duration of the project.
- Home economics and industrial arts: Hold an exhibition of previously finished products.
- Physical education, dance, and drama: Get older students to put on a performance, or show a performance on video.
- English: Read aloud the work of other students and ask the class to deconstruct it.
- History and geography: Pass around examples of students' projects, essays, or completed test papers.
- Math: Let the class watch an older student perform a calculation on the board.
- Science: Interview an older student in front of the class about the topic at hand.

Why Do It?

- Most students enjoy rising to a challenge. If you suggest that they might be able to do better than so-and-so, they will make sure they do. The approach is motivating.
- "Inspiration" creates high self-expectation, which focuses attention and drives perseverance. Consequently, students often perform better than they previously thought they could, which in turn has a positive effect on self-esteem.
- This approach creates self-sufficiency. There is an external source of authority, a yardstick other than the teacher, against which progress can be measured. The exemplar material replaces the teacher as the standard-bearer and helps to wean students off dependency on the teacher.
- It also creates self-direction. Rather than the teacher having perpetually to give feedback, to tell students what to do next, the exemplar material provides the direction and the destination. Self-sufficiency and self-direction are fundamental components of learning to learn.

Variations

- With older classes, instead of relying on previous students' achievements, put yourself on the line. Demonstrate to the class yourself what "quality" is like: Do a demonstration or show "something you made earlier." This introduces an element of "beat the teacher" and adds a bit more spice to the challenge.
- Get students to envision their own outcomes, rather than depend on other people's models. Encourage them to consider what they would love to be able to achieve. What do they see themselves doing? What does the achievement look like or sound like? Ask students to visualize their success, then draw it, describe it to someone, or write it down. Encourage them to return to their personal visions whenever they start to lose heart.
- Use "Inspiration" to help students improve grades on tests. Ask students to envisage being more successful than they have ever been before on formal assessments. What will their grade be? What will it feel like? What will they be able to do as a result of such achievement?

Mantle of the Expert

Everybody likes to show off once in a while. This is a golden opportunity for students to show what they know.

Purposes	
Thinking	★★★★
Emotional intelligence	★★
Independence	★★★★ (expert)
Interdependence	★★ (audience)
Multisensation	
Fun	★★
Articulation	★★★ (expert)

Skills Used	
Individual work	★★★★★ (expert)
Group work	★★ (audience)
Moving	
Speaking	★★★★ (expert)
Listening	★★★★ (audience)
Reading	
Writing	
Looking	★★ (audience)
Choice	★★★

Specific Room Layout?	
Yes	(No)

How?

1. Bring into class a shawl or scarf for a student to wear as a mantle. With younger students, you can ham this up by using a wizard's cloak, for instance, to imply that the expert has magical powers.

2. Explain that students will be tackling a new topic. Give the learning objectives, offer an outline of the content, and connect to the bigger picture of the unit (good practice at the start of any new topic, of course).

3. Ask students to jot down what they already know, or can do, regarding *any* aspects of the topic, and ask them to exchange these details in pairs.

4. Ask for a volunteer to come out to the front, wear the mantle of the expert, and tell the class what she knows or can do.

5. The class can ask questions, and the expert has the right to say "pass" if she's not sure of the answer. You can add comments.

6. Then another volunteer is sought—"Who can add to what Sharon has just told us?"—and the process continues.

Application

At the start of any topic.

Why Do It?

- It provides a student-centered starting point. It enables you to plan (or adjust your plans) based on what students know, rather than move ahead with the idea of covering the curriculum or getting through the book regardless.
- It hooks students. It says, "This learning is going to be relevant to you."
- Students who don't know much at the beginning will already have learned a lot from the experts' descriptions or demonstrations—it tends to have an equalizing effect.

Variations

- Use it to assess learning at the end of a lesson or topic (see also "Spotlight," on page 133).
- As experts show and tell what they know to the class, note key points to come back to—inaccurate information, half-explained ideas, misconceptions, missing pieces, and so forth. Tackle these right away so that students don't form the wrong impression, or use them to revise your teaching plan for the next few lessons.
- Don't limit "Mantle of the Expert" to knowledge: What about skills? Invite students to demonstrate a technique in physical education, a procedure in science, how to draw an arithmetic graph in math, a movement in dance, a convention in drama, or the procedure for an experiment in science. You can even prepare a couple of students by giving them warning and coaching the lesson before.

Masterminds

Masterminds do it together! Why not try a little collaborative research to spice up everyone's learning life?

Purposes	
Thinking	★★★★
Emotional intelligence	★
Independence	★★★★
Interdependence	★★★★
Multisensation	★
Fun	★★★
Articulation	★★

Skills Used		
Individual work	★★	
Group work	★★★★	
Moving		
Speaking	★★★	
Listening	★★★	
Reading	★★★★	
Writing	★★	
Looking	★★	(variable)
Choice	★★	

Specific Room Layout?	
Yes	No

How?

1. Discuss with the class the next topic to be tackled, dividing it up with them into manageable and, as much as possible, equal chunks.

2. Ask class members to organize themselves into small research groups. Some of the options for different types of groupings can be found under "Groups Galore" (page 172). You might suggest that *mixed skill* is likely to be the most appropriate type of grouping for "Masterminds." You will also need a student volunteer to be the timekeeper.

3. Each research group takes a different aspect of the topic and is expected to research it thoroughly by a common deadline. They may use resources both in and out of the classroom. You will be available to advise on information sources and research methods. Ask each group to ensure that every member fully understands the material. As they research, prepare questions that reflect the standards of whatever official assessment the students are facing, such as a standardized state test. Write the questions down.

4. At the appointed time, groups enter the "Masterminds" competition as experts in their field of research.

Rules

1. The contestants have to answer as many questions as they can within a specified time (say, two minutes). They get one point for every correct answer.

2. The question master (you) has all the questions written out in advance so that they can be asked in quick succession. As soon as an answer is given by the contestants, say whether it is right or wrong. If it is wrong, give the correct answer. Either way, move on to the next question quickly, trying to get in as many questions as possible before time is up.

3. The timekeeper strikes a gong (or makes any other kind of sound) when the time is up. If a question is under way when time is called, it has to be finished.
4. The team's score is the number of questions team members have answered correctly. Then the next team takes the stage.

Applications

- Any subject: Use with any age as long as resources can be found for the learning at hand.
- Foreign languages and ESL: Have students research different verb patterns, different parts of speech, or the basic vocabulary for various topics (using audio or video as well as print resources).

Why Do It?

- This strategy demands a variety of study skills: finding, selecting, and recording information, as well as speed reading if tight deadlines are set for the research.
- A range of social skills is required for successful teamwork and, if outside resources are used, for working with adults outside of school. Such skills are acquired only by practice, through exercises like this.

Variations

- Groups could put forward just one person to be their entrant; the others just applaud and cheer wildly.
- Instead of being allowed to confer, students must answer questions in turn, individually. This will sharpen the group's resolve to ensure that every member understands all the material beforehand.
- Groups could devise the "Mastermind" questions for other groups. This way they have to research two topics.
- Give very structured research sheets as opposed to open-ended research instructions, cutting down the degree of independence. This is important when students are just learning the skills of resource-based learning.
- Have students work in groups with others at a similar level of performance, and vary the degree of structure and help given—in other words, differentiation.
- Rather than being used to start a new topic, "Masterminds" is an excellent review strategy using textbooks and students' notes as resources. A limited amount of time can be given for preparation for the competition—say, 20 minutes—or make the preparation homework.
- After the game, the research could be used for peer teaching. Get the students to form mixed groups, one person from each of the original teams, and take turns teaching each other.
- Afterward, you could clear up any unanswered or wrongly answered questions in the game.
- Once the game is over, the class could spend some time reflecting on what has been learned about learning to bring out the double benefit, content *and* process.

Memory Board

A quick and easy game to help students remember technical terms and definitions. No, they won't be bored with "Memory Board"!

Purposes	
Thinking	★★★★
Emotional intelligence	
Independence	★★★★
Interdependence	(variable)
Multisensation	
Fun	★★
Articulation	★★★★

Skills Used	
Individual work	★★★★
Group work	(variable)
Moving	
Speaking	
Listening	
Reading	★★★
Writing	★★★★
Looking	★★★
Choice	

Specific Room Layout?	
Yes	**No**

How?

1. Write a dozen or more technical terms on the board, taken from the topic just completed or a topic being reviewed after some time. Better still, write the terms in advance on an overhead transparency.
2. Give the students a minute to remember the list.
3. As soon as the time is up, erase the words, turn the board around, or switch off the overhead projector.
4. The students have to write out not the terms themselves, but their *definitions*, remembering as many as they can in a specified length of time.
5. Go over the terms and discuss the different ways in which students have defined them.

Applications

- Use in any subject where knowledge of technical or specialized vocabulary is expected: science, math, geography, English, physical education—is there any subject that doesn't qualify?
- Foreign languages and ESL: Use the game for straightforward translation of words or phrases.
- Math: Use equivalent fractions. One-quarter could be written as two-eighths, for example. Or write random numbers on the board and have students write calculations to which the numbers are the answers.

Why Do It?

- The exercise requires an active engagement of the mind.
- It teaches memorization by making two points. First, the conversion of material from one form (technical term) into another (definition) forces understanding. Deep learning can occur only when material is understood. Rote learning is superficial and inefficient. Second, when the brain tries something, then compares the attempted version with the accurate version (when you go over the answers), memorization occurs naturally.
- If you try the fourth variation, the exercise teaches a further point about review—the need to go over material several times in order for it to stick (based on the Ebbinghaus effect). This is excellent training in basic review technique.
- Games such as these add spice to otherwise dull learning chores. They make learning, and life, a bit more bearable.

Variations

- Have students work in pairs rather than on their own.
- Use pictures or diagrams rather than words on the memory board. For example, stick up flash cards in foreign language and ESL classes, photographs in geography, diagrams of apparatus in science, geometric drawings in math, or materials or tools in home economics or woodworking. Or show a slide sequence using a projector or computer, during which the students are not allowed to write anything down.
- Make it a cooperative exercise by having so many items to remember in so short a time that no one person could possibly get them all. Students work in groups and organize their strategy in advance for the successful collaborative completion of the task.
- Use the exercise to teach the importance of revisiting material several times. Imagine you are using an overhead projector. Show the technical terms for a minute. Switch off. The students have half a minute to go over them in their heads. Switch the projector back on for another minute. Switch off. Again, the students have half a minute to go over them in their heads. Switch back on for the third and final time. Then the students are allowed to write the definitions. Discuss how much clearer and more complete their memories are after the third viewing compared to the first. Relate this to the need for review.

Now You See It . . .

Now you don't. Memories made in the blink of an eye.

Purposes	🔧
Thinking	★★★★★
Emotional intelligence	
Independence	★★★★
Interdependence	
Multisensation	★
Fun	★★★
Articulation	★★★★

Skills Used	🌡️
Individual work	★★★★
Group work	
Moving	
Speaking	
Listening	
Reading	★★★
Writing	★
Looking	★★★
Choice	

Specific Room Layout?	✏️
Yes	(No)

How?

This is a basic memory technique, the foundation of many variations. When students first use it, they are often delighted that learning occurs as if by magic.

1. Supply to each student, or have students each make for themselves, a pack of small blank cards, about the size of business cards.
2. On one side of the cards, students write the items to be learned, one per card, and on the reverse, the meanings or definitions of the items.
3. Student spread out their cards on their desks, with the meanings or definitions face down.
4. Explain to students that they will look at a card, give its meaning or definition in their heads, then turn it over to see if they are right. If they are, they turn the card over. If not, they leave it face down and may not return to it until they have tried the same procedure with all the other cards. They may turn a card over only when they have given the correct meaning or definition. Ask students how long they think it will take them to turn all the cards over.
5. Of course, learning occurs effortlessly when students compare the answer in their heads to the answer on the back of the card.
6. Once all the cards are turned, ask students to reverse the process. How long will it take them to turn the cards back again?

Applications

- Foreign languages and ESL: Have students use it to learn or review vocabulary.
- History: Have students use it to learn or review dates and the significance of key events and policies.
- Science: Students could use it to learn or review formulas, diagrams of apparatus, and technical terminology.
- Math: Students could use it to learn or review symbols, rules, and conventions.
- Physical education and health: Students could use it to learn or review the names of muscles and bones.
- Art: Have students use it to learn or review key features of artists' styles.
- Music: Have students use it to learn or review musical genres and examples of works and instruments from around the world.
- Geography: Have students use it to learn or review weather graphs and climate names.

Why Do It?

- It's a very efficient and natural way of memorizing information.
- It teaches the students an invaluable technique they can apply to many subjects, adding to their repertoire of independent learning skills.
- It helps students to realize that success can be achieved with a little effort and a little fun—it creates motivation for future learning.

Variations

- Use pictures, diagrams, or symbols on one side, words on the other.
- To aid memorization, use different colors of cards for different aspects of the topic, for example, for different parts of speech in English and foreign languages, or for positive and negative consequences of a historical event.
- Students could put the pack in an envelope for use as a review aid at home.
- Encourage students to make further packs for other topics; assign pack-making homework.
- Raise the level of challenge by getting students to set time targets for themselves. Then encourage them to beat their best time for turning a whole pack over.
- Ask students to work in pairs. They put two identical packs together, one face up, the other face down; shuffle the cards randomly around the desk or table; and then take turns to match pairs. When a pair is successfully matched, the player keeps it and goes again until a mismatch is made. The player with the most pairs at the end wins.

On Tour

Give students a chance to get out and about. They all get there in the end, but the route has many twists, turns, and stops along the way.

Purposes	
Thinking	★★★★★
Emotional intelligence	★
Independence	★★★
Interdependence	★★★★
Multisensation	
Fun	★
Articulation	★★★★★

Skills Used	
Individual work	
Group work	★★★★
Moving	★★★★★
Speaking	★★★
Listening	★★
Reading	★★★
Writing	★★★★
Looking	★
Choice	★★★

Specific Room Layout?	
Yes	No

How?

1. Decide on a series of challenging questions that require long, detailed answers. These could be actual questions from past papers or exams.

2. Write each question at the top of a large sheet of poster paper or flipchart paper and put the sheets on desks around the room. Create more question sheets than there are pairs of students, to avoid congestion.

3. Explain to students the overall goal: to ensure that all the questions are answered as fully and accurately as possible within a given time limit. The class has collective responsibility for this, and everyone is asked to keep going until satisfied that all the answers are as good as can be.

4. Students work in pairs. At the word "go," each pair starts on the question nearest to them. They are allowed to work at it for a few minutes, then you shout, "Move!" From here on, for the rest of the time, pairs move freely around the class, deciding which questions to tackle in which order and for how long.

5. Pairs are encouraged to add, delete, and redraft in the collective attempt to create a set of perfect answers. The only rules are only one pair at a question at a time, and pairs may spend no more than five minutes at a question. Of course, they also have to keep their eyes on the clock.

6. When time is up, pairs return to their original questions and grade them. You will need to explain the assessment criteria first. Alternatively, each pair writes up a polished version of the answer. These are collected, photocopied, and distributed to everyone. A third option is for you to collect all the large sheets, go through some of them with the class, and bring out key teaching points, both about the content and about exam technique.

Applications

Any subject that can be tested through long answers, even math, with long complex calculations.

Why Do It?

- Exam technique: The exercise trains students to answer questions precisely and fully, and it simulates the pressure of an exam in presenting a number of diverse questions to be answered within a set time.
- It contains peer teaching at two levels. First, the two students in each pair are pooling their expertise, discussing and making decisions together. Second, they are learning from the work of others as they move from paper to paper scrutinizing contributions.
- The corporate and ultimately anonymous nature of the exercise makes it inclusive.
- It provides a diagnostic assessment for you, enabling you to work on aspects of content and exam techniques that emerge as weak.

Variations

- Instead of allowing free movement around the questions, move pairs on at set times (say, every five minutes) and perhaps in a set order.
- Reverse the management of the exercise. Instead of having students move, the question papers move. You decide when to take a paper away from a pair and which pair to give it to next. This enables you to build in fairly precise levels of differentiation and challenge.
- To begin the exercise, allow pairs a substantial amount of time to answer their initial questions as accurately and fully as possible. The rest of the time is spent moving around and grading, not adding to, answers. Each pair could be responsible for a particular assessment criterion or aspect, such as content, spelling, grammar, paragraphing, use of tense and voice, and so forth. This is ideal for foreign languages, ESL, and English, or for subjects that have particular writing conventions, such as describing experiments in science.

One to One

The simpler the better. When it comes to peer teaching, you can't get simpler than "One to One."

Purposes	🔧
Thinking	★★★★
Emotional intelligence	★
Independence	★★★
Interdependence	★★★★
Multisensation	
Fun	★
Articulation	★★★★

Skills Used	🌡
Individual work	★★★
Group work	★★★
Moving	★
Speaking	★★★
Listening	★★★
Reading	★★★★
Writing	★★★★
Looking	★★
Choice	

Specific Room Layout?	✏️
Yes	(No)

How?

1. Divide the class into halves.
2. Divide the topic under study into halves. For example, the Native Americans' perspective on the colonization of the Midwest and the settlers' perspective. Or series circuits and parallel circuits. Give one subtopic to one half of the class and the other one to the other half, along with appropriate study materials.
3. Give a reasonable deadline, by the end of which every student must have mastered their topic and produced a teaching aid to use at the next stage. During this initial study period, students may work individually or in pairs. They may seek help from others in their half or, as a last resort, from you. The teaching aid should be on 11" x 17" paper, and students should use a range of colors and a mixture of words and images.
4. Pair students up across the halves, either randomly or by taking into account learning styles, reading and writing abilities, personalities, and confidence levels. Students move to sit by each other in their new pairs. Alternatively, you could pair up the first two students to finish, then the next two, and so on. This means you can then set differentiated extension tasks to the faster workers while the rest catch up.
5. Pairs now teach each other using the teaching aids they prepared earlier. Reasonable deadlines are given. You move around monitoring, supporting, and providing input where students are stuck or inaccurate.

Applications

Use this activity for any subject that can be divided into two subsections:

- Ideal for exploring two halves of a debate, two interpretations, or two horns of a dilemma in history, political science, or physical education and health.
- English: Use to study two key characters in a novel, or two quite different interpretations of a character.
- Art: Use for critical studies—the life and work of two artists, the characteristics and significance of two art movements, or two examples of an artist's work to be studied in detail.
- Excellent for review in any subject.

Why Do It?

- It requires everyone to learn. In order to teach something, you have to understand it. If you understand something, you remember it. Also, research suggests that students learn more efficiently from peers than from teachers.
- It requires everyone to take responsibility and therefore trains students in independent and interdependent learning.
- It's easy to set up and manage.
- It prepares students for more advanced forms of peer teaching, such as "Corporate Identity" (page 76).

Variations

- After the paired peer teaching, a test can be given under exam conditions. Students take the test without reference to notes or to each other. The pair's scores are added together and divided by two, giving each the same score. This reflects the quality of their teaching as well as their learning. Before the test, you could provide the opportunity to check understanding with the rest of the class and with you in an open forum for five to ten minutes.
- Instead of just teaching each other the material, pairs have to do something with it. For example, they have to compare the properties of two materials (in home economics or a shop class) and decide which one will be best for the job. Or they have to rank all the causes of an event (in history), or decide which of two experimental methods to use (in science), or choose which settlement site to vote for (in geography), or write a business plan once all the factors are known (in business studies).

Pairs to Fours

This is a classic active learning strategy—simple, effective, and collaborative.

Purposes	
Thinking	★★★★★
Emotional intelligence	★★
Independence	★★★
Interdependence	★★★★
Multisensation	
Fun	★★
Articulation	★★★★★

Skills Used	
Individual work	★
Group work	★★★★
Moving	★
Speaking	★★★★★
Listening	★★★★★
Reading	★★
Writing	
Looking	
Choice	

Specific Room Layout?	
Yes	(No)

How?

1. The students form pairs.
2. Each pair has a task to complete, involving the need to discuss and make decisions together. For example, a ranking exercise, choosing which mock business plan to accept, sequencing a narrative, creating headings for paragraphs in a text, proposing the design of an experiment, deciding on captions for a series of photographs, putting forward a proposal for a drama, or deciding the order in which topics will be covered.
3. As pairs finish (or after a set time), they come together into groups of four. That is, two pairs join up, just by turning their chairs, and each pair shares the results of its labors with the other. The four then enter into further debate in order to arrive at an agreed-on version, which they will then share with the whole class.
4. Any one of the four should be able to explain and defend the decisions made by the group. You may want to spontaneously choose any of the four to do this, rather than have the group decide who the spokesperson will be, just to keep them all on their toes.
5. Debrief students on the content and the process, focusing on the nature of decision making and on the pros and cons of consensus, compromise, and voting.

Applications

The applications are endless. Use whenever tasks can be devised that require debate and decision. For example:

- "Here are five possibilities. Which one will be the most efficient?"
- "Figure out how these two sets of cards match up."
- "You are such-and-such a group. If you had only this much time/money/material, how would you use it?"
- "Predict the declension of this verb you have not come across before."
- "Put these quotations in order of significance."
- "What do you think will happen if I mix these two materials/turn on the power/add this component?"
- "Given what we know about the stated beliefs of this person, which of his actions was most hypocritical/characteristic/expedient?"
- "Which observation and recording techniques will be appropriate for the field trip?"
- "To what extent was John F. Kennedy a good president?"

Why Do It?

- Deep learning occurs when the brain sorts things out for itself. The process of creating a personal construct is powerfully aided by discussion. The more a learner talks and listens, the more ideas are settled in the mind.
- The technique promotes cooperation and helps students practice oral and listening skills as well as debating and decision-making skills. Together, these strengthen interpersonal, linguistic, and logical intelligences. They are also among the subskills of independence.
- Presenting and defending a position, arguing and compromising, exercising group responsibility—these are all key citizenship skills.

Variation

If numbers (and nerves) will stand it, the groups of four could move into groups of eight and so on until a whole-class decision has been reached.

Pass the Buck

Why not pass the buck and let someone else do the work? But, to mix metaphors, when the buck stops, all your chickens come home to roost.

Purposes	
Thinking	★★★★★
Emotional intelligence	★
Independence	★★★
Interdependence	★★★
Multisensation	
Fun	★★
Articulation	★★★★★

Skills Used	
Individual work	
Group work	★★★★
Moving	
Speaking	★★★
Listening	★★★
Reading	★★★
Writing	★★★★★
Looking	
Choice	

Specific Room Layout?	
Yes	(No)

How?

1. Students work in pairs and have five minutes to begin a draft answer to a difficult question. It's best if they work on large poster paper or flipchart paper with felt-tip pens.
2. As soon as time is up, they pass their partial answer to the pair behind them and receive the work of the pair in front (or pass around the circle, if that's how the desks are arranged).
3. They now have five minutes to continue, not their own answer, but the received answer from the pair in front, picking up from wherever that pair left off. They are encouraged not just to add, but also to cross out parts they don't agree with and redraft others.
4. Again, when time is up, papers are passed backward or around.
5. The newly received answer is continued for a further five minutes, and so on until the process has served its purpose.
6. Papers are then returned to their original authors, who, using the several contributions, draft the final, polished version of the answer.

Applications

- Exam preparation: Pairs tackle SAT, ACT, or state standardized test questions to show how much precision and detail can be achieved in exam answers when they really think about it.
- English: Use to bring out the difference between rushing an essay and planning an essay; extended creative writing; or writing about the same subject for different audiences.
- Foreign languages and ESL: Use for translations; writing open-ended stories; or writing a story in the target language from a storyboard.
- Home economics and industrial arts: Use for generating or evaluating different designs to given specifications.
- Math: Use for solving substantial problems or carrying out investigations.
- Art: Use for developing drawings and paintings in the style of a variety of artists (with longer times).
- Review: In any subject, ideal for getting students to recall material already taught.
- Use for processing ideas such as "What shall we do about bullying?"; "How shall we organize ourselves?"; "What are the arguments for . . . ?"; or "How should the classroom rules be revised?"

Why Do It?

- This activity trains students in crucial exam techniques, particularly the art of writing precise and full answers.
- It promotes a more conscious approach to writing, including planning, accuracy, attention to time and speed, and awareness of audience.
- Even though the material might be heavy and serious, the activity itself is light. No one gets too bogged down. The pace and the passing make it sparky and fun.

Variations

- Vary the time for each round. Give four minutes for the first round, five for the second, six for the third, and so on to allow enough reading and thinking time as the answers become fuller.
- Vary the length and complexity of the tasks. Differentiation can be built in.
- Vary the questions, so that each pair starts with a different question—this really keeps people on their toes. Students have to switch their thinking to a new subject every round. This simulates the pressure of an exam.
- In the first round give people enough time to write a complete answer. Then, the pair behind don't *continue* it but *redraft* it.
- The pair behind *assess* the answer according to set criteria. This is particularly powerful if exam criteria are used. Students will need to know beforehand how their tests will be assessed.
- As work is passed on, different pairs mark different features: One pair marks spelling, the next marks grammar and syntax, the next content, the next style, and so forth. In foreign language or ESL, students could mark tense, voice, gender, and so forth.

Prediction

Fortune cookies? Horoscopes? Crystal balls?
No, just some good, honest forward thinking.

Purposes	
Thinking	★★★★★
Emotional intelligence	★★
Independence	★★★★
Interdependence	★★★
Multisensation	★
Fun	★
Articulation	★★★★

Skills Used		
Individual work	★	
Group work	★★★★	
Moving	★	
Speaking	★★★★	
Listening	★★★★	
Reading	★	(variable)
Writing	★★	
Looking	★	(variable)
Choice		

Specific Room Layout?	
Yes	(No)

How?

1. Before starting a topic, turn the information or concepts you want the students to learn into problems for them to solve or a challenge for them to meet. In pairs or small groups, the students have to come up with solutions that are directly connected to the learning for the topic. Effectively, they are trying to predict the right answer. For example:

   - Foreign languages: Ask students to create a theory to explain why the same adjective is spelled differently in different parts of a text. Is there a rule for all adjectives?
   - History: Ask students to solve three or four actual problems faced by a historical leader, before studying the politics of that period.
   - English: Ask students to propose ten features of discursive writing and suggest how they can be grouped, by analyzing two or three examples, before giving them your list.
   - Science: Ask students to predict what the results of an experiment will be before conducting the experiment.

   In each case, the key question is "What do you think (or predict) . . .?"

2. The task you give the students needs to be complex enough, and the time allowed must be sufficient, for students to get into the material. They must have the chance to become intrigued and feel some ownership of their solution.

3. It is important that you give students only minimal information to help them. Aim for students to use maximum imagination, lateral thinking, and creativity. If they are stuck, prompt them to think of parallel cases or point them to other resources.

4. When time is up, ask them if they want to know the "real" solution. They will inevitably say yes. Then hand out an information sheet, tell them where to look it up, demonstrate the answer, show them a presentation, or just explain it orally. At this point, the students will be almost totally attentive and will absorb the material naturally.

Applications

- Math: Use for estimation, an important part of mathematics that has many applications.
- English: Students predict the continuation of a story that has been partly read; how a character will behave in a different situation; what grade a piece of work was given.
- Foreign languages and ESL: Students predict rules of grammar; the declension of a verb the students have not met before; how to say or write something that is just beyond the students' current capabilities.
- Geography: Students predict the processes of erosion and deposition under given conditions; the results of a survey; the effects of specific natural disasters; the consequences of pursuing certain political or economic policies; the best location for a settlement.
- History: Students predict the consequences of certain historical decisions, policies, or treaties; the outcomes of battles; the wisest courses of action in given historical situations; the conclusions historians have drawn given certain sources.
- Business studies: Students predict the decisions that a business should make in certain circumstances; the best roles and responsibilities for a given business; changes in productivity when certain conditions are modified; the results of applying a new business process.
- Home economics and industrial arts: Students predict the tools and materials required for a particular job; the performance of certain materials; the way in which a certain machine is operated.
- Science: Students predict the outcome of an experiment; the behavior of certain chemicals; the consequences of phenomena; the commercial application of scientific processes; the changes in outcome when certain variables are modified.
- Physical education and health: Students predict the outcome of a game if certain tactics are used; the effect of certain exercises on the body.

Why Do It?

- It is universally true that people want to know whether they are right or wrong once they've guessed something. The human brain always wants to know how well it's done. "Prediction" sets up an open mind for learning. When students have put some effort into devising a solution, or have just guessed at something, they are interested in knowing the real answer. Even dull, dry, and trivial material can seem fascinating once a "mental investment" has been generated using the prediction principle.
- Consequently, this approach usually results in material being absorbed in more detail and being retained longer.

- In the process, students exercise a range of thinking skills, including analysis, application, and synthesis.
- The collaboration in pairs or small groups requires students to converse, which is vital to concept formation.
- Students are sharing knowledge and perceptions with each other, and thus a degree of peer teaching is built in. We know that students usually learn well from each other.

Variation

Instead of predicting *content* issues, students can predict *process* issues, such as how long it will take to complete a task, which group will finish first, what questions are likely to come up on a test, and what problems will be encountered along the way. This is good training in learning to learn and develops an attitude of responsibility for learning.

Question Generator

Question the teacher? What is the classroom coming to? This approach will easily generate lots of learning.

Purposes	
Thinking	★★★★
Emotional intelligence	★
Independence	★★★ (variable)
Interdependence	★★★ (variable)
Multisensation	
Fun	★
Articulation	★★★

Skills Used	
Individual work	★★★ (variable)
Group work	★★★★ (variable)
Moving	
Speaking	★★★
Listening	★★★
Reading	★
Writing	★★
Looking	
Choice	★★★

Specific Room Layout?	
Yes	(No)

How?

1. Describe the topic to be studied.
2. Ask students to generate as many questions as they can about the topic. This can be done as a whole-class brainstorm, as an individual list, or in pairs or small groups.
3. The questions then need to be sorted. If the generation was done by individuals, pairs, or small groups, they simply rank the items, putting the questions they are most interested in at the top. If the generation was by whole-class brainstorm, ask a student to propose a question he is interested in, then gauge general interest by using "Thumbometer" (page 137), "Calling Cards" (page 70), or just a show of hands. Then another question is proposed, and soon a rough ranking is established.
4. Build your teaching and materials around the questions, beginning with the most popular. The first few questions might last for a couple of lessons. Later, minority-interest questions can be dealt with quietly with individuals or small groups while the rest of the class is working.

Applications

- Use when the students have enough general knowledge to frame intelligent questions about the topic; it may not be appropriate for highly technical material of which they have no prior experience.

- Ideal for addressing meaty chunks of the syllabus that could be rather dry, for example, in humanities and social science subjects.
- Perfect for practical and vocational courses, in which students need to know how to carry out certain procedures accurately: for example, child care, home economics, business studies, and industrial arts.
- In physical education and computer courses, use when students are eager to get going.

Why Do It?

- It increases students' interest in, and curiosity about, the topic—this raises their level of motivation and opens their minds for learning.
- Information students ask for enters the memory more readily than material that comes out of the blue.
- The brain is self-rectifying. If it receives information that doesn't confirm but challenges its preconceptions and prior knowledge, it will naturally adjust. Learning feels easier to the student, and to the teacher.
- It gives students practice in an important study skill: framing appropriate questions.

Variations

- **Lucky Dip:** Instead of answering the questions yourself, have the students do so. They write generated questions on small cards—one question per card. Collect all the cards in a box. The box is passed around, each student taking a card until no cards are left. Students are then called on to offer answers, which are checked with you and the whole class. If appropriate, give students research time before answering begins. They could refer to books and confer with each other. They could work in small groups to share questions and answers before "going public." The exercise could be extended into a substantial piece of research, especially if it is an entirely new topic.

- **Scrambled Groups:** The students are divided into groups of, say, five. Only the top few questions are taken, and each is given to a different group. The groups are expected to research their question by a common deadline. You can inject supplementary or extension questions from the list if necessary. Each student is expected to have a clear understanding of her group's question and to have prepared a teaching aid by the deadline. Groups are then rescrambled, making new groups each containing a delegate from the original groups, and students teach each other.

Quick on the Draw

This research activity has a built-in incentive for teamwork and speed.

Purposes	🔧
Thinking	★★★★
Emotional intelligence	★
Independence	★★★★
Interdependence	★★★
Multisensation	★★
Fun	★★★★
Articulation	★★

Skills Used	🖌️
Individual work	★
Group work	★★★★★
Moving	★★★
Speaking	★★★
Listening	★★
Reading	★★★★
Writing	★★★
Looking	★★
Choice	

Specific Room Layout?	✏️

Yes   Ⓣ   No

How?

1. This is a straightforward race between groups. The goal is to be the first group to work its way through a set of questions. Begin by preparing a set of, say, 10 questions about the topic under study. Copy enough sets for each group of three or four to have its own set. Each question should be on a separate card. Each set of questions should be in a distinctive color. Put the sets out on your desk, numbers facing up, with number 1 on top.

2. Divide the class into groups of three (four if necessary, although this invites passengers). Allocate a color to each group so that group members can identify their set of questions on your desk.

3. Give each group source material that contains the answers to all the questions—one copy per student. This could simply be selected pages from the regular textbook. After the first couple of questions, the answers shouldn't be too obvious: The idea is for students to have to search the text.

4. At the word "go," one person from each group "runs" to your desk, takes the first question only of the group's color, and runs back with it to the group.

5. Using the source material, the group finds and writes down the answer on a separate piece of paper.

6. A second person from the group takes the answer to you, and you check the answer. If it is accurate and complete, the group collects the second question from the color pile, and so on. If any answer is inaccurate or incomplete, send the runner back to the group to try again. Writers and runners should rotate.

7. While one student is running, the others should be scanning the resource and familiarizing themselves with its contents so that they can answer future questions more efficiently. It's a good idea to make the first couple of questions fairly easy and short, just to get momentum going.

8. The first group to complete all their questions wins.

9. You then go over all the answers with the class, while students take notes.

Applications

- Endless applications from sixth grade on. The depth and complexity of questions can be varied to suit many different contexts. Run the contest over a week with questions that demand out-of-classroom research.

- Science: In addition to straightforward questions on text, run the activity with apparatus. Groups may collect their next pieces of equipment only when they have the earlier parts set up correctly. Alternatively, try it with step-by-step instructions for an experiment.

- Math: Each card could be a separate problem, or each card could be one step in a series that leads to the completion of a more complex task. This trains students to check that each stage of a process is correct before moving on to the next.

- English, social studies, and business studies: The source could be text, pictures, or artifacts.

- Foreign languages and ESL: The source material could be text, such as a story, making the activity a straightforward comprehension exercise. Or the material (or the questions) could be pictorial. Or it could be an exercise in sentence construction, matching one half with the other, or simply an exercise in learning new vocabulary.

- Study skills: Debrief students on the range of skills used in the exercise, including skim reading, scanning, close reading, keyword identification, and collaboration, and the ways in which students can organize more effective resource-based learning in the future.

- "Quick on the Draw" is ideal for review.

Why Do It?

- The activity encourages teamwork—the more efficiently the team works, the faster the progress. Groups learn that dividing labor is more productive than duplicating labor.

- Students experience a variety of reading skills, driven by the pace of the activity, plus a host of other independent learning and examination skills—reading the question carefully, answering the question precisely, distinguishing between crucial and peripheral material, and so on.

- The exercise helps to get students used to basing their learning on resources other than you.

- It suits learners with a kinesthetic disposition who can't sit still for more than two minutes.

Variations

- The activity could be played as a race against the clock, rather than against other groups.
- The activity does not have to be competitive at all—groups could check answers with each other to ensure detail and thoroughness.
- Groups could collect visual pieces to build up a finished picture. For example, in biology, anatomy, physical education, and health, bones can be collected to build up a whole skeleton. Each of the pieces must be named and a question about its function or vulnerability in sports must be answered correctly before the next piece can be collected.
- A shortcut: Instead of copying a set of questions on cards for each group, whisper the question to each runner.
- The questions could be graded: The first ones deal with essential information *(must)*; the next few embellish or deepen understanding *(should)*; the final ones extend understanding *(could)*.
- Rather than all groups having the same questions, each group could have its own. If you carefully compose the groups, you can differentiate learning to a precise degree.
- Different groups could have questions on different aspects of the topic. Afterward, this would lead to peer teaching.

Randomizer

Playing cards in the classroom? You'll be lucky.

Purposes	
Thinking	★★★★
Emotional intelligence	★★
Independence	★★★★
Interdependence	★★★
Multisensation	
Fun	★
Articulation	★★★

Skills Used	
Individual work	★★★★
Group work	★★ (variable)
Moving	
Speaking	★★★
Listening	★★★★★
Reading	
Writing	
Looking	★★
Choice	

Specific Room Layout?	
Yes	(No)

How?

1. Bring two decks of playing cards to class. Take one deck and count out the same number of cards as there are students in the class. Take the second deck and choose exactly the same cards, so that you end up with two identical packs.

2. Shuffle the *first* pack in front of the class and then invite a student to cut the deck. This public shuffling and cutting shows everyone that the cards are now completely random.

3. Deal the cards, one per student. Ask the students to hold up their cards briefly so that they know that you know what they've got. They then hold their cards close to their chests.

4. Shuffle the *second* deck and choose another student to cut, randomizing the pack as before.

5. Explain that the first card you draw from the top of this deck will determine who makes the first contribution to the discussion. Explain that the next card will determine who has to sum up what the first speaker said. After she has summed up, the second person adds her own contribution to the discussion. The third card determines the next summarizer and contributor, and so on.

6. Every time a new card is drawn, the student has to sum up the contribution of only the person before him (not the whole chain) and then say his own piece.

7. Once a student has finished his summary and contribution, his card is placed at the bottom of the pack. However, this means that students who have had a turn are out of the running and may be tempted to lose concentration. It's a good idea to continuously shuffle the pack, which means that everyone always has a chance of being picked. The luck of the draw continues to add spice to the proceedings.

Applications

For any class discussion:

- to explore a range of opinions or feelings.
- to assess prior knowledge.
- to work on difficult concepts and iron out misconceptions.
- to consolidate or review a completed topic.

Why Do It?

- It's engaging because the element of luck keeps people on their toes. It's engaging also because of the degree of concentration required—on the whole, students don't want to look silly in front of their peers, so they tend to pay full attention to the speakers, just in case they have to do the summing up.
- The activity provides training in the disciplines of listening, patience, and self-control, which are central to citizenship and, in fact, all relationships.
- "Randomizer" levels the playing field and equalizes participation. The reticent students are no longer at the mercy of the loud-mouths who normally hog discussions. This is an inclusive strategy.
- Future learning is improved. Think of how much time is usually wasted through unproductive discussions in which no one listens to what anyone else says. This activity begins to establish better habits. It also provides the foundational training required before more complex group work and peer teaching activities can be used.

Variations

- If you can't get your hands on two packs of playing cards, just make two sets of numbered cards.
- If you fear that the cards might "disappear," you could have one playing card permanently taped to each desk. The randomization occurs by having students change their places each lesson, which isn't a bad thing in itself.
- Once students have been shown how to play "Randomizer," they can use it in small-group work to ensure that people listen to each other.
- Instead of being used for discussion, the cards could be used for a peer-led question-and-answer session. The first card drawn by the teacher determines who will ask the first question; the next card drawn determines who has the pleasure of answering it. Having given the answer, this student then asks the next question—the cards will determine who answers it. If a student can't answer the question fully or accurately, a new card is drawn to determine who will continue the attempt.
- Alternatively, the teacher could use the cards to select who should say whether a given answer is right or wrong, or *why* the answer is right or wrong, or give an alternative answer, or expand on the given answer. In these variations, a variety of thinking skills is being developed.

Ranking

This activity ranks high in anyone's list of active learning strategies. It requires, as the saying goes, engaging the brain while putting the mouth into motion.

Purposes	🔧
Thinking	★★★★★
Emotional intelligence	★
Independence	★★★
Interdependence	★★
Multisensation	★★
Fun	★
Articulation	★★★★

Skills Used	🥄
Individual work	
Group work	★★★★
Moving	
Speaking	★★★★★
Listening	★★★★
Reading	★★
Writing	
Looking	★ (variable)
Choice	

Specific Room Layout?	✏️
Yes	**No**

How?

1. Prepare pieces of information, ideas, pictures, or statements—whatever is appropriate to the learning at hand—as a collection of separate items, perhaps on cards. For example, the causes of World War Two, the paintings of van Gogh, the evidence for global warming, or the scientific discoveries of the twentieth century.
2. The class works in pairs or small groups. Present each pair or group with the information.
3. Explain the criterion for distinguishing between the items (for example, "With hindsight, how significant were these discoveries?" or "Which are the most convincing . . . ?"). Ask each group to debate the relative merits of the items and place them in rank order according to the criterion. This is most easily done if the items can be moved around on the desktop or floor.
4. Once the exercise is complete, the whole class can compare and discuss the results.

Applications

- Use this activity in any subject that requires judgments to be made between different options.
- Ranking is a decision-making process; it can be used to decide between differing proposals at a meeting or where to go for a field trip. It is a positive alternative to voting.

Why Do It?

- Ranking is an *academic* exercise: Through the exchange of opinion, students exercise thinking and achieve personal understanding of key issues and concepts. This results in deep rather than shallow learning.
- Ranking is also a *democratic* exercise that encourages debate, listening, compromise, and consensus. It contributes to citizenship education.

Variations

- Have students order all the items from most favored to least favored.
- Have students choose just the top three in order, or just the top two and the bottom two.
- Have students rank using a pyramid (one at the top, two on the next row, three on the third row, and so on) or a diamond shape.
- Once the original pairs have completed their rank order, use "Pairs to Fours" (page 112).

Silent Sentences

Classrooms are usually noisy places. This activity is one way for students and teacher alike to get an unusual period of peace and quiet.

Purposes	
Thinking	★★★★★
Emotional intelligence	★★★
Independence	
Interdependence	★★★★★
Multisensation	★★
Fun	★★★
Articulation	

Skills Used	
Individual work	
Group work	★★★★★
Moving	
Speaking	
Listening	
Reading	★★★★
Writing	
Looking	★★★★★
Choice	

Specific Room Layout?	

Yes (circled)   No

How?

1. Prepare sets of envelopes, one per group, each envelope containing a different selection of words or phrases on pieces of paper or index cards. The selections are such that no one can make correct, logical sentences from their own pieces. They need other people's and other people need theirs. The activity works best when there is only one solution, only one correct permutation.

2. Students work in groups of four. The challenge is for each player to have complete, grammatically accurate and meaningful sentences in front of her within the given deadline.

3. The rules:
   • Total silence: No one may speak or use sign language.
   • Players may only give; they may not take or beckon for others to give them cards.
   • If a card is offered, it cannot be refused.
   • Players must stay in their seats.

4. The exercise gets under way. Students look to see who might need a card, and they offer it. There's no need to take turns because there isn't time—groups are working against the clock.

5. When a student has a set of finished sentences, he has not necessarily finished. He might have the wrong solution or hold cards still needed by other players, and so he must remain actively involved.

6. The exercise is complete only when everyone has an accurate set of logical sentences.

Applications

- English: Sentences must be grammatically correct, make logical sense, and contain specified parts of speech. Give clear instructions as to which parts of speech must be included in all sentences.
- Foreign languages and ESL: Use as in the above point, but in the target language. Variables can include gender, singular and plural endings, tenses, and voices.
- Math: Students make balanced equations. Or use shapes instead of sentences. For example, each person has to make a square equal in dimensions to everyone else's from various cut-up pieces.
- Science: Use with circuit boards and components—working circuits have to be made to certain specifications. Or have students make chemical equations.
- Art: Use jigsaw puzzles of paintings, perhaps in different styles, to train students in looking closely.

Why Do It?

- With speaking eliminated, observation and mental processes are heightened.
- Those with dominant interpersonal and spatial intelligences and those with Concrete Sequential or visual learning styles are in their element.
- Students' understanding is put to the test. By wandering around the room, you will easily see where confusions and uncertainties occur. The exercise offers informal formative assessment.
- It provides a strong lesson in true group work, cooperation, and above all, self-discipline.

Variations

- Vary the number of sentences per person. For older or more able groups, many sentences each will be needed to ensure enough complexity.
- At a simple level, use colored cards. For example, all the verbs are on red cards, all the nouns on blue, and so on. Then discuss the patterns with the students: "What do we notice about the colors in every sentence? Why are they like this? What would happen to the sentence if we . . . ?"
- Play in groups of varying sizes.
- Each player could have a different specification to meet. For example, if you use circuit boards, each player has to make a specific circuit to do a specific job. In this case, all players need to know the various specifications.
- Discuss the exercise with students at two levels: the *content* of the material—misconceptions and confusions that were exposed; and the *discipline* of the exercise—learning about group work, collaboration, good citizenship, and silence!

Sorting Circles

These sorts of circles certainly sort your thinking.

Purposes	
Thinking	★★★★★
Emotional intelligence	★
Independence	★★★
Interdependence	★★★★
Multisensation	★
Fun	★
Articulation	★★★★

Skills Used		
Individual work	★	
Group work	★★★★	
Moving	★	(variable)
Speaking	★★★★	
Listening	★★★★	
Reading	★★	(variable)
Writing		
Looking	★★★	(variable)
Choice		

Specific Room Layout?	
Yes	No

How?

Students are asked to sort items into categories by physically putting them in different places. For instance, have three or four colored card circles on students' desks so that they can place on them different words, ideas, facts, pictures, texts, proposals, designs, or whatever. "Sorting Circles" is best explained through an example, but please read the applications and variations sections—they are as important as the following model:

Prepare a good number of questions about the topic that you are about to start. The questions should vary in difficulty and be printed on small cards so that each group can have a set.

1. Make three differently colored "sorting circles" out of cardboard or construction paper for every two or three students in your class. Each circle should be about 12 inches in diameter. Prepare a pack of question cards for every two or three students, with questions related to the topic at hand.

2. Organize students into pairs or small groups. On each group's desk or table, place three differently colored sorting circles and a pack of question cards.

3. Explain that in their groups, students should designate the sorting circles:
   • one for questions that everyone in the group can answer
   • one for questions that no one can answer
   • one for questions about which there is some uncertainty or disagreement

4. Ask the students to shuffle the cards and place them face down on the desk. They then take turns picking up a card, reading aloud the question, and asking the group for the answer. This is a cooperative exercise; students are expected to pool their knowledge with the group.

5. Cards are then placed on the appropriate sorting circles. Cards that no one can answer are clear cut. If one or two students can answer and are able to explain to the others so that they genuinely understand, then the card is placed on the "everyone in the group can answer" circle.

6. At the end of the exercise, ask groups to offer examples from different categories. With the class, create lists of items that still have to be learned and check each item off as the class covers it over the next few lessons.

Applications

- English: Sort poems according to style; characters; parts of speech; dramatic tensions according to type; model essays according to the grade students would give them.
- Art: Sort pictures according to different schools, artists, periods, or other criteria; materials and media for different effects.
- Science: Sort elements; animal characteristics; mixtures and solutions; properties; predictions (definitely will happen, might happen, definitely will not happen).
- Math: Sort questions according to type or complexity; geometric shapes according to properties; equations.
- History: Sort sources; leaders; decisions; causes and effects; bias.
- Geography: Sort physical features; land use; fieldwork techniques; questions into different types.
- Home economics and industrial arts: Sort materials; equipment; processes; needs; design proposals; constraints; products.
- Foreign languages or ESL: Sort words into parts of speech; verbs into types; pictures and text; tenses.
- Physical education and health: sort drugs; opinions over a contentious issue (we all agree with this; no one agrees with this; some agree and others disagree and neither side can persuade the other; we're not sure whether we agree or not); rules; types of games and sports; parts and systems of the body; warm-up exercises.
- Computer science and technology: Sort software (pros and cons, features); do's and don'ts; locations of various types of data ("Where would you find . . . ?").
- Any subject: Conduct evaluations through "Sorting Circles," for example: what was done well and what can be improved; what meets the criteria and what doesn't; what is not understood, what is half understood, and what is completely understood. Use to sort any topic in any subject about which students have some prior knowledge or experience, as in the main example above. Review any topic that has just been covered. Prepare questions to check varying levels of understanding and retention. The circles might be "we absolutely know this," "we don't have a clue," and "we're somewhere in between." In other words, "Sorting Circles" can be used as a group-based assessment, or just to consolidate what has been covered.

Why Do It?

- As items are discussed, students automatically clarify their thinking and teach each other what they know. Talk is vital to the process of conceptualization.

- Students also come to realize what they don't know or are not sure about. This creates a sense of anticipation. It's a neurological fact that when people try or assert something, they want to know whether they are right or wrong, and they become curious about the answers to questions they couldn't answer. This generates the motivation to learn even dull material.
- As the teacher, you can gain important information about the levels of knowledge and understanding in the class. This can inform what you do next and lead to greater levels of differentiation.
- "Sorting Circles" requires students to categorize, to identify similarities and differences, and therefore promotes a number of important thinking skills.
- The activity also promotes collaboration and the component skills of listening, debating, and decision making.
- "Sorting Circles" is a kinesthetic activity and as such is appealing to many learners.

Variations

- The items to be sorted don't have to be prepared by you; the students can do it for themselves.
- The circles can be hoops on the floor and the exercise can be conducted in large groups or as a whole class.
- Students can themselves be the items to be placed. For example in science, each student can be an element. Different parts of the classroom become the different categories and students physically move to these different areas.

Spotlight

When you're caught in the spotlight, all is revealed.
This is one way for everyone to shine.

Purposes	
Thinking	★★★★★
Emotional intelligence	
Independence	★
Interdependence	
Multisensation	
Fun	★★
Articulation	★★★ (volunteer)
	★ (class)

Skills Used	
Individual work	★★★★★
Group work	
Moving	★
Speaking	★★★ (volunteer)
Listening	★★★★ (class)
Reading	
Writing	★
Looking	
Choice	

Specific Room Layout?	
Yes	(No)

How?

1. A volunteer student comes to the front of the class and stands "in the spotlight." This means standing on a special spot, or sitting on a "celebrity" chair, or wearing a scarf denoting the "mantle of the expert" (see page 100).

2. All the other students turn to the backs of their books, or use scrap paper, and list numbers 1–10, ready to respond to questions.

3. You ask 10 questions of the spotlight volunteer about the topic just covered. The student answers each one in turn out loud. After each answer, the rest of the students individually decide whether the response was right, or wrong, or if they weren't sure.

4. If they think the answer was right, they put a check against the number; if wrong, they put an X. If they weren't sure (or the spotlight volunteer couldn't answer the question), they put a question mark.

5. To conclude, the spotlight student is applauded, and you go over the responses. For each question, ask how many people gave which response. This gives you feedback about who has learned what. It also gives precise feedback to individual students about the issues they need to work on further.

Applications

- This activity is ideal as an end-of-lesson check on learning in almost any subject.
- Conduct a more substantial version at the end of a unit.
- Use it for predictions; in science, for example, "What do you think will happen when . . . ?"
- Use it to gather whole-class opinions quickly. Students mark whether they agree with the spotlight volunteer's views and suggestions, whether they disagree, or whether they have no strong feelings either way.
- Use it to make whole-class decisions.

Why Do It?

- It's a novel way of doing diagnostic assessment. You can then plan further learning in light of what is revealed.
- It's immediate—you and your students get instant feedback. The brain is a self-rectifying organ, thrives on immediate feedback, and automatically makes adjustments when it knows what it should have thought.
- It gives show-offs a chance to show off constructively.

Variations

- Vary the number of questions or the number of volunteers.
- Instead of writing checkmarks, X's, and question marks on paper, students could hold up one of three response cards as soon as an answer is given. The cards give an immediate visual impression of who understands what. (See "Calling Cards" on page 70.)
- Students could ask questions too.

Stepping Stones

One step at a time. That's the safest and surest way to make progress.

Purposes	
Thinking	★★★★★
Emotional intelligence	★
Independence	★
Interdependence	★★
Multisensation	★★★
Fun	★★★
Articulation	★★★ (volunteer)

Skills Used	
Individual work	★★★★ (volunteer)
Group work	★★★★ (variable)
Moving	★★
Speaking	★★★★★ (volunteer)
Listening	★★★★ (class)
Reading	
Writing	
Looking	★★★
Choice	★★

Specific Room Layout?	

Yes — — No

(T)

How?

1. Move the desks aside and sit the class in a circle.
2. In the center of the circle, place several sheets of poster paper or flipchart paper and a thick felt-tip pen or a marker.
3. Discuss with the class the number of steps in the process under discussion. For example, a procedure (carrying out an experiment or making a recipe), or the stages of a physical phenomenon (the water cycle, for example), or the logical steps of a thinking process (the calculation of quadratic equations, or the identification of a piece of rock).
4. Number the pieces of paper and set them out in sequence across the circle to represent the stages of the process. These are the stepping stones. If necessary, add keywords to each one. For example, for the water cycle, you would write "evaporation," "condensation," "precipitation," and so on.
5. Ask for a volunteer who thinks she can get across the circle on the stepping stones. She stands on the first "stone" and explains the first step of the process accurately and fully. If you are satisfied, she moves to number two, attempts to explain the second step to your satisfaction, and so on.
6. The successful student is applauded loudly. If a student gives an incomplete or inaccurate answer, she has fallen off the stone and sits back down. Another volunteer takes up the challenge.

Applications

- As a review exercise, several different processes can be covered at one sitting.
- Home economics and industrial arts: Use it for the design-and-make process—students become clear about what they have to do before they go off and do it.
- Science: There are endless applications from simple experiments to chain reactions involving complex formulas and molecular structures.
- Math: Use it to study the conventional ways to carry out a whole range of calculations.
- Physical education, particularly dance and gymnastics: Use it to review a sequence of movements.
- Geography and other social studies: Use it to review the water cycle, the processes of glaciation, settlement growth, industrialization, and so on.
- History: Review any sequence of events, such as key moments in the Cold War, and the various causes and effects.
- Economics: Use it to review cycles of economic growth and depression.

Why Do It?

- It's a novel and fun way of dealing with potentially dry material.
- It's multisensory, using auditory, visual, and (for volunteers) kinesthetic learning channels.
- It requires students to articulate and clarify their understanding, either orally as they cross the stones or in their heads as they compare what the volunteer is saying with their own thoughts.

Variations

- Let the class judge whether steps have been explained accurately and fully.
- Have rules to speed up and spice up proceedings: no repetition, hesitation, or deviation. If the volunteer does any of these, he's off.
- To keep everyone on their toes, you can choose people (or pull names from a hat) to repeat a successful crossing.
- Instead of using it to consolidate or review material, use it to introduce material. Ask students to try it, using prior learning, general knowledge, logical thinking, and guesswork.
- Use it as an arena for teaching. You move from stone to stone, explaining the concepts involved. This gives a strong visual impression to complement your oral exposition.
- Students could take written notes once the fun and games are over.
- Students could divide into teams. Each team puts forward a "champion" to give it a shot. You describe the list of stepping-stone challenges in advance and allocate them randomly to teams. Each team then coaches its champion before the competition begins.

Thumbometer

What are they thinking? How much do they understand? Are they awake? It's easy to gauge the situation—just take a reading with the "Thumbometer."

Purposes	
Thinking	★★★★
Emotional intelligence	★★
Independence	★★★
Interdependence	
Multisensation	★
Fun	★★
Articulation	★★

Skills Used	
Individual work	★★★★★
Group work	
Moving	
Speaking	
Listening	★★★
Reading	
Writing	
Looking	★
Choice	★★★★

Specific Room Layout?	
Yes	(No)

How?

1. Demonstrate how to present the thumbometer: arm out, fist clenched, thumb up.
2. Show how to use the thumbometer to indicate a personal response. Thumb straight down is a downright negative; thumb straight up is a maximum positive, with all positions in between.
3. Whenever you want to gauge whole-class understanding, thinking, feeling, or opinion, ask students to get their thumbs out.

Applications

- Use it to check how well an instruction or concept has been understood: for example, "How confident are you that you've understood what I've said?" or "How well would you be able to explain this to someone else?"
- Use it to test knowledge: for example, "How sure are you about the following statements . . . ?" or "Are the following statements true, or false, or don't you know?"
- Use it to gauge thoughts and feelings: for example, "How are your concentration levels?" or "How interested are you in this new topic?" or "How prepared are you to try this new learning technique?"

- Use it to gather opinions: for example, "How much do you support the idea that we . . . ?" or "To what extent do you agree with . . . ?"

Why Do It?

- It gives you immediate feedback so that you can tailor your teaching accordingly.
- It gives students a genuine sense of participation.
- It requires all students to be on the ball—there's no hiding place.
- It promotes the notion of shared responsibility and demonstrates democracy.
- It includes those who can't speak or who are shy and feel awkward about speaking in public.

Variations

- If peer pressure is a problem, ask students to close their eyes during "Thumbometer."
- Have "Thumbometer" ongoing during the lesson. Students can indicate the points at which their understanding or concentration wanes. They can silently tell you which parts they understand clearly so that you can move on, and which parts you need to spend more time on. They can indicate when they can't take any more, and when it's time to change the activity.
- Instead of using their thumbs, students can indicate the strength of their responses by showing a number of fingers on a scale of one to five. Make sure that their palms, not the backs of their hands, are facing you!

Value Continuum

This rather technical-sounding term describes a strategy that encourages students to express their views in complete emotional comfort.

Purposes	
Thinking	★★★★★
Emotional intelligence	★★★★
Independence	★★★
Interdependence	★★
Multisensation	★★
Fun	★
Articulation	★★★★★

Skills Used	
Individual work	★★★
Group work	★★
Moving	★★★
Speaking	★★★
Listening	★★★★★
Reading	
Writing	
Looking	★★★★
Choice	★★★★

Specific Room Layout?	
(Yes)	No

How?

1. Clear the desks to the side and arrange the chairs in a semicircle.

2. Across the open end of the semicircle, ask students to imagine a line (or use chalk, masking tape, or a rope) and place a chair at each end.

3. Introduce the issue to be discussed (such as vegetarianism) and outline the two opposite positions. Do this by sitting on one chair and speaking as if you held this extreme view: "I never eat meat. Meat eating is an abomination—unhealthy, unnatural, and uneconomical. I campaign daily to persuade others to give up this immoral habit. A law should be passed banning the eating of meat, on pain of death." Then sit on the other chair: "I am a devotee of meat . . ."

4. Ensure that the two views are *extreme* and *balanced*—one is not obviously more right (in your eyes) than the other. Explain that everyone's view will fall somewhere on the sliding scale between the two chairs.

5. Explain the rules: "You choose whether to participate or not. The person who is on the line is guaranteed that her view will be listened to. There will be no agreeing or disagreeing (there will be time for that later)—no reaction, verbal or otherwise from the audience. Honesty is expected."

6. After you sit down in the semicircle, anyone may begin by taking her chair and sitting in a position on the continuum that represents her view. The volunteer is expected to say a few words to the class about her position and then stays in her chosen spot.

7. The process is repeated, with volunteers going out and speaking, one after another. If one person's view is identical to that of an earlier speaker, she can sit in front of him. (Alternatively, of course, you might have students standing instead of sitting.)

8. If, after the first few brave souls, the rest of the students are reluctant to take part, then you might use two softer strategies: "Come and stand on the line, but you don't have to say anything." If there is further reluctance, you can say, "Stay where you are and just point to your position on the line." This way everyone makes a statement of some kind. These options might be needed with shy or fearful students initially, but the goal is to encourage bolder participation in the future, which is why protective ground rules are so important (see section 3).

9. The process is likely to come to a natural end.

Applications

- Use it to discuss any issue about which there can be polarized, but equally plausible, views. Health and political science classes are obvious contexts.

- Science: Use it to discuss ethical dilemmas, such as genetic engineering, nuclear energy, or animal experiments.

- History: Use it to explore questions of judgment, for example, "Was Catherine the Great an enlightened despot?" Students have to defend their positions with evidence.

- English: Use it for character studies, for example, "What was Curly's wife in the novel *Of Mice and Men*: simple flirt or the most complex and tragic character in the story?" Or use to introduce nonfiction text about an issue such as animal rights. Once initial positions on the line have been established, students read the arguments for and against, then reposition themselves with increased awareness.

- Use it in any subject to assess what students know about a topic before it is begun. From "I know absolutely everything there is to know about this topic" to "I know nothing at all about it."

- Use it to assess how much support there is for a proposal.

- Use it in any subject to evaluate learning: from "This was the best possible way to solve the problem/fulfill the assignment/conduct the experiment/learn the topic" to "This method was completely useless. It had no merit at all."

- Try conducting the exercise in a foreign language or ESL class.

- Use it to establish a timeline, in which case each student will be given a card with an event, invention, breakthrough, character, or clue.

- Math: Set up a line of probability from zero to one. Distribute cards with possible events written on them such as "Our school football team will make it to state within the next three years." Students take turns to come out and position their event on the line. Once several students are on the line, adjustments to some positions will be inevitable as relative probability is debated.

Why Do It?

- It's good training in self-discipline, group cooperation, and courage. It therefore promotes both independent and interdependent learning.
- The activity develops listening skills as well as patience, tolerance for differences of opinion, management of feelings, and other aspects of emotional intelligence.
- "Value Continuum" raises self-esteem when conducted in strict accordance with the rules, because each student receives the full attention of the class. This usually translates into increased confidence to speak and participate in the future.
- It requires students to consider a range of opinions and is excellent preparation for the art of debate, essential for all active citizens.
- It requires and helps students practice a range of thinking skills as they interpret, compare, and contrast positions.

Variations

- Use a two-dimensional continuum to explore two related issues at once. In this case, students will need to sit in a circle. Draw a cross on the floor using chalk, masking tape, or string. For example:

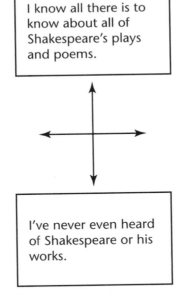

I know all there is to know about all of Shakespeare's plays and poems.

Shakespeare's work is without a doubt the very finest literature in the English tongue ever.

As literature, Shakespeare's work is completely worthless.

I've never even heard of Shakespeare or his works.

- When all or most people are on the line, or at least have made their mark by pointing, you can break the line in half and make two debating teams. The teams face each other and take turns to make points. It might be helpful to give each team an object, a pencil and a felt-tip pen, for example, with the rule that students may speak only if they are holding it. The same person cannot make two consecutive contributions. The goal is to persuade people to change sides, and the team with more converts at the end wins the debate. In the process, of course, the finer points of the arguments should emerge. Partway through, teams could go off and research their arguments in more depth and detail.
- The "Value Continuum" could initiate, or could be the culmination of, an extended period of research about an issue.

Verbal Football

Physical skills are replaced by mental in this action-packed, fast-paced game of two teams.

Purposes	
Thinking	★★★★
Emotional intelligence	★
Independence	★★★
Interdependence	★★★★
Multisensation	★
Fun	★★★★★
Articulation	★★★

Skills Used	
Individual work	★★
Group work	★★★★
Moving	★
Speaking	★★★★
Listening	★★★★
Reading	★★★★
Writing	★
Looking	★
Choice	★★

Specific Room Layout?	
Yes	(No)

How?

1. Explain that the purpose of the game is to test knowledge and understanding. Divide the class into two teams. Each team should appoint a captain. Choose one student to be the referee, or do this yourself.

2. Explain that success in the game will depend on serious training. Training involves the team going over a given topic, checking facts and understanding with each other, and memorizing details to be ready to answer your questions.

3. When the training period is over, students put away all books and notes, the captains are called together, a coin is tossed to see who receives the kick-off, and the game begins.

4. The receiving team gets a question from you. Anyone on the team may answer within five seconds. If the team answers correctly, it retains possession. You ask another question. Again, if someone on the team answers correctly within five seconds, the ball has been passed successfully and possession has been retained. Put together a string of three correct answers (to equal three passes), and it's a touchdown. Once a person has answered a question, he cannot answer again until everyone else on the team has had a try. It's up to players, and especially the captain, to monitor who has and who hasn't taken part.

5. If a player answers incorrectly, that's a tackle, and possession moves to the opposition. You ask the other team the questions. If no one answers within five seconds, that's a loose ball. If the opposition can answer within a further five seconds, that team picks up possession and begins to receive questions.

6. Shouting out answers when it's the other team's turn, answering when one is ineligible, and, especially, arguing with the referee are all fouls.
7. The winning team is the one with more touchdowns at the end of the session.

Applications

- Use to consolidate learning at the end of a topic or to review later on.
- Use to introduce a new topic. "Verbal Football" enables you to check how much students already know.
- Use to conduct informal diagnostic assessment partway through a topic. The exercise roughly reveals how much has been understood and how much detail has been retained so far. This enables you to adjust subsequent lesson plans.

Why Do It?

- It's fun and adds variety to the teaching and learning diet. Students hardly notice that they are being tested.
- The "training" phase encourages students to look back at the work in some detail. This establishes the idea that long-term memorization requires that material be revisited again and again. The exercise demonstrates the value of review.
- There is an incentive for the students with more knowledge and understanding to ensure that those on their team with less have mastered the information and concepts.
- It appeals to students who don't settle down well to concentrated desk work.

Variations

- During training each player could prepare several questions to ask the opposition. During the game, instead of you asking the questions, students ask each other. A student may not ask a second question until everyone else on the team has contributed. In this case, fouls are committed by asking incomprehensible questions and for not knowing the answer oneself. Captains organize the order in which players ask questions.
- Teams could be given either the same topic in training or different topics.
- Instead of using it for consolidation or review, use it to introduce a topic. In this case, the training involves research, either open-ended if the class has the skills, or structured. Both teams will need to research, and prepare questions on, the same material.
- After a touchdown, a team could kick a field goal—answer a particularly challenging extra question—for an extra point.
- Instead of football, use basketball, baseball, hockey, soccer, or another sport.

Verbal Tennis

Love, sets, and matches. They're all part of school life. Make them a productive part of learning with a quick bit of banter.

Purposes	
Thinking	★★★★★
Emotional intelligence	
Independence	★
Interdependence	★
Multisensation	★
Fun	★★★★
Articulation	★★★★

Skills Used	
Individual work	★
Group work	★★★
Moving	
Speaking	★★★★★
Listening	★★★★★
Reading	
Writing	
Looking	
Choice	

Specific Room Layout?	
Yes	(No)

How?

1. Students sit facing each other in pairs. No books or notes are allowed.
2. You set a topic. Each pair tosses a coin to see who "serves" first. The server begins by saying a word or phrase associated with the topic; the partner immediately gives a second word or phrase; the server gives a third; and so on back and forth in rapid succession. It has the pace and feel of a word-association game.
3. When a student hesitates, gets stuck, repeats a word or phrase already given by either player, makes an off-topic contribution, or gives an inaccurate contribution, her partner gains a point. The scoring follows the rules of tennis.
4. Some topics can be sustained for a number of games, even a whole set, because they are sufficiently wide. Otherwise, write a list of topics on the board and ask students to change to a new topic at the start of each game.

Applications

- Ideal for review in any subject: names of twentieth-century artists; safety procedures in the workshop; key moments in the Civil War; chemical formulas; words associated with *The Crucible*; numbers divisible by nine; and so on.

- It makes a perfect lesson starter.
- It could be done as an informal test.
- Foreign languages and ESL: Use it to build vocabulary with topics such as adjectives, sports and hobbies, pluperfect constructions, store names, and goods.
- Use it to brainstorm creative ideas, such as possible ingredients in a healthy snack; ways of finding information about an assignment; or where to go on a field trip. Can be preparation for a whole-class brainstorm.

Why Do It?

- Students often need to warm up before they are ready to take part in open discussion. This exercise is structured and non-exposing.
- It raises energy levels in a flagging class.
- It focuses attention on the topic at hand at the beginning of a lesson, especially after a break or lunchtime.
- It switches on the brain and gets creative and lateral thinking going.
- It's fun and helps to create an environment conducive to learning.

Variation

Play according to squash or racquetball rules instead of tennis.

Wheel of Fortune

It won't tell their fortune; it won't make their fortune; but, for those who are fortunate, it will make them take part.

Purposes	
Thinking	★★★★
Emotional intelligence	
Independence	★
Interdependence	★★
Multisensation	★★
Fun	★★★
Articulation	★★★★

Skills Used		
Individual work	★★★	(variable)
Group work	★★★	(variable)
Moving	★★	
Speaking	★★★★	
Listening	★★★	
Reading	★	
Writing		
Looking	★	
Choice		

Specific Room Layout?

Yes / No

How?

1. Make a set of large cards with prompts or questions on one side and numbers on the other.

2. Make the "wheel of fortune" out of cardboard. Divide it into as many sectors as there are question cards and number the sectors. Make a spinner using a cardboard arrow and a brass paper fastener. The finished product should look like a Twister wheel.

3. The students sit in one large circle. The cards are spread face down, covering most of the floor space, with the numbers clearly visible.

4. A volunteer begins, takes the wheel, and spins it. The student gets up, picks up the card corresponding to the number shown when the wheel stops, and responds to the prompt or question.

5. A brief discussion takes place between you and the whole class. If class members judge that the student has responded fully and accurately, the card is placed back on the floor face up. That number is now void. If the answer is incomplete or inaccurate, the card is placed face down again for someone else to try his luck.

6. The wheel passes to the next person. As time goes by, more and more cards are turned face up. Whenever a void number is spun, the player is off the hook and simply passes the wheel to the next student. So, the game speeds up.

Applications

- Any subject: Students could define technical terms or use the activity for review. The cards could have very demanding questions, with strict criteria for a successful answer before the card may be turned over.
- Foreign languages and ESL: The cards could have pictures that must be described accurately in the target language or phrases to be translated.
- English: Use stanzas from poems—students have to give the poem and poet, context, imagery, symbolism, and meaning of keywords.
- Math: Use calculations to be solved on the board or have students name the rule or procedure to be applied to such-and-such a problem.
- History: Use dates or have students give the details of an event or the main achievements of such-and-such a figure.
- Science: Students name the equipment, procedures, and safety regulations for various processes.

Why Do It?

- It encourages reluctant students to take part—they tend to accept the random selection of the wheel.
- It is a game with a challenging edge, like many TV game shows. This is a familiar and motivating genre for most students.
- At an advanced level, it is excellent preparation for an exam.
- It helps students practice recall and speed of thought.

Variations

- Reverse it. Take the question cards in sequence and let the wheel decide which student is going to answer next. For this, you don't need to reorganize the room; simply number the students.
- Playing with a large class can be tedious. Instead, break students into three or four groups, each with its own set of cards and wheel. Or stay as a whole group and divide the students into teams. When the team turns a question up, team members have to decide quickly which of them is going to answer. Each team member may have only two turns.
- Beat the clock—each player has only 30 seconds to give the answer.
- The cards on the floor are roles. The student has to answer questions from the class in character for one minute. For example, roles within a company in business studies, characters in a novel or play in English, key players in a military or political engagement in history, famous designers or artists in art and design.

Tools for Managing Group Work, Behavior, and Personal Responsibility

Introduction

Everyone is concerned about behavior. Naturally. We all know how our best-laid plans can be wrecked by one or two disruptive students. What prevents many teachers from using innovative and interactive classroom techniques? Discipline.

Even when they are convinced by the theory and can see that the practical idea is a good one, most teachers will still refuse to try a technique if they suspect that discipline and control will be undermined. The reasons for this are understandable. First, there is a biological explanation. Whenever a person perceives threat—physical, emotional, or psychological—the blood supply to the ancient, instinctive parts of the brain is dramatically increased. Survival behaviors are instantly and automatically activated, and rationality goes out the window. The brain's job, first and foremost, is to ensure survival. It will go for the safest option, the tried-and-tested solution. When the chips are down, when it is fearful, the brain will instinctively protect itself, its reputation, its job.

Second, we live in a culture in which there is little acceptance of personal responsibility. On the whole, parents, the media, school administrators, and certainly most students, think that it is the teacher's job to control the class. A teacher's reputation rises or falls by his ability to master difficult groups of students. There is little belief in self-discipline. Otherwise we wouldn't be so dependant on rewards and punishments, which perpetuate students' reliance on extrinsic behavioral motivators (for further discussion of this point, Alfie Kohn's book *Punished by Rewards* [1993] is excellent). The role models portrayed in most walks of real and televised life suggest that getting away with it if you can and blaming someone, or something, else is normal. The job of reversing these norms appears enormous.

However, this section bravely tries to do just that. It draws on humanistic rather than behavioristic psychology and presents a series of strategies that attempt to transform your average classroom into a self-regulating minisociety. Given the forces at work, though, the section also offers a number of fallback positions and pragmatic techniques that may not be ideal, but at least help us make progress.

The goals are

- to create sufficient self-discipline for teachers to feel confident about using active and interactive learning strategies
- for students to feel that they can take part enthusiastically in whole-class and small-group activities without fear of negative consequences from their peers

The reptilian response of the brain, described above in the case of fearful teachers, applies to fearful students, too. They also tend to play it safe when they sense ridicule or marginalization. Acceptance by the peer group is all-important to most students, and they will not sacrifice their standing with their friends for the sake of the teacher's fancy classroom techniques. So, basic work has to be done on attitudes to learning, to each other, and to the teacher. "Murder Mystery" (page 152), "Framed" (page 156), "Observer Server" (page 159), "Learning Listening" (page 161), "Sabotage" (page 164), and "Games" (page 166) are all designed to begin the process of creating new behavioral norms through direct experiential means. "Maintenance" (page 169) suggests ways of maintaining momentum toward the new order.

Apart from creating the conditions in which risky learning strategies are most likely to work, there are three further and noble reasons for investing time and effort in these matters. First, inclusion. Enabling *all* learners to be physically present in a classroom is only the first step toward inclusion. Full participation in learning occurs only when each student is genuinely accepted, and *knows* that she is genuinely accepted, by the whole group. This requires students to behave toward each other in an acceptant and inclusive manner. In concrete terms this involves

- letting each other speak without background snickers and sarcastic remarks;
- listening;
- inviting;
- encouraging;
- and, most fundamental, *eliminating all types of put-downs.*

Such behaviors are reassuring, encourage participation, and build self-esteem, which increases confidence. These are the deep-seated needs of all students, not just those with identified "special needs."

Second, good citizenship. These inclusive behaviors are also the foundation stones of democracy. People are allowed—no, *encouraged*—to have their say. Everyone is heard. Opinions are respected. These are the preconditions of open debate. Beyond this, every student is asked to accept responsibility for his own and for the group's behavior. Crucially, the society of the classroom is of the students' making. The teacher does not allow the class to cop out by shoveling all responsibility onto the one person with the positional power, whom they can then resist, fight, and blame.

Third, emotional intelligence. Daniel Goleman's internationally renowned work has once more brought to prominence the importance of personal and social development. Being able to identify, name, describe, and manage one's own feelings; being able to read and accommodate the emotions of others; and developing key personal qualities such as perseverance and self-restraint are all hallmarks of an emotionally intelligent person. Such intelligence can be developed; it can be taught. It will be easy to see how such learning can occur through the activities in this section.

All in all, then, the campaign for self-discipline and collective responsibility is well worth the effort.

Murder Mystery

It's a mystery. What kind of ground rules will the group create? The plot thickens . . .

How?

1. Print the following 30 clues individually on small cards (make up more clues if you need them):

    - Only one bullet had been fired from Mr. Azir's gun.
    - Clare Smith saw Jamil go to Mr. Azir's apartment building at 11:55 p.m.
    - The workman had been with the company for years and was regarded as completely truthful and trustworthy.
    - The workman said that he often saw Jamil's sister walking down the road with Andrew Scott.
    - The workman reported to the police that he saw Jamil with no injuries at 11:50 p.m.
    - Jamil had destroyed Mr. Azir's business by stealing all his customers.
    - Jamil's sister disappeared after the murder.
    - The workman saw Jamil's sister go to Andrew Scott's house at 11:30 p.m.
    - It was clear that Jamil's body had been dragged a long way.
    - Clare Smith worked at the same school as Andrew Scott.
    - Jamil's bloodstains were found in Andrew Scott's car.
    - When he was found dead, Jamil had a bullet hole in his leg and a knife wound in his back.
    - Andrew Scott's ex-wife was regarded as a very jealous woman.
    - Mr. Azir disappeared after the murder.
    - Clare Smith often followed Jamil.
    - Jamil's body was found in the park.
    - The police were unable to find Andrew Scott after the murder.
    - The workman saw Jamil go to Andrew Scott's house at 12:25 a.m.
    - Mr. Azir had told Jamil that he was going to kill him.
    - Andrew Scott was a teacher and outdoorsman.
    - When the workman saw Jamil just after midnight, Jamil was bleeding but did not seem very badly hurt.
    - Mr. Azir shot at an "intruder" in his apartment building at midnight.
    - Jamil had been dead for an hour when his body was found, the coroner said.
    - A knife with Andrew Scott's fingerprints on it was found in Clare Smith's garden.
    - Jamil's bloodstains were found on the carpet outside Mr. Azir's flat.
    - Jamil's body was found at 1:30 a.m.
    - In the local community, Mr. Azir was regarded as a cheerful and kind man.
    - The bullet taken from Jamil's leg matched the gun owned by Mr. Azir.
    - The workman said that nobody left Andrew Scott's house between 12:25 a.m. and 12:45 a.m.
    - Jamil had very strong religious beliefs.

2. Explain to students that a murder has been committed and it is their responsibility to solve the mystery. The answers to these six questions have to be found within the next 15 minutes (adjust the time to suit the class):

- Who was murdered?
- Who committed the murder?
- When?
- Where?
- What was the weapon?
- Why?

3. The class sits in one large circle. Give every student a clue card and explain the rules: "You have to keep your own card—you may not give or show your card to anyone. Only one person in the group is allowed to write. You may not leave your places. When, as a group, you think you have all six answers, let me know, and I'll tell you how many you have right and wrong, not which ones. If you don't get them all right within 15 minutes, I win!" From this point on, you don't intervene, no matter how badly the group does, unless violence is about to be committed! You merely act as timekeeper and give the students a reminder halfway through.

Consider asking one or two members of the class to be "Observer Server" (see page 159). The job of observers is to note, and report back to the class, helpful and unhelpful behaviors during the exercise. Whether you use observers or not, "Murder Mystery" is designed to lead into a discussion about group behavior, and then to the formation of ground rules.

The Answers

- Victim: Jamil
- Murderer: Andrew Scott
- When: 12:30 a.m.
- Where: Andrew Scott's house
- Weapon: Knife
- Why: It seems as though Jamil interfered in a relationship between his sister and Andrew Scott. Presumably they did him in so they could carry on undisturbed. (This question, by its very nature, cannot be answered with the same degree of certainty as the others.)

Application

This is a classic way to get students to appreciate the need for basic rules and procedures. More often than not, when the teacher's controlling hand is removed, a class behaves in a disorganized way. Left to their own devices, students generally have little understanding of how to give and take leadership, how to organize discussion, how to include everyone, how to process information collectively, how to make decisions, and how to manage time. At worst, the group disintegrates—some people withdraw, others shout, others argue. Mocking, name calling, and wise cracking rise to the surface.

Therefore, the experience is likely to be frustrating for the students (and very frustrating for the watching teacher). However, this is the intention. The exercise creates the motivation to identify the current behavioral norms of the class, and to propose the changes needed if group work and interactive learning are to be successful in the future. A discussion with the students about these issues can now be precise and concrete—it is about a common experience that just happened. "Framed" (page 156) and "Observer Server" (page 159) can help with this debriefing process.

The intention is to arrive at a new set of behaviors that everyone agrees to uphold. They might include:

- We will take turns.
- We will let people finish what they are saying.
- We will be quiet when people are speaking.
- We will look at the person who is speaking.
- We will cut out rude comments and gestures.
- We will not make fun of anyone.
- Each of us will be able to sum up what other people have said.

Sometimes, though, the students never get this far. They strongly resist the idea that they should take this amount of responsibility for their own behavior. They fiercely cling to the belief that it's the teacher's job to make them behave. At this point, you will need to judge whether you have the skill and strength to persevere, or whether a combination of the students' upbringing, the culture of their local society, the modus operandi of your colleagues, the behavior policy of the school, and other factors simply make it too hard a task.

You may need to back-pedal and take a number of preliminary steps, such as increasing your own assertiveness, changing classroom language, and campaigning to raise students' self-esteem (see page 205). Beyond this, it will be important to raise self-discipline as a whole-school issue and seek agreement among all staff members about new approaches to behavior management.

Ultimately, "Murder Mystery" is daring because it allows the truth about students' behavior to surface. It confronts students with the challenge to be self-disciplined, and it takes away their usual dependency on carrots and sticks, which means asking some of them to change the habits of a lifetime.

Why Do It?

- The overriding purpose of "Murder Mystery" is to establish agreed-on behaviors that support self-esteem and collaboration. It confronts students with the idea that they should accept both personal and group responsibility, self-discipline, and the creation of a self-regulating classroom society. Such learning can occur only experientially.
- The activity exercises a wide range of thinking skills, especially because only one person is allowed to write and so much has to be held and processed in the mind.

Variations

- Instead of leaving the students to conduct the exercise on their own, and probably do a bad job of it, lead it for them. Demonstrate the processes of good group leadership and get them to adopt the desired behaviors such as taking turns, listening, inviting contributions, summing up, building on each other's suggestions, giving way, being persistent, keeping their eyes on the time, and checking that all information has been gathered. Give them a good and positive experience. Then ask them to adopt the behaviors that worked well and to take responsibility for ensuring that they happen even when you aren't in charge.
- Instead of running "Murder Mystery" as a whole-class exercise, do it in small groups. In this case, each student will have a number of cards that she holds close to her chest, just like a hand of playing cards. This increases everyone's participation.

Framed

It's not very comfortable being framed, but sometimes we just have to face up to what we have, or haven't, done. Still, we can always do it better next time.

How?

1. Have the students carry out a collaborative exercise. This may be a genuine learning activity about the topic at hand using "Corporate Identity" (page 76) or "Quick on the Draw" (page 121), for instance. Or it could be an artificial exercise designed to test cooperative behaviors. "Murder Mystery" (page 152) is ideal for this.

2. Then ask students to reflect on the experience and examine their behaviors. The first step is for them to recall what happened. This might be done by hearing feedback from an observer server (see page 159), or by watching a video recording of the lesson, (which is ideal because there's no argument; the camera doesn't lie), or by listening to an audio recording of themselves. Otherwise students' and teacher's memories will have to be relied upon.

3. Whatever recall device is used, ask students individually to record their own and other students' helpful and unhelpful behaviors in this simple frame. The rule: Name behaviors; don't name people.

What I did that helped the group	What I did that hindered the group
What other people did that helped	**What other people did that hindered**

4. Discussion follows. It is crucial that no one be criticized. Don't focus on the past (What should we have done?), but on the future (What should we do differently from now on?). Be tough. Don't let students play down the damaging effects of behaviors. Insist that improvements will be identified and agreed on. Explain why. It's best to tackle *whole-group* issues first, looking to secure everyone's commitment to a few general changes. For example: "Everyone will speak one at a time."

5. Individuals can then be encouraged to make *personal* changes: for example, "I will ask people what they think more often" or "I will not interrupt."

6. The whole-group rules should be immediately written large and posted on the classroom wall, so that they are in the students' faces for the foreseeable future.

7. Both the group and the personal agreements can be recorded by everyone on the team action plan, and, after a few more lessons, an assessment of progress can be carried out. To do this, set up another cooperative whole-class or small-group exercise. After discussion, everyone marks with a checkmark on the right-hand side of the sheet the progress made—or not made.

TEAM ACTION PLAN

Progress

As a whole group we agree to . . .

No different than before | We've kept the agreement completely

_____

_____

_____

_____

Personally I agree to . . .

_____

_____

_____

_____

Name: _____

Signed: _____   Date: _____

Application

Use for vital foundation work with any class in any subject.

Why Do It?

- It's pragmatic. A great deal of time is often wasted during group work—students not taking part, annoying each other, being marginalized, retaliating. Likewise, whole-class activities are often sabotaged by unthinking, clumsy, or malicious behavior. It is more efficient to tackle these issues up front, in advance, than it is to fight a running battle during lessons.

- Students keep their heads down and play it safe if they suspect that they might be embarrassed for taking part. Few students admit this, but brain scans show that the blood flow to the ancient, instinctive parts of the brain is automatically and instantly increased when a person feels threatened. This tends to trigger survival (fight, flight, freeze, or flock together) behaviors and reduces rational thought. So, to maximize participation and therefore learning, it is vital that students regard the classroom to be emotionally and psychologically safe. They know that they will be protected from each other's hostility. They are confident that they will not be ignored, called names, mocked, belittled, laughed at, or joked about for having an idea, attempting an answer, volunteering, or being smart. Until these norms are proven (and students will test them!), the teacher is likely to struggle to get widespread participation, which means that a lot of *Toolkit*-type ideas will collapse.

- Making a big deal about interpersonal behaviors and their effect on feelings raises the status of emotional intelligence. This whole aspect of being human is hugely underplayed in most schools these days, where pursuit of narrow attainment still tends to dominate proceedings. Only if they are able to recognize and manage emotions can students be fully successful within themselves and with other people. This is most likely to happen if the key concepts of emotional intelligence are explained and *lived* in classrooms.

- Social inclusion can become a reality only if hostile and excluding behaviors are eliminated.

Variation

Instead of students recording helpful and unhelpful behaviors in the "frame" individually, ask them to call them out while you build up a whole-class record on the board or on an overhead projector.

Observer Server

Out of sight, out of mind. It's easy for everyone to slip back into old ways—unless, that is, you have an "Observer Server."

How?

1. Assign the students a collaborative task, either in small groups or as a whole class. It's important that they have to work together. It's best if this is a genuine task, a natural development of the ongoing topic, though an artificial task will do, such as making a bridge out of a few sheets of newspaper, some straws, and string; or dropping an egg from a second-floor window with a device that will enable it to land without breaking. Ask for one or two volunteers to opt out of the task and be observer servers. Explain that this involves watching what goes on during the activity and reporting back to everyone at the end.

2. The observers look at how well the students work together. You might give them a general instruction: "Write down everything you see and hear that helps the group to get the job done and everything you see and hear that undermines and spoils their efforts (without using names)." Or you might have more structured questions for them to answer, such as

   - Did you notice any of the following behaviors (and, if so, what effect did they have)?

interrupting	asking someone a question
inviting someone to contribute	summing up
shouting out	congratulating
ignoring	being rude
making fun	withdrawing
adding to someone else's idea	giving way to someone else
contradicting	standing up for one's self

   - What were people doing apart from the job they were supposed to be doing?
   - Were there any leaders? What did they do?
   - How did they become leaders?
   - How equally did people take part? What effect did this have on getting the job done?
   - What did the teacher do to help or hinder the group?
   - What advice would you give to the class and the teacher for next time?
   - Whether observers use a structured list of questions or follow the more open instruction, they must follow the rule of naming behaviors, not people.

3. Ensure that there is enough time left at the end for the observers to share their findings with the class and for discussion about lessons learned. It is easy for this to be done badly because many students are not used to giving and receiving feedback constructively. If you have time, train them; if not, try one or two rules that might help:

   - Observers do not name students; they just describe behaviors.
   - Observers simply say what they saw and heard.

- To avoid any hint of accusation, feedback sentences begin with "I" (for example "I saw . . .", "I noticed . . .", "I observed . . .", "I heard . . ."), not "You" ("You did such-and-such" or "You didn't do . . .").
- If observers give an opinion or advice, the sentence begins with "I think . . ." or "In my opinion . . ." rather than "You should . . ."
- In fact, observers never use "should," "ought," "must," or "have to."
- The class and the teacher do not interrupt the observers—there will be time for discussion later.
- In any discussion that follows, speakers begin all sentences with "I" (for example, "I disagree . . ." or "I'd like to add . . ." or "I saw something different . . .")
- Actually, there's no need to persuade anybody. If a student doesn't agree with some of the feedback from the observers, she can just put it in her mental waste-basket.

4. To make the best use of the feedback, play "stop, start, continue." Ask each student to decide on one behavior she will stop, one she will start, and one she will continue doing. These could be written in personal journals.

5. You could end with a "Round" (page 170) of "What I personally intend to improve next time is . . ."

Applications

- Use in any class, in any subject. Observers provide a mirror for the class. Use the strategy to create ground rules by highlighting what needs to be done differently.
- Refresh ground rules by pointing out the difference between what was previously agreed to and what is actually happening now.

Why Do It?

- With so much pressure these days to cover content, it is easy to neglect the process of learning in general and the quality of group interactions in particular. However, we know that for optimum learning to occur, the brain requires a sense of security, well-being, and the absence of threat—emotional, psychological, and physical.
- The "Observer Server" strategy promotes the habits of self-appraisal and personal reflection. These are lifelong learning skills.
- The technique also helps to establish the skills of giving and receiving feedback. As students grow older, they will discover that these life skills are crucial to the health of all substantial personal and professional relationships.

Variations

- Use a video recording of the activity rather than human observers for feedback to the class.
- Swap observers partway through the activity or lesson, so that you get more people involved and more perspectives.
- Make the role of observer server a high-status one: To undertake the role, students must be willing to catch up with the classwork later. It's not a cop out.

Learning Listening

This is an effective and fun way to get students to listen. I said, this is an effective and fun way to get students to listen.

How?

This activity is conducted over four rounds. Organize people to sit in pairs facing each other. Ask each pair to decide who is A and who is B.

Round One

A's and B's are to speak to each other simultaneously, without hesitation, repetition, or deviation, nonstop, for two minutes. Ask the class for a topic or give a suggestion (for example, favorite TV programs, music, places, holidays, food, clothes, sports, and so forth). While talking nonstop, each partner also has to listen to what the other is saying.

Debrief. Ask students how it went, how they felt, and how successful they were at listening and speaking simultaneously. Ask: "How often does this occur in real life? When do you see people talking *at* each other rather than listening *to* each other?"

Round Two

The A's speak for two minutes about a new topic (such as family and friends or what they'd do with $100,000), while B's turn to stone, showing no movement or response of any kind, not even in the eyes. Before they begin, ask the statues to get comfortable and look just past their partner's face at a point on the other side of the room.

Debrief students on the feeling of being completely ignored, the effect this has (for example, running out of things to say, wanting to smack the statue), and the occasions when this kind of thing happens in everyday life.

Round Three

B's now have their turn to speak for two minutes on a new topic (for example, people, places, events, and things that matter to them or their favorite memories), while A's use subtle behaviors to show that they are not really paying attention (for example, glancing at their watch, yawning, making their eyes glaze over, and looking over the speaker's shoulder). Alternatively, you can ask A's to try to steal the show and take over the conversation with comments like "Oh, yes, of course that happened to me . . . ," and "Yes, I know, that reminds me of . . ."

Debrief, focusing on the feeling of not being *really* heard. How can they tell? What did they do about it? When does it happen, both in and out of school, that people are being polite but not really attentive?

Interval

Based on the first three rounds of poor listening, ask the class to list the hallmarks of quality listening. What do good listeners do? For example:

- Maintain eye contact.
- Respond nonverbally as appropriate using nods, frowns, smiles, quizzical looks, and so forth.
- Use grunts, yeps, ahas, and other sounds to signal their continued attention.
- At an advanced level of listening, *mirror* the gestures, body language, and facial expressions of the speaker.
- At intervals, sum up and repeat what has been said (this is the acid test of listening).

Active listening does not involve asking questions, except for clarification.

Round Four

Pairs practice active listening of the quality described above, with topics that are fairly serious and personal (such as what they'd like to do with their lives, what they worry about, or what they think about education, ghosts, politics, aliens, and so forth). It is important that both A and B get a chance to speak and listen and have enough time to do the job well, say, seven or eight minutes each, and that they are not allowed to take notes. At the end of each turn, the listener sums up what his partner said. This really brings home to students the degree of concentration needed to listen properly and take in what people say. This last round also gives students experience of the feel-good factor, the feeling of worth, the boost to self-esteem, generated by someone paying them exclusive and total attention.

Debrief. Ask about successes and difficulties. What were the feelings? When is it important to listen properly—with friends, family, and in class? Finally, ask students to consider making quality listening a feature of every lesson. Ask them to commit themselves to making it the rule.

Applications

- Use it to make or refresh ground rules with a class. This is the main purpose of the activity.
- Use it to open up discussion or to conduct review in any subject—the topics talked about would be relevant to the unit or lesson.
- Use as a vital foundation for health education and tutorial work, central to good citizenship, and crucial to group-based and interactive learning in any subject.
- Teach listening as part of a conflict-resolution strategy, such as peer mediation. Most arguments are resolved by first asking students to listen to each other and summarize what the other has said.
- At an advanced level, the exercise could be conducted in a foreign language.

Why Do It?

- Listening has an immediate and positive impact on self-esteem. People who are genuinely heard universally say that they feel valued and respected. Self-esteem cannot be raised superficially through smiley faces and the like, but it can be by allowing people to feel that they matter enough to be listened to.
- Listening is the basis of quality discussion, negotiation, conflict resolution, peer assessment, decision making, and the tutoring process.
- Listening is therefore the feature of classroom life most generally required for nondidactic methods to work. Many teachers feel confident about trying more adventurous techniques only once self-discipline (through firm ground rules based on listening) has been established. Likewise, most students want to feel the protection of firm ground rules before they will participate in risky learning activities.
- Listening is the life skill at the core of all personal, professional, and civic relationships. If you value achievement beyond exam success, teach and model listening.

Variation

Begin the "Interval" stage by asking for a volunteer to help you demonstrate active listening. They talk; you listen. Show how to give total attention, putting everything else out of your mind, and demonstrate all the verbal and nonverbal listening behaviors. Ask the rest of the class to watch and then list the skills you use.

Sabotage

Poor behavior wrecks learning. Here's a nifty way to sabotage the sabotage.

How?

1. Write the word "sabotage" on the board and ask students what it means. Provide dictionaries if necessary and hold a discussion to ensure that everyone gets the idea of subtly wrecking, spoiling, or undermining.

2. Ask the students, in pairs, to list all the ways in which learning is being (or could be) sabotaged by members of this class. They may need some encouragement to be honest and should not write students' names—just list the behaviors.

3. Students then take turns calling out behaviors from their lists while you write these behaviors on the board.

4. Now be open about how difficult it is for the teacher to control all these. In some cases, they're difficult to pin on anyone: Sometimes they're behind the teacher's back, under the desk, or outside the classroom. Therefore it's up to students to decide: Do they want to carry on these behaviors and spoil their own and other people's learning or cut out these behaviors and do well? The responsibility is actually theirs. Discuss the consequences of this decision and give the upbeat message that you want them all to succeed and that you bet they all want to too, secretly. Allow some discussion. Resist their attempts to shovel all the responsibility back onto you.

5. Ask which of the listed behaviors do the most damage. Select the top two or three. Challenge the class to tackle these first. Suggest that students agree with each other to cut these out from now on.

6. If agreement can be reached, write up the new "expectations" (avoid the word "rules" if you can) in large letters and display them prominently in the classroom. Resist the idea of punishments, even though the class might want them. Instead, establish the idea that it is the joint responsibility of teacher and students to remind and challenge each other.

7. If agreement cannot be reached easily, suggest that the class try cutting out specified behaviors for a trial period, after which the effects of the experiment will be reviewed.

Application

To create workable ground rules directly and quickly with any class, in any subject.

Why Do It?

• It locates the responsibility for students' behavior where it actually belongs—with the students.

• It makes sharp points about personal and collective responsibility, which are the stuff of good citizenship.

- It makes equally strong points about life being a series of choices and consequences, that no one can escape responsibility for her own actions. It uncompromisingly points out the immaturity of looking for people to rescue others from their actions (expecting the teacher to hand out punishments, for example). Consequently, it deals with some tough aspects of emotional intelligence.
- Your openness and honesty usually result in more respect for you and a more wholesome relationship with the class.
- If it works, it reduces your stress because you no longer have to control the class single-handedly.

Variation

Give students behaviors on cards to rank, rather than expect them to come up with their own lists from scratch.

Games

Life's a funny thing. Well, it could be. Here's a way of creating some serious rules with some serious fun.

Classroom games are currently out of fashion, which is a pity. So much potential benefit is lost. Well-chosen games can

- create more flexible working relationships among students
- break the ice between students and teacher
- raise or lower energy levels
- refocus attention
- help students practice a range of thinking skills painlessly
- stimulate the brain, connect left and right hemispheres, and accelerate learning

But the particular use of games described here is to create an acceptance of basic ground rules. (The following four games are just examples. Many more can be found in myriad classroom game collections available online and in bookstores.) Such games effectively alter the dynamics of the classroom and usually create a greater willingness to learn and behave. These benefits can be increased substantially if time is taken to debrief the class on the experience. There are two levels of debriefing:

Level 1

Debrief students on the effects of the experience. Prompts might include

- Why do you think I chose this game?
- What have we learned from it?
- What real-life issues are mirrored in this game?
- How can games like this affect the way you feel about being in this classroom?
- How can games like this alter our relationships with each other and the way we see each other?
- What might be the benefits of playing such games in the future?

Level 2

Debrief students on the workings of the game and the transferability of these workings to regular classroom life. Prompts might include

- How did the game work?
- What can it teach us about the way we operate in this classroom?
- What part did rules play in the success and enjoyment of the game?
- What effect would or did breaking the rules have on the game?
- How could the rules be improved?
- How could we improve our rules to make sure that our classroom is purposeful and fun at the same time?

Tick Tock

1. Everyone sits in a circle, including you. You hold two objects (for example, a felt-tip pen and a ruler), one in each hand.
2. Turn to the student on your right (student 1) and offer the object in your right hand, saying, "This is a tick." Student 1 says, "A what?" and you repeat, "A tick." Only then may student 1 take the object.
3. Student 1 then immediately turns to student 2, on her right, saying, "This is a tick." Student 2 asks, "A what?" Student 1 repeats the question to you. You answer, "A tick" to student 1, who in turn says, "A tick" to student 2. Only then may student 2 take the object.
4. Student 2 offers the tick in the same way to student 3 and so on around the circle. Each time, the question "A what?" must pass from student to student back to you, and each time the answer "A tick" must go out from you along the chain.
5. Once the group has had a chance to practice, explain the challenge: "The idea is to pass the tick around the circle one way at the same time as passing the tock around the circle the other way. Eventually I should get them both back."
6. The game starts for real. You send the tick out to the right and the tock to the left. If all goes well, you sit there sounding like a clock until the crossover point really throws a wrench into the works.

This game can be a bit slow to get going with a large class, so explain to two students how to lead it, divide the class into two circles, and have two separate games going while you supervise.

Key debriefing points might include teamwork; everyone playing a part; sticking to rules and routines; supporting each other when stuck; and having fun but avoiding the temptation to make fun of others. In addition, this is a mental exercise that stimulates concentration and prepares the mind for further learning.

Giants, Dwarfs, and Wizards

1. Divide the class into two equal(ish) teams five or six feet apart, perhaps separated by a line of rope, masking tape, or chalk.
2. Explain: "You live in a world inhabited by warring giants, dwarfs, and wizards. Giants always beat dwarfs by stamping on them. Wizards naturally beat giants by casting spells, and dwarfs beat wizards by, I'm told, tickling their legs. You're about to do battle with each other. Your team must decide, collectively, which of the three beings you are. Everyone in your team must agree to be the same thing and you must keep your joint decision secret—whatever you do, don't let the other team know!"
3. Each team huddles together to make their decisions, then line up and face each other.
4. Continue: "On the count of three, you will all display what you've decided to become. Giants will stand on tiptoes with their hands stretched above their heads. Dwarfs will crouch down, and wizards will step forward with their spell-casting hands outstretched."

5. You count, the teams display their characters, and points are awarded: two for a win, one each for a draw. Further rounds follow, and the first team to 10 points wins.

The debriefing can include a discussion about competition versus cooperation (both elements are present in the game), making and upholding group decisions, inclusion, exclusion, and the various us-and-them divisions in the classroom.

Caterpillar

1. Students sit in a tight circle with the sides of their chairs touching. One person volunteers to be "on" and stands in the middle, leaving her chair free.
2. At the word "go," everyone shuffles around clockwise, with their bottoms sliding from chair to chair as fast as possible. While the person in the middle desperately tries to sit back down on any seat, the rest keep the motion going, so there's never a chair free.
3. If the circle is too slow moving, try two spare chairs instead of one. Become adventurous and have two people in the middle, then go for three people with three spare chairs. Upgrade to four as the game builds momentum.
4. If a person who's "on" does manage to sit down, then someone else takes her place in the middle.
5. To add spice, whenever you clap your hand, the movement changes direction.

Lots of debriefing potential here about being left out, ganging up, in-crowds and out-crowds, humiliation, and the potential escalation of conflict.

Control Tower

1. Clear the desks and chairs to the sides of the room. Ask for two volunteers, one to be the control tower, the other to be the airplane.
2. The control tower stands on a chair in one corner of the classroom, and the plane, blindfolded, stands in the opposite corner awaiting instructions.
3. The rest of the class clutter the runway (the rest of the classroom) by standing one arm's length away from one another with their arms by their sides and feet together, in total silence so that they don't give their positions away.
4. The control tower's job is to give oral instructions to guide the plane down the runway to the tower without its hitting any human obstacle. For example: "Right a bit, stop, two steps forward . . ." and so on. One penalty point for each obstacle touched. Three penalty points and the plane crashes.
5. After the first try, new volunteers are the control tower and airplane. Each time there's a new control tower and airplane, all the obstacles change position.

As for debriefing, this game works because one person is allowed to speak and everyone else is quiet: an obvious lead-in to listening, taking turns, and other classroom ground rules.

Maintenance

Maintain your sanity with these five easy-to-use techniques for reinforcing listening skills and maintaining ground rules.

Even when classroom rules have been successfully created with a class through experiential means, behavioral norms are not significantly changed without continued effort. Agreeing on ground rules with students is only the start of the process. In middle and high schools, when you see a class at intervals and sometimes only once a week, it is hard to build momentum. Changes secured in one lesson will often be reversed in the interim, and behaviors will then be back to square one next time. This sounds depressing, but with determined optimism and the skillful use of some pragmatic techniques, you can create in just one classroom norms that might not apply elsewhere in the school.

Use whatever means you can to support the cause. For example, in addition to modeling the key behaviors yourself, pay attention to seating arrangements. Are students looking at the back of one another's head? Arranging desks so that they form three sides of a square creates a common arena for speaking and listening. Alternatively, pushing desks to the sides of the classroom means that students can turn their chairs inward for input, discussion, and activities and can turn their chairs to the desks facing the walls for individual work. Another standard layout would be to have desks pushed together in blocks to form working groups of four, six, or eight students.

Naturally, it's important to arrange the space to suit the activities. This will often mean moving the furniture several times a week, a day, or even within one period. Students can help and are often willing to come in a few minutes before the end of break or lunchtime. An outgoing class can quickly rearrange desks and chairs for the next group in the final couple of minutes before the bell. Or an incoming class can be challenged to get the furniture reorganized within two minutes, following a plan you've drawn on the board.

Now that the rearrangement of furniture is an established principle, use pragmatic techniques that encourage, or even require, the new behaviors. Here are some suggestions.

Circle

Create an open circle of chairs with everyone, including you, taking part. The goal is for the circle to be a place where people can speak freely, ask and answer questions, express opinions, suggest solutions, share feelings, and contribute ideas—or not—without fear of ridicule, marginalization, or punishment. It is an ancient and universal meeting format. There are several reasons for using a circle:

- It is a powerful statement in itself about making the group feel united: "We are each responsible for this group's learning and behavior. We are in this together."
- It shows that you are flexible enough to adopt different roles—in a circle, you are more of a supporter and tutor than a deliverer and controller.

- A circle is open, even exposing, and it consequently challenges students to be more relaxed and confident with each other.
- A circle encourages participation from the whole group—there's no hiding place.
- A circle is practical. It creates an open space for games, for drama, and for many of the learning activities described in the *Toolkit*.

One or two practicalities: Bags and coats should be left outside the circle, perhaps on the desks that have been pushed to the sides of the room. Naturally, students will immediately want to sit with their friends. Initially, this might not be a bad idea because it provides familiarity in an unfamiliar setting. Before long, though, mix them up. This can be done randomly by giving out shuffled playing cards, one per person, then asking students to sort themselves into straights, flushes, or suits. In a cramped space, students often get left outside the circle, or the circle takes on an amoeba shape, around science benches for example, with people in odd nooks and crannies. It's better to have two concentric circles with everyone involved than to have a few students marginalized. Finally, some students, out of nervousness or mischief, may deliberately push their chairs out of the circle. They should be challenged to come back in before proceedings continue.

The circle is an ideal way to begin a lesson—to conduct a learning review, the explanation of learning objectives, connecting the lesson with previous and forthcoming learning experiences, or re-establishing the big picture. It is also an ideal way to end a lesson—to review and check on progress. The following examples illustrate a few ways to use the circle.

Round

This is a time when everyone in the circle has an opportunity to speak, in turn, without being forced to do so.

Explain the rules: "Anyone may start, then each person will have a chance to speak in turn around the circle. No one may comment, verbally or nonverbally, negatively or positively, on what anyone says; no one may interrupt. Anyone may say 'pass' when it's his turn." Explain the spirit: "This is an opportunity to listen to each other. Discussion can come later." Decide whether the round will go clockwise or counterclockwise and ask for someone to begin.

The round provides a structured and calm way of encouraging students to speak to each other and to you. No one has to fight for airtime, because everyone is guaranteed a fair share. It encourages participation by removing the fear of being ridiculed or ignored; everyone will be heard. It challenges shy and retiring students to speak by momentarily putting them in the spotlight and presenting the expectation that they will have something to say. The round acknowledges that everyone has an equally valid and valuable contribution to make, which helps to raise self-esteem.

Use it to find out what students know about a topic in advance, or what they have learned afterwards. Use it to get students' opinions, thoughts, and feelings out in the open. Use it to generate ideas, to air grievances, or to make decisions.

Variation: Paper Round

Useful when class members are not confident enough to express personal opinions in public, perhaps because the material is sensitive or because the students are very shy.

1. Give everyone a piece of paper and a pencil.
2. Ask for contributions to be written individually and privately but not signed.
3. Papers are folded, collected in a container, and shaken.
4. Pass the container around the circle. Each person takes out one piece of paper.
5. Take turns reading the papers out loud, each person reading the comment as if it were her own.

Conch

Choose an object (a felt-tip pen, small box, ruler, ball, or similar) to use as a conch. (The idea of "Conch" is taken from the novel *Lord of the Flies*.) Explain that a person may speak only when she is holding the conch. When a speaker has finished, she passes the conch directly to the next person who wants to speak.

This usually brings order to a discussion. It's amazing how much authority the innocent object can have! A single conch can be used in whole-class discussions, two conches used in formal debates (one for each side), or several conches used for several small groups. With younger students, use a "magic microphone."

Tokenism

Give everyone three tokens (such as buttons, blocks, a card). Each time a person makes a constructive contribution to the discussion by making a point or asking a question, he surrenders a token, putting it in a box in the middle of the circle. Vary the number of tokens per person according to the size of the group and nature of the discussion.

This simple device starts to equalize participation, to limit the outspoken and encourage the shy. If someone is out of tokens and desperate to speak, she may buy back a token by summing up the main points of the discussion so far.

Sum Up and Speak Up

When a person wants to contribute to a discussion, he must first sum up what the previous speaker said and then give his own opinion: "So-and-so said . . ."; "I think . . ." Every so often you shout, "Sum up and speak up," and someone volunteers to sum up the main points of the discussion so far, drawing applause from the whole group.

Groups Galore

Teachers often ask what kind of small groups work best. There are many options, and they serve different purposes.

There are at least nine types of groups. Ask yourself:

- Which type will work best for this activity?
- Which will work best given the current state of the class?
- Which type will move them on socially?
- Which haven't we used for a while?

1. Random Groups

These are composed by chance. For example, you can

- pull names out of a hat
- stick pins randomly in your class list
- number around the class
- give out differently colored cards as the students come in

2. Friendship Groups

Students get together with their friends.

3. Interest Groups

Students get together because they want to work on the same topic or use the same approach.

4. Skill Groups

Students with the same skills form groups. For example, all the readers, all the speakers, all the artists, and all the dramatists.

5. Mixed-Skill Groups

Students with *different* skills get together, so that every group has a mixture. For example, an organizer, a confident speaker, a fast reader, a motivator, and a creative writer.

6. Learning-Style Groups

Students with the same learning style get together. For example, a discussion group, a role-play group, a reading and notetaking group, a worksheet group, a trial-and-error group.

7. Mixed-Style Groups

Visual, auditory, and kinesthetic learners get together, or AS, CR, AR, and CS learners get together, to form the ultimate team.

8. Support Groups

Students who know they can do something well get together with students who need some help. For example, good readers get together with poor readers and help them, or experienced interviewers work with students who've never conducted an interview before.

9. Performance Groups

Students with similar levels of current performance in the subject get together. This enables them to work at a common level and pace. It allows you to differentiate the tasks and challenges.

What about Ability Groups?

Ability? Is there such a thing? The answer is probably no, not in a crude sense. In the past we tended to think of ability as fixed and consequently used it to define students. We now know that intelligence is fluid—it can be increased, students can become cleverer. Intelligence also comes in all shapes and sizes—nowadays we recognize and value a whole range of abilities. Therefore, a student who is poor at reading and writing, but highly skilled interpersonally, might still be regarded as "able." With our current knowledge of the brain, it is neither easy nor desirable to define and measure ability in the narrow way we once did.

A further problem with labeling students as "more" or "less" able is the effect of the message on performance. Since Rosenthal and Jacobson's *Pygmalion in the Classroom* (2003; originally published in 1968), we have known that teachers' internalized expectations of students directly affect the quality of those students' learning. Students tend to live up or down to expectations. Finally, labels tend to stick. Most students regarded as less able at school continue to think of themselves as less able throughout life. The hold that categorization has on self-image, and therefore on self-esteem, is sometimes unshakable.

So there are many problems with the idea of ability groups. A positive way forward is to replace the word "ability" with the phrase "current performance" or "current competence." These terms suggest, even invite, improvement. They also refer to particular skill sets, rather than making generalized judgments. A student's current performance in algebra might be quite different from her current performance in geometry, and this might reflect her different levels of logical and spatial intelligence. Therefore, "performance groups" might be created only in relation to the subject matter and particular task at hand.

What about Group Size?

Does size matter? The answer is definitely yes! Obviously it depends on the nature of the activity. In the *Toolkit*, different sizes of groups are required for different exercises. For general purposes, though, when you want students just to discuss, read, brainstorm, think, plan, define, or decide something together, it seems that groups of four are too big, pairs are too small, and groups of three are just right.

How to Avoid Creating Passengers

- If the group is supposed to produce some sort of flipchart presentation or poster, give each of the students a differently colored felt-tip pen, which they are not allowed to swap. As you move around the room, you will be able to see who is contributing what by the colors on the paper.
- Let the class know that at the end of the group activity, you will ask each student secretly and anonymously to submit effort percentages for all group members. (See "Proportional Representation" on page 182.)
- Let the class know that during the group work you will be moving around, dropping in on individual students at any time and asking the student to explain what has been discussed. If she can't do it, the group is in big trouble.

Step On It

Managing individual or group projects can be a slow and painful process. Students sometimes meander and take the most tortuous route or leave the beaten track completely. If it's all too slow, get them to step on it.

How?

The basic idea is to help students identify the short steps they need to take in advance and always to keep ahead of themselves.

1. Prepare a "Step On It" recording sheet, like this.

Date and time written	Step to be taken	How long the step should take	How long it actually took

2. Each student has his own copy. The student decides what he has to do first. The step should be small and specific: for example, "Use the history-of-art CD-ROM and draw a timeline of Picasso's life," "Write and send a letter to a city's visitor's center, asking for pamphlets on the top 10 attractions in that city," "Select the three most useful books on this topic from the school library," or "Read the information sheet from the teacher and turn it into a flowchart."

3. The date and time of writing the step are recorded in the first column and an estimate of how long it will take is entered in the third column. The deadline should be challenging, giving no opportunity to mess around. Then, afterwards, the time the job actually took is entered in the final column. This sometimes gives students an incentive to beat their prediction. If, however, it ended up taking longer than estimated, this invites a debriefing with the student. Was there a subskill to master, such as knowing how to write a business letter or knowing how to take notes? Or were the resources inadequate—students had to take turns with the only CD-ROM, for instance? Or was the problem lack of motivation or too many distractions? At this point you are operating as a tutor rather than a teacher.

4. For "Step On It" to work properly, though, defining and doing a single step at a time is not enough. Students are asked always to be at least one step ahead of themselves. So, when they have written the first step, they decide on and record the second step *before* they actually do the first. Likewise, before they move on to the second step, they think through and record the third step and maybe the fourth as well. This helps them to stay on track and keep their momentum up. They are always looking beyond the immediate; there's always something else to do. Also, as you move around the classroom, you can see where each of them is going. This enables you to anticipate problems, select resources, organize equipment, and prepare teaching materials on particular facts, concepts, or skills. No one ever runs out of things to do.

5. The predictive nature of "Step On It" also enables you to adjust steps with certain students and even write steps for others. Some members of the class can get along with little help. They know what to do and how to do it. You can trust them to write realistic steps and to be self-directing. Others need more support. You may want to rewrite vague steps such as "Find out about the Crusades" or "Investigate ingredients" or "Read the book." You may need to sharpen  timeframes. Or you may need to delete some of the steps ahead because they would take the student off on an unproductive tangent. At the other end of the scale, with highly motivated and capable students, you may want to encourage them to make their steps more complex, long term, and challenging. Finally, you may wish to suggest alternative ways of doing a step, to bring it more in line with the student's learning style. For example, "Find out about the Crusades by watching the first 20 minutes of such-and-such a video" or "by talking to the teacher about it," rather than "by reading a book," which is what the student originally wrote. So the process allows for a high degree of differentiation in regard to detail, depth, pace, and style of learning.

6. Have students leave out the "Step On It" sheets on their desks, always available. They follow continual cycles of plan-do-review with your tailormade support.

Applications

- This can be used in any situation when students are expected to sustain a piece of learning over a long period of time: a research project; a piece of homework; retaining learning for a final exam; or preparing for a final paper.
- It is also a very useful way of managing group work (see "Variations" below).

Why Do It?

- It's pragmatic. In the hustle and bustle of a busy classroom, with a million different things going on at once, it helps to keep things on track and on time.
- It's educational. Many students find individual or group research difficult, usually because they haven't done much of it before. "Step On It" trains them in some of the basic procedures of self-management and personal or group organization.
- It's idealistic. The procedure helps to develop personal responsibility for learning, one of our long-term goals.

Variations

- If the class is working in small groups, the "Step On It" sheet might look something like this:

Date and time written	Name of group member	Step to be taken	How long the step should take	How long it actually took

This central record sheet is kept by the group leader or manager, who meets periodically with you. From time to time, the group meets to decide on the next round of steps, remembering always to keep at least one round ahead.

- Alternatively, this recording device might be filled in each time the group meets:

Date and time of meeting	Next step	Time	Then	Time	Then	Time
Name		Estimate Actual		Estimate Actual		Estimate Actual
Name		Estimate Actual		Estimate Actual		Estimate Actual
Name		Estimate Actual		Estimate Actual		Estimate Actual
Name		Estimate Actual		Estimate Actual		Estimate Actual

The group will meet again on _____ at _____

Help! How Do We Hold a Group Discussion?

Talking? People do it all the time, even when they shouldn't! This advice is designed to bring a little order and calm to small-group proceedings.

In all group discussions, rules are important.

- They encourage people to take part.
- They stop arguments.
- They make sure time is used well.

Here's some advice for students. It could be given to them as a handout.

Get Organized

Most groups find these two golden rules helpful:

- We will give our complete attention to the person who is speaking.
- We will respect other people's opinions even when they are different from our own.

Instead of adopting these, you might want to make your own. If you do, be sure that they say what people should do, not what they shouldn't do. The rules should enable you to have organized discussions and should make sure that no one's feelings get hurt. Don't have punishments. Write the group rules on a piece of paper or cardboard large enough for everyone to see. Make sure they are displayed every time the group meets together.

If a member of the group breaks the rules, simply remind her of what has been agreed on. Help students get into new habits.

Ideas for Organizing Your Discussion

What's the best way to organize your discussion? Here are five possibilities.

1. **Sit properly.**
    Everyone needs to see and hear each other easily. So make sure you are sitting in a circle or around a desk. Sitting in a line along a desk or bench doesn't work.

2. **Appoint a chairperson.**
    Signal to the chairperson that you want to speak. The chairperson will call on you when it is your turn.

3. **Use a round.**
   This means taking turns, one after another, around the group. You may speak only when it is your turn—this eliminates interruptions and sarcastic comments. If you don't want to make a contribution when your turn comes, just say, "Pass." Go around the group as many times as necessary.

4. **Use tokens.**
   At the start, everyone gets five tokens: for example, buttons, pieces of paper, or playing cards. Every time a person speaks, she gives up a token. When people have no tokens left, they may not say any more.

5. **Use a "microphone."**
   Choose an item to be a "microphone": for example, a pen, a ruler, a box, or a book. You may speak only when you are holding the microphone. When you have finished speaking, pass the microphone to the person who wants to speak next.

Other Useful Tips

- Face the person who is speaking.

- When you are speaking, make eye contact with the other members of the group.

- From time to time, sum up what other people are saying. This lets them know that their contributions have been heard.

- If you don't understand someone's comment, ask for it to be explained.

- If you don't feel that *you* have been understood, ask someone else in the group to sum up your point of view. If no one can do it, you will need to try to make your point again in a different way.

Civilized discussion and debate lie at the heart of the political process, so the guidelines above make a significant contribution to citizenship education. They give students a taste of the dynamics of debate and will prepare them in general for life in the United States. Apart from political applications, the guidelines apply equally to family, social, and business discussions.

What's more, the national drive for inclusive education must come down to this: attention to detail. Simply allocating a student to a group does not guarantee inclusion within that group. The procedures above are designed to make inclusion a genuine rather than a superficial experience.

Help! How Do We Make Decisions?

Give this advice to small groups when they are struggling to agree. Or before!
After all, prevention is better than cure.

Groups often face questions such as

- What shall we do and how shall we do it?
- Who's going to do what?
- How can we make sure that everyone is happy with the decision?

The steps in the following handout will help students answer such questions efficiently.

Step 1

Make sure that everyone in the group understands the question or problem. Try writing it down large enough for the whole group to see. Use the board, a flipchart, or a large piece of paper. Check that everyone understands by asking each person to explain it in his own words.

Step 2

List all the possible answers or solutions. Brainstorming and rounds are good ways of doing this. Write down all the possibilities for everyone to see.

Step 3

Now you have to choose one solution from your list. Strive for everyone to agree. Give yourselves a time limit for discussion, perhaps 5 or 10 minutes. If you all agree at the end of this time, then congratulate yourselves. If you don't all agree, then move on to Step 4

Step 4

Now try for a compromise. This involves some give and take. Look at the two or three most popular solutions and ask yourselves:

- What changes would we have to make to one of these solutions for everyone to accept it? or

- Which one of these would we all be willing to try for a short time only, then review it?

Again, give yourselves a time limit. If you are still stuck, go to Step 5.

Step 5

It's now time for the last resort: voting. You could go for a straight vote with a show of hands, or a secret ballot in which everyone writes anonymously on a piece of paper. You'll have to decide beforehand what percentage is needed for the vote to be carried. The snag with both of these methods is that they create winners and losers. There is another way of doing it:

1. Label the different solutions A, B, C, D, E, and so on.

2. Go around the group asking each person in turn for her top three, while someone tallies the votes.

3. The solution with the highest number of votes is accepted; second and third choices will also emerge.

This method should give you the favored solutions without splitting the group.

Collective decision making is a large part of good citizenship. The steps above explore ways of doing this and train students in good practice.

Proportional Representation

Groups are notorious for carrying passengers, but students should beware:
The proportion of their representation will be represented proportionally.

How?

1. Let students know that at the end of the group work, each group member will be expected to judge the percentage contribution of all the others. Show them the sheet that they will have to fill in:

Name of group member	Member's % of the total group effort
Name	
Name	
Name	
Self	
	= 100%

2. As soon as the group work is finished, ask each student to complete the form secretly and anonymously, judging the relative contribution of each member over the whole period of group work. For example, a student who shone at the end because he is a confident and engaging presenter would still be given a low percentage if he did little of the initial thinking and research—and vice versa. Remind students to include themselves in the equation and that the percentages should total 100.

3. Collect the forms and look for patterns within groups. If people have been honest, it will enable you to see who's contributed what. Dishonesty will usually show as discrepancies among students' returns. Either way, the information will give you a lot to talk about with the class about how to handle group work in the future.

Applications

- Do this rating whenever you suspect that students are not pulling their weight in group work.
- Do it anyway, just to keep students on their toes.
- Do it to strengthen people's resolve to challenge their lazy peers. The exercise brings the issues out into the open, breaks the ice, and gives people an agenda to talk about more candidly.

Why Do It?

- It makes group work more productive by encouraging everyone to do a fair share of the work. Few students want to be exposed as lazy and antisocial.
- It contributes to your campaign for all students to accept personal responsibility for their behavior. It's not possible to hide behind the group.
- It encourages group responsibility by making very explicit the idea that "we are all in this together."
- On a practical note, it helps you to allocate grades or comments to individuals when group work has been used for some kind of assessment.

Variations

- Don't do it anonymously. Ask students to own their judgments by putting their names on the forms. This promotes the concept of personal responsibility and explores conflicting loyalties between individual friends and the group.
- Students don't fill in the form individually but as a group. Each small group discusses and agrees on an accurate distribution of points.

Triple Check

If at first you don't succeed, check and check again.

Here are three checklists for high-quality small-group work in the classroom, lab, workshop, studio, or gym. Be explicit with students about the quality of group work you want to achieve, perhaps by showing them and explaining these checklists. Make spot checks—or stop the lesson and ask students to carry out spot checks—on the quality of group work. Every now and then, spend a few minutes before the end of a lesson asking how much group-working progress has been made. Set new goals for high-quality group work: for example, "By the end of next week, let's make sure that we're all brave enough to ask for something to be explained again if we haven't understood it the first time."

When a Group Is Working Well

- The group sits so that each group member can see and hear all the others easily.
- One person at a time speaks during discussion.
- Everyone turns to face the person who is speaking.
- Individual group members remind others if they break agreed-on ground rules.
- Any member at any time is able to explain:

  what she is doing
  how this contributes to the overall group task
  what other group members are doing and why
  what the next step will be

- The group always works to agreed-on and explicit deadlines—each member should be able to answer the question, "When will this be finished?"
- A group member who finishes a task early offers to help others or negotiates the next step with the group manager.
- Everyone contributes equally to looking after resources, to cleaning up, and to moving furniture.

If Group Work Isn't Going Well, Check That . . .

- time has been given to creating ground rules and making clear the behavior expected of everyone within a group
- there is a designated leader, or manager, for each group
- there are clear procedures for discussion (see "Help! How Do We Hold a Group Discussion?" on page 178)
- the manager is the main channel of communication between you and the group
- over a long period of group work (an industrial arts project, for example) there are group meetings at intervals, chaired by the manager, at which agreements are made about division of labor, deadlines, and use of resources
- apart from short-term tasks, notes are kept of who should be doing what by when
- you are unbending about the keeping of agreed-on ground rules
- the group has procedures for making decisions and solving problems (see "Help! How Do We Make Decisions?" on page 180)

Still Problems? Check . . .

- classroom layout: Is the furniture arrangement conducive to group work?
- resources: Are they appropriate for the task (content, readability)? Are they sufficient for the number of students? And do the students know where to get them and how to use them?
- time: Has enough time been invested in setting up group work properly in the belief that it will be recouped later? Do you need to go back a step or two?
- trust: Is it believed that students will, in the end, handle group work well and use it to achieve great things? Do the students know your high expectations of them?
- safety: Are safety requirements, where they exist, built into the ground rules?
- tasks: Have the tasks been designed and structured for collaboration so that they cannot be achieved by any individual alone?
- ground rules: Do they need revisiting, or even re-creating?
- skills: Do the students need to acquire certain subskills, for example, scan reading or notetaking?
- teacher: Do you need to learn how to operate differently, for example, getting around to the groups and always being there to check on deadlines when you say you will?

Smooth Starts

The first few minutes of a lesson are crucial. They set the tone for what is to come. Here are 10 terrific tips for getting off to a smooth start.

1. Act as gatekeeper—stand at the door, letting students in one at a time, instead of letting them come in en masse with all their "baggage." You can smile, frown, have a quiet word, give a warning, hold a student back, separate students, or direct students to particular seats.

2. Have a simple task for everyone to do as soon as each enters the room—expect everyone to settle down immediately. This gives you a chance to deal with individuals and get your head together. Introduce the lesson only when you are ready.

3. Have learning objectives that are expressed in this form: "By the end of this lesson you will be able to . . ." This suggests to students that the lesson is purposeful and that they will have experienced success by the end. Have the objectives written up on the board or on a handout before the students come in.

4. Link the learning objectives to the big picture of their learning—what's gone before and what's coming after and how it all adds up to success on the forthcoming assessment.

5. Have learning objectives that are differentiated, using, for example, the must-should-could model (that is, must know or be able to do this; should know or be able to do this; and could know or be able to do this). This lets students know that they will be able to achieve, and it encourages them to aspire.

6. Have the lesson plan written up on the board, on an overhead projector, or as a flow-chart, timeline, or time circle (like a clock face), showing the timeframe. Talk through the plan with students and ask them to help you stay on time.

7. Instead of standing at the front, position yourself near potential troublemakers and introduce the lesson from there.

8. Ask one or two students to explain to you (and therefore to the whole class) what everyone has to do before anyone is allowed to start.

9. Give a tight deadline for the first task. This creates a fast pace and a sense that you are firmly in charge. Make sure you have a clearly visible clock in the room.

10. Give upbeat messages about the students' abilities and the learning planned for the lesson. Say things like, "I know today's work is challenging, and I also know we can all master it, so let's get cracking," and "I've designed some exercises that will challenge you, but once they're done, you'll feel really good about what you've achieved." Don't give the impression that you are reluctantly accepting learning that is being forced on the class from above: "Oh, well, if I had my way we wouldn't be doing this . . ." Instead, let the students know that you are in charge and have reworked state curriculum and standards, tailoring activities just for them.

Tricks of the Trade

Dealing with low-level disruption can be tricky.
Here are 13 ways of outsmarting the smart alecs.

1. Set deadlines for specific tasks. Create a sense of urgency. Write public, whole-class deadlines on the board. Jot down individual deadlines in the margin of your grade book. Break the learning into short steps and challenge reluctant students to complete the next step within a tight timeframe: "I think you can do questions 2 and 3 within the next 10 minutes. I'm jotting that down and I'll be back to check at 2:25 p.m." (See "Dreadlines" on page 88.)

2. Use traffic lights. Have red, green, and yellow cards on hand. Stick the green card on the board when you are happy for students to chitchat as long as they are doing their work. Stick the yellow one up to signal that silence will be expected in one minute. Naturally, red indicates total silence. Red and yellow together mean only one more minute of silence before chitchat will be allowed again.

3. Use tokens. Everyone starts off with three tokens each (such as buttons, pieces of paper, or small cards). Each time a person speaks when she shouldn't, she surrenders a token. Students may win tokens back for particularly impressive contributions. The goal is for students to make sure that they are never without a token. For the reverse of this idea, see "Tokenism" on page 171.

4. Rearrange the room. Make sure it promotes the kind of listening you require. For example, having tables in groups with some students' backs to you is not a good idea until self-discipline has been firmly established.

5. Have a time-out area in the back of the room, where work is laid out for students to work on individually. Students who have been reminded once or twice are given a choice: Either settle down and pay attention or go to the time-out area and work alone. They may come back into the main learning activity as soon as they are prepared to behave.

6. Never talk over chatter. Wait until you have complete silence.

7. Play "eye-to-eye." Require everyone to turn and look at the person who is speaking, whether it's you or a student.

8. Have a chatterbox, a sealed shoebox with a slit in it (like a ballot box), on your desk. Each time a person disrupts, jot his name down and pop it into the chatterbox. Open the box each month; names that appear more than five times are in big trouble.

9. Have rotating "talk police." Choose a couple of people each day to be on the lookout for low-level disruption and to issue reminders to students. People can be "booked" for more serious offenses.

10. Play the waiting game. Stop and wait for silence. Don't say anything. Some teachers have a signal, for example raising a hand or holding a pen, to show that they are waiting. It's important not to look bored, angry, or frustrated—this only gives the disruptive students the incentive to keep being disruptive.

11. Record instructions or passages on tape. Curiously, students will often settle down to a *recording* of the teacher's voice more than to a live performance. The recording also frees you to watch students while they listen.

12. Don't stand at the front. Stand next to likely interrupters when you are addressing the whole class. Move around, making sure that you make eye contact with potential disrupters.

13. Don't raise your voice—lower it.

SECTION 4

Audit Tools

Introduction

I wasn't sure whether to call this section "Audit Tools" or "Tools for Guidance." The items are a mixture of the two. You will find checklists, suggestions, questions, tips, and recommendations, all designed to bring a number of key issues down to earth. The goal as ever is to be concrete and practical, even with the more nebulous concepts such as self-esteem.

You may use the tools as genuine audit instruments, in which case you will allow them to ask stiff questions of your current practice. This testing process will identify precise practical steps that you could then take to enhance your teaching. On the other hand, you don't have to be so rigorous and systematic. Just use the tools informally to guide and stimulate your thinking about the issues. Read through them. You may disagree with some of the stronger suggestions, but at least you'll be thinking about practical manifestations and implications rather than leaving matters vague.

Remember, it's only when people know exactly what to do and how to do it that change ever takes root. Working out the practical details of big ideas is the change agent's job, whether you're changing yourself, your department, your school, or just the whole world!

Check Your Lesson Plans

This audit tool has two purposes:

1. to summarize all the thinking behind *The Teacher's Toolkit*—in other words, to present current ideas about learning in a way that readily translates into the design of lessons and units
2. to put the *Toolkit*'s individual practical ideas into context so that they don't appear to be just small ways to spice up a lesson; the purpose and potential of the individual techniques are understood only once it's clear how they fit into a whole

This section presents the sorts of questions that might run through your head when you're planning a series of lessons. The questions are divided into five sequential parts:

1. learning objectives
2. learning method
3. learning environment
4. assessment
5. recording

You can use this tool to

- audit existing lessons and units
- design new lessons
- observe other people's lessons and give constructive feedback

This checklist is intended to be organic. Delete things, modify some, add others. In other words, use it just to get you going, then customize the list to represent your own understanding of high-quality teaching.

Part 1: Learning Objectives

1. **Do you express learning objectives as outcomes, using the phrase "learners will be able to . . ."?**

   For example: By the end of this lesson, you will be able to . . .
   - recognize series and parallel circuits on circuit boards and in diagrams
   - predict the brightness of bulbs in one circuit compared to another
   - connect an ammeter into a circuit correctly
   - explain the effect of changing the resistance in a circuit.

2. **Are the learning objectives clearly related to the big picture?**

   In other words, are they related to the syllabus as a whole, what has been covered already, and long-term learning goals and deadlines? For example, see the applications section of "Assembly" (page 62) as well as "Mantle of the Expert" (page 100).

3. **Are the learning objectives differentiated?**

   Do they have two or three levels of sophistication? For example: By the end of these three lessons you
   - *must* be able to describe representative democracy and explain why it is like it is
   - *should* be able to list the main similarities and differences in democracy as practiced in four different countries
   - *could* be able to explain why these differences exist

4. **How do you make the learning objectives clear to the students?**

It is important that the objectives are explained and understood, not just read and received. For example, you could show students the assessment they will have to take; you could show them some of the achievements of students who have already taken the class; or you could ask them to guess the learning objective from some cryptic clues you give them.

5. **Do the students have input into defining the learning objectives?**

For example, use "Calling Cards" (page 70), "Sorting Circles" (page 130), or "Thumbometer" (page 137).

6. **How will you check individual students' learning against the learning objectives, and when?**

Will this happen during the lesson, at the end of the lesson, for homework, at the beginning of the next lesson? For example, see "Beat the Teacher" (page 66), "Bingo" (page 68), "Calling Cards" (page 70), "Center of the Universe" (page 72), "Dicey Business" (page 78), "Dominoes" (page 84), "Guess Who" (page 90), "Masterminds" (page 102), "Memory Board" (page 104), "Spotlight" (page 133), "Stepping Stones" (page 135), "Thumbometer" (page 137), "Verbal Football" (page 142), "Wheel of Fortune" (page 146), in addition to the more usual types of tests and assessment tasks.

Part 2: Learning Method

1. **How do you communicate high expectations?**
   - Through the learning objectives?
   - Through your energy and optimism?
   - Through your interaction with individual students?
   - Through the nature of the activities?
   - Through deadlines?

2. **What account do you take of students' prior knowledge, experience, and performance?**

For example, see "Calling Cards" (page 70), "Center of the Universe" (page 72), "Discussion Carousel" (page 80), "Mantle of the Expert" (page 100), "Question Generator" (page 119), and "Value Continuum" (page 139).

3. **What can students figure out for themselves during the lesson or topic?**

For example, see "Assembly" (page 62), "Conversion" (page 74), "Ranking" (page 126), and "Silent Sentences" (page 128) .

4. **What are students encouraged to find out for themselves from**
   - text sources such as books, information sheets, leaflets, newspapers, magazines, letters, journals, and other students' work?
   - visual sources such as charts, pictures, photographs, advertisements, slides, posters, exhibitions, and demonstrations?
   - technological sources such as CD-ROMs, slide show software, the Internet, television, videotapes, radio, audiocassettes, DVDs, and video conferencing?
   - human sources such as their own experience, each other, you, and other adults?
   - physical sources such as places and artifacts?

For example, see "Double Take" (page 86), "Hot Seating" (page 95), "One to One" (page 110), and "Quick on the Draw" (page 121).

5. **Are the students sufficiently active, mentally and physically?**
   For example, see "Back to Back" (page 64), "Discussion Carousel" (page 80), "Sorting Circles" (page 130), and "Verbal Football" (page 142) .

6. **Do the students need to consolidate preliminary skills before activities can be successful?**
   For social skills, see the whole of section 3. For research skills, see "Conversion" (page 74), "Distillation" (page 82), "Hierarchies" (page 92), and "Question Generator" (page 119).

7. **How do you provide variety so that different learning styles are satisfied?**
   Do you use a sequence of different styles within the lesson or over a number of lessons, or different learning strategies operating simultaneously so that students have choice? For guidance you could use:
   - the sensory model: visual, auditory, kinesthetic
   - Gregorc's model: Abstract Sequential, Abstract Random, Concrete Sequential, Concrete Random
   - Gardner's model: verbal-linguistic, logical-mathematical, visual-spatial, bodily-kinesthetic, musical-rhythmic, interpersonal, intrapersonal, naturalistic

8. **How is learning made multisensory or emotionally strong?**
   For example, see "Stepping Stones" (page 135) and "Center of the Universe" (page 72).

9. **To what extent are students involved in making decisions about learning strategies?**
   Level 1: You adjust activities as a result of feedback from students.
   Level 2: Students choose between different preset activities.
   Level 3: Individual students propose and negotiate their personal learning strategies.
   Level 4: You ask the class the open-ended question: How shall we tackle these learning objectives?

10. **How are students encouraged to make their own meaning?**
    For example, see "Conversion" (page 74), "Corporate Identity" (page 76), "Hierarchies" (page 92), "Hot Seating" (page 95), "Pairs to Fours" (page 112), "Ranking" (page 126), "Stepping Stones" (page 135), and "Value Continuum" (page 139).

11. **How does the lesson develop the students' use of language?**
    For example, see "Back to Back" (page 64), "Distillation" (page 82), "Dominoes" (page 84), "Guess Who" (page 90), "Now You See It . . ." (page 106), "Memory Board" (page 104), "On Tour" (page 108), "Pass the Buck" (page 114), "Silent Sentences" (page 128), and "Verbal Tennis" (page 144).

12. **How does the lesson support the development of independent learning and thinking?**
    For example, see "Beat the Teacher" (page 66), "Calling Cards" (page 70), "Conversion" (page 74), "Double Take" (page 86), "Dreadlines" (page 88), and "Guess Who" (page 90).

Part 3: Learning Environment

1. **What else can you do to make the environment *emotionally* conducive to learning?**
   Check . . .
   - that you have ground rules that guarantee listening and no put-downs
   - your use of language
   - your use of conflict diffusion and resolution strategies
   - your use of humor

2. **What else can you do to make the environment *biologically* conducive to learning?**
   Check . . .
   - fresh air
   - plants
   - temperature
   - hydration—access to water
   - ionizer

3. **What else can you do to make the environment *psychologically* conducive to learning?**
   Check . . .
   - color
   - aesthetics
   - aromas
   - music
   - displays

4. **What else can you do to make the environment *physically* conducive to learning?**
   Check . . .
   - room layout: Is it appropriate to the learning activities?
   - clarity of board and overhead
   - sufficiency and accessibility of learning resources

Part 4: Assessment

1. **How do students prove what they have learned?**
   Ideas: take a formal test; write an explanation; conduct an interview; be interviewed; teach someone else; explain to parents and test them; make a model; create a quiz; give a demonstration; sequence jumbled information; label a blank diagram; construct a diagram; undertake a challenge against the clock; give a commentary; mime the knowledge; spot the deliberate mistakes; predict what will happen if . . . ; provide questions to given answers; fill in missing keywords; write an essay; make a presentation, create a worksheet; mount an exhibition; be hot seated; complete an unfinished chart, table, or timeline; present a still image; match words with definitions; conduct an experiment; answer past exam questions; make a Mind Map; draw a storyboard; or create and grade a test for the teacher.

2. **How quickly will students get feedback on their progress?**
   The sooner the better!

Part 5: Recording

How do students record what they have learned for future reference?

Options include bulleted or numbered list; keyword plan; Mind Map; diagram; storyboard; written questions and answers; flowchart; journal; letter; annotated picture; script; table or chart; audio recording; video recording; photographs; flashcards; fill-in-the-blank writing frame; magazine or newspaper article; completed worksheet; photocopy; report; headed paragraphs; timeline; index-card summaries; and crossword puzzles.

Check Your Students' Learning Styles

Why check your students' learning styles? Because people are different. They learn in extremely different ways, and this has a profound effect on their levels of achievement and self-belief. (For more information about learning styles theory and research, see page 31.)

So how can you detect students' learning styles so that they can operate effectively? There are at least four ways of doing it, though these suggestions come with serious health warnings. See "But Is It Desirable to Try to Identify Students' Learning Styles?" on page 203.

Through Observation

Perhaps the most natural, and certainly the least intrusive, way of identifying students' preferences is to watch them at work and play. Notice the frequency of movement, the tendency to be with others, the desire to follow or break with convention, the amount of silence they enjoy or endure, the way they put things on their desks and on paper, the types of activities they go for when there's choice, when they are most easily distracted, how often they check the time, how carefully they follow instructions, whether they operate from oral instructions or need to see them written down, and so on.

Most teachers say they can get a sense of these things during the natural course of events as one lesson follows another. However, it's not easy to teach and observe at the same time, so the conclusions we come to can be way off the mark. This is partly because we catch only glimpses of behavior while busy with lessons, and prominent incidents stick in our minds and color our judgment. And it's partly because we are observing without a purpose. Mike Hughes (1999) explains that teachers will have difficulty seeing student learning preferences if they don't know what they are looking for during a lesson. Left to our own devices, we tend to see the things that bother us (such as when students chew gum, rock back on a chair, or shout out instead of putting their hands up), and we miss the essential signs of style. Therefore, prepare an observation schedule based on one of the learning-style models—it's easy to customize one of the questionnaires mentioned below—and stick to it.

Observing against a schedule is a full-time job; it requires total concentration, so give yourself the opportunity to do it well by

- videotaping some of your lessons and watching them afterward in the comfort of your own home
- visiting other teachers' classes where you are completely free from the responsibilities of teaching and managing behavior
- having a colleague come into some of your lessons to operate the schedule—you have to be sure that she is skilled enough to put her own agendas aside; otherwise you'll be letting yourself in for a lot of unwelcome feedback

Naturally, an accurate picture of students' styles can be built up only over time. A quick observation won't do: There are too many variables skewing the behaviors that indicate style. However, you can short-circuit the process by deliberately assigning a series of open tasks that allow for a variety of personal responses. For example:

- "Explain how to get from school to your house." Some students will draw a map; others will write a series of instructions; others will explain orally with lots of gestures and hand signals.
- "How would you find out how a battery-operated clock works?" Some will want to consult a book; others will want to ask an electronics expert; others will want to take a clock apart and figure it out for themselves; others will want you to explain it with diagrams and components.
- "Present a proposal for reorganizing the classroom." Natural preferences will be revealed at two levels. The first is the way they go about it—on their own, with a partner, or in a group; drawing rough sketches; closing their eyes and visualizing; measuring the space and plotting the furniture on graph paper; conducting a survey of what people want; getting up, walking around, and weighing options; or wanting to move the furniture and try it out in different positions. The second is what they come up with—a circle of chairs with desks to the walls, tables blocked into groups, separate desks in rows, café style, and so on.

Through Structured Choices

Prepare several ways of studying the next topic, each based on a different learning style. Introduce the topic to the class, explain the various options, and ask students to make individual choices.

For example, if students are studying career choices, after a general introduction to the topic, offer four options (based on Gregorc):

1. Study the life of a person in the career of your choice by following a structured research guide that refers to books at the library. You will end up with a written report: "Highlights of This Career." You will work on your own. (Abstract Sequential)

2. Invite into school, entertain, and interview a couple of people who work in your chosen field, then present "A day in the life . . ." in a series of still images that will be photographed. You will need to add captions and labels. You will work in small groups. (Abstract Random)

3. Find a way of presenting to us "The Steps Necessary to Pursue a Career in This Field." You may use whatever resources and methods you like, but you may not use any spoken words in your presentation. You may choose to work on your own, in a pair, or in a small group. (Concrete Random)

4. Make a detailed and professional-looking chart showing the job functions, advantages, disadvantages, and career ladder of your chosen job. Follow the example given and work on your own. (Concrete Sequential)

Another example of choices (this time based on VAK), for studying percentages:

1. You will work outside in pairs (or in the gym, depending on weather). Follow the instructions on the sheets for bunny hopping, throwing a baseball, and running 100 yards. Take all the measurements, and then calculate the shortest and slowest possible hop, throw, and run as percentages of the longest and fastest possible. Then you will hop, throw, and run to given percentages. (whole-body kinesthetic)

2. You will work in small groups. Push a couple of desks together and follow the detailed instructions for measuring, cutting, and assembling different shapes of different relative proportions. (tactile kinesthetic)

3. You will listen to my explanation about percentages and the instructions about what to do on audiocassette. You may listen to the tape, or parts of the tape, as often as you like until you feel sure that you have understood. If you're still stuck, ask each other and, as a final resort, ask me. (auditory)

4. You will watch me showing you how to do percentages using diagrams on the board, posters, and a variety of objects from around the room. In pairs you will then prepare colorful visual aids for teaching these points to elementary school children. (visual)

If students are not used to making these sorts of choices, their initial decisions might be influenced by peer pressure (they'll choose what their friends are doing) or by sheer laziness—which one will be the least work? To minimize the first problem, students could be asked for a show of hands with their eyes closed, or could be asked to write their names and selections on pieces of paper that they fold and hand in.

The only way to counter the second problem is probably to let "bad" choices be made, then, once work is under way, challenge students as you move around the classroom. Focus on the learning outcomes and ask students to show you how far they've gotten; ask them to explain what they've understood so far. If it's clear that not much progress has been made, ask them to choose a different strategy.

At the end of each unit of work, it's important to debrief students on the whole experience, focusing on what they've learned about themselves as learners. Discuss how demanding, comfortable, natural, forced, satisfying, boring, or motivating the choices felt. Ultimately, ask each student to get a sense of how efficient her chosen strategy turned out to be. How much was achieved with what amount of time and effort? Would she choose it again? This way students become more self-aware and more likely to choose wisely next time. After giving them several opportunities to make choices of this kind, consider asking confident students to stretch themselves by deliberately working in less comfortable ways at the next opportunity. It's probably a good idea to keep a note of who chose what so that a picture of individuals' styles can be built up over time, and you can operate effectively not just as a subject teacher but as a personal tutor.

Through a Questionnaire

There's a lot of debate about the use of learning-style questionnaires with students (see the discussion on page 203). On the whole, the younger the students, the greater the risks. If you plan to use questionnaires, then follow these seven rules, which have stemmed from some bitter experiences:

1. The person administering the questionnaire must have a good understanding of its intentions and underlying rationale. Only then will she be able to explain its purpose to students and answer their questions.

2. The person administering it must also be committed to the exercise. If the questionnaire is given out casually as "just another worksheet" to be filled in, students will complete it carelessly and the results will be invalid. Fully explain the reasons for doing the questionnaire and how you will use the results.

3. The instructions you give to the students must be in keeping with the instrument. For example is a gut reaction to each prompt required, or a carefully considered response?

4. The model must not be used for illegitimate purposes. All models are simplifications of reality. They cannot be used to categorize or label students. They are not the last word on someone's character. They don't sum someone up. They simply provide insights that lead to increased understanding of self and others.

5. Individual results must be shared with individual students. It is not OK to take the results away and use them secretly, nor is it OK to share the results publicly with the class, colleagues, or parents without students' permission. The prime purpose of the questionnaire is to help students understand themselves better, so that they might become increasingly successful as learners. The secondary purpose is to help teachers plan learning strategies that will give everyone an equal chance.

6. Give enough time for reflection and discussion. Students benefit from talking with each other and with you about the results: the extent to which they are accurate, context-specific, and changeable. How much of the feedback from the questionnaire is being accepted and how much resisted? Students often want to know what types of learners are best, who will do well on tests, and what they can do to better their chances. Lots of reassurance is usually needed.

7. Do not administer a test unless you are determined to do your professional best to accommodate all learning types in the future. It is very damaging to expose the issue of learning differences, to raise students' expectations, and then not deliver.

If you are still determined to use a student questionnaire after all this, then have a look at the options on page 199. I have developed a questionnaire based on insights derived from information-processing models. I hesitate to use it for reasons that will be discussed in a moment, but I have found that it can be illuminating for students and teachers if administered in accordance with the rules above. Here it is.

Learning-Styles Questionnaire

1. In each row (A–G), rank the four statements. The statement that fits you best gets a score of 4, next best 3, next best 2, and the one that fits you least gets a score of 1. You cannot use half marks.

2. Add the scores in each column. Put the total at the bottom.

3. Plot your scores on the Learning-Styles Profile. You will end up with a kite shape. The kite shape shows the ways in which you most naturally learn.

4. Compare your kite shape to those of other people.

		score		score		score		score
A	I like to be given open-ended problems to solve.		I like group work so that I can talk things through with other people.		I like to do practical work.		I like reading.	
B	I like to figure out answers in my own way and in my own time.		I want to use my imagination.		I don't like thinking and talking too much—I want to get on with it.		I am happy to work alone.	
C	I have a lot of ideas.		I want the freedom to create my own ideas.		I want to be told exactly what to do.		I like to find things out from books, talks, and other sources.	
D	I like to try my ideas out even if people think they are weird.		I am happy to trust my instincts.		I like to tackle things one step at time.		I like reasons and theories; it is important for me to understand.	
E	I like to find things out for myself.		I like to use drama, art, dance, and music to learn.		I like to be organized.		I weigh different ideas.	
F	I want to be allowed to make mistakes and learn from them.		I do not like to be given too much detail.		I pay attention to detail.		I am happy to do written work.	
G	I like to have something to show for my efforts.		I often do things on the spur of the moment.		I like to get things right the first time.		I like my studies to be organized carefully.	
	Red		**Blue**		**Green**		**Yellow**	

199

Learning-Styles Profile

The rationale for these four categories arises from the work of David A. Kolb (1984), Bernice McCarthy (1980), Kathleen Butler (1986), and Anthony Gregorc (1998), who is firmly opposed to student questionnaires, perhaps rightly. They share the basic idea that there are two mental processes involved in learning, one concerned with *acquiring* and the other with *sorting and storing* new data. They agree that there are big natural differences among people on both counts, and therefore the two processes can be seen as continua, with extremes at each end and shades in between. In my model, acquiring runs from highly *physical and sensate* to highly *abstract and reflective*. The sorting-and-storing continuum runs from extremely *structured and linear* to extremely *random and diverse*. If these two continua are set at right angles to each other, four possible learning modes are created.

Red	physical, hands-on, unstructured, open-ended, practical, investigative
Blue	creative, unstructured, open, reflective, artsy, human
Green	structured, practical, guided, hands-on, precise
Yellow	thoughtful, structured, academic, reasonable, research-based

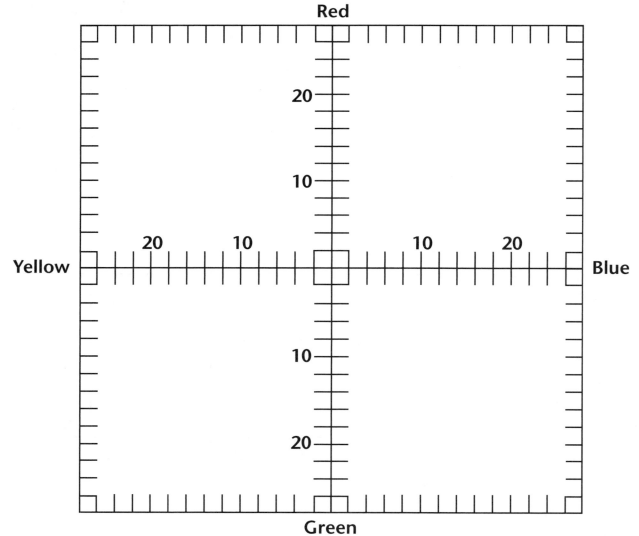

Through Reflection on Multiple Activities

This approach requires you to set up a number of diverse learning activities for all students to do. Once they've been through them all, you lead a reflection in which students identify their preferences. The diverse learning activities should be designed against a learning-styles model, so decide this first. You might use VAK (in which case I recommend that you design four activities: visual, auditory, tactile, and whole-body kinesthetic), Gregorc (in which case you will design four activities: Abstract Sequential, Concrete Sequential, Abstract Random, and Concrete Random), or Gardner (in which case you will design eight activities: verbal-linguistic, logical-mathematical, visual-spatial, musical-rhythmic, bodily-kinesthetic, interpersonal, intrapersonal, and naturalistic).

There are four formats in which this approach can be delivered.

Format 1

Take a series of lessons and make each one different. Follow your usual curriculum, but deliver it in diverse ways. For example, the first lesson will be auditory, the second visual, and so on. The advantage of this format is that each learning style is sustained over a whole lesson, giving all students a chance to feel genuine reactions. The disadvantage is that you have to find a section of the curriculum that lends itself to delivery through different styles.

Format 2

Change learning-style activities within a lesson. There might be an auditory exposition and discussion, a visual development such as a traditional or computer slide show, and a kinesthetic reinforcement, such as a skit. The advantage of this format is that no one gets bored. The disadvantage is that no one has to put up with a distasteful style for long enough to feel the incompatibility. Therefore, run several varied lessons of this type before moving on to the reflection.

Format 3

This is a circus. Set out the various activities around the room and have students move among them, either randomly (individuals are responsible for getting through all the activities, in any order, before the bell) or orchestrated by you.

Format 4

This final format is more ambitious. Collapse the timetable for an entire grade for a day and run a "learning-style experience." During the day, students work with others in the same class and go through a series of activities, each in a different style. At the end of the day, the final lesson is given over to reflection led by all grade-level teachers. Clearly this requires a good deal of organization and the cooperation of many colleagues.

You might follow the example of a school that organized such a day around the theme of "Healthy Living for Healthy Learning" with eighth graders. The event began with all eighth graders in the auditorium for an Abstract Sequential lecture and worksheet from a visiting dietician; then individual classes explored various activities: Concrete Random creative cooking; Abstract Random theater to explore temptation; and Concrete Sequential fitness planning.

Another school ran a similar day with sixth graders based on "Pirates." There was a fact-finding lesson involving a research guide and several in-class texts (Abstract Sequential), an empathetic small-group exercise exploring piratical encounters and tensions through still images (Abstract Random), an outdoor orienteering exercise around a fictional treasure island (Concrete Sequential), and a communications problem—figure out a way, without using spoken words, of getting messages to the group across the room that no other people would be able to understand (Concrete Random).

Reflection

Whichever format you use, allow plenty of time for reflection, probably a minimum of 45 minutes. One tried-and-true way of doing it is to clear the desks aside, arrange the chairs in a circle, and make a cross with masking tape on the floor, with the two axes stretching across the circle. This gives four sectors (vary depending on which learning-style model you are using and how many categories it has). In each sector of the circle, place a large piece of cardboard or poster paper with details of each style written big and in different colors in students' language. For example, if you are using my four categories as presented in the Learning-Styles Questionnaire on page 199, then the cards would read

Abstract Sequential	Concrete Sequential
• You like reading. • You are happy to work alone. • You like to find things out from books, from talks, and from other sources. • You like reasons and theories; it is important for you to understand. • You weigh different ideas. • You like to do written work. • You organize your homework carefully.	• You like to do practical work. • You would rather get on with it than talk and think about it too much. • You like to be told exactly what to do. • You like to tackle things one step at a time. • You like to be organized. • You pay attention to detail. • You like to get things right the first time.
Concrete Random	**Abstract Random**
• You like to be given open-ended problems to solve. • You like to figure out answers in your own way and in your own time. • You have lots of ideas. • You like to try your ideas out even if other people think they are weird. • You like to find out things for yourself. • You want to be allowed to make mistakes and learn from them. • You like to have something to show for your efforts.	• You like group work so that you can talk things through with other people. • You use your imagination a lot. • You want the freedom to create your own ideas. • You like to use drama, art, dance, and music. • You trust your instincts. • You do not like being given too much detail. • You often do things spontaneously.

Students first discuss which of the day's activities belong to which sectors, then place paper or placemarkers on the floor to show where each lesson is located on the learning-style map. The nuances are important. For example, was the lesson entirely such-and-such a style, or did it tend toward or cross over into another? How extreme (toward the outer edge of the circle), or how mild a version of the style was it (toward the middle)? This discussion should be allowed to continue until sufficient understanding has been created for the next step.

Now give students three colored index cards. They write their names on each. Give them time for quiet personal reflection prompted by a series of questions that you might write on the board, have prewritten on an overhead transparency, or talk through, for example:

- During today's lessons, when did you feel most comfortable?
- Where did you feel you were learning most naturally?
- What did you find hard to understand?
- What did you enjoy?
- Which parts of the day were a struggle?
- Where did you feel you achieved most?
- What seemed to come naturally to you?
- Which activities were you excited to do?
- What would you choose again if you had the chance?
- What would you avoid if you had the chance?

After a few minutes of individual thought, ask students to place their cards according to their learning preferences. They may put all three in one sector if they feel strongly that this is their single dominant style, or they may spread them two and one, or three ones. There is a quicker and cruder version of this self-assessment step: Instead of using cards, students simply stand up, move around, and sit down in the sector that represents their dominant style. Then, students write down their individual preferences in their planners, and the whole-class distribution is recorded by taking a photograph or by plotting the positions on a large wall chart.

Finally, discuss the teaching implications of the findings. What needs to change? How feasible are such changes given your curriculum and resources? What can students do for themselves to use their preferred styles at home? What changes do students need to make to behavior and attitudes if a wider range of teaching styles is to be used?

But Is It Desirable to Try to Identify Students' Learning Styles?

There are serious concerns about both the validity and potential side effects of "testing" for students' styles. First, in questionnaires and self-confessions, students might not tell the truth—for understandable reasons. Many tend to give answers that will please the teacher, demonstrate their conformity to institutional expectations, be acceptable to a peer group, or that arise from an illusory view of themselves.

Second, in questionnaires and self-confessions, the prompts often have to be too simple to be of much use. The kind of abstract and general terms often found in adult questionnaires are too unfamiliar, and younger students haven't had sufficient life experience to be able to give accurate responses. This means that the prompts have to describe context-specific situations that don't necessarily give insight into the all-important generalities of the mindsets that underlie the styles. In fact, in the end, they might report only preferred behaviors in particular circumstances, not styles at all. The students' liking for the subject, their relationship with the teacher, a mood swing, a falling out with friends—all these can affect the results. Which means that on a different day, a different set of preferences might emerge from the same student. The best way to counter these first two difficulties is to go for skilled observation (the first two strategies, pages 195–97), rather than questionnaires.

Third, a human tendency is to categorize and label. This applies to both teachers and students. Although it is true that no one is ever entirely one style, once a student's dominant score is revealed, that's the category that sticks. Students start to talk of themselves as being that type of learner or, worse still, that type of person. Teachers quickly pigeonhole and label students, usually with the good intention of providing appropriate support. Some schools and colleges offer self-help booklets to students containing tips for mastering material according to style, no matter how it's presented by the teacher. Such resources are well intentioned and are in many cases helpful, but they do reinforce the idea that students are either one thing or the other. So, the discerning teacher is left with a tough decision—to test or not to test?

Check Your Impact on Students' Self-Esteem

Self-esteem is notoriously difficult to define. It can't be reduced to glib terms such as "self-confidence" or "feeling good about yourself." According to Tony Humphreys (1998), feeling lovable and capable are central to self-esteem. The *Student's Dictionary of Psychology* (Stratton and Hayes 1993) describes self-esteem as "the personal evaluation that an individual makes of her or himself; their sense of their own worth or capabilities" (175).

So we see that self-esteem is a personal *judgment*—a gut feeling about how worthy I am, how happy I am to be me—based on the extent to which I feel lovable and capable. Clearly, the conclusion I come to will be fed by the extent to which I am *actually* loved and am *actually* able to do things. The judgment can, of course, shift either way over time.

What about Self-Image?

> The internal picture that an individual has of her or himself, a kind of internal description, which is built up through interaction with the environment and feedback from other people
>
> —Stratton and Hayes, *A Student's Dictionary of Psychology*

Moment by moment we get feedback about ourselves. Some comes from other people, who react to what we say and do, or who tell us what they think of us. Some feedback is in the form of results—were we successful or did we fail or were we somewhere in between? Feedback comes from looking in the mirror; from comparing ourselves to and with other people, real and fictional; from reflecting on our lives; from undertaking formal assessments; from noting how our plans work out; from trying something new and seeing what happens (for example, attending a voice workshop for the first time to discover "Oh, I never knew I could sing like that!"). The countless messages we receive about ourselves are woven into a *picture*: This is the person I am.

And Self-Concept?

> The sum total of the ways in which the individual sees herself or himself. Self-concept is often considered to have two major dimensions: a descriptive component (known as self-image) and an evaluative component (known as self-esteem)
>
> —Stratton and Hayes, *A Student's Dictionary of Psychology*

Therefore, in crude but helpful terms: self-image + self-esteem = self-concept. In other words, the kind of person I see myself as being, plus the extent to which I feel it's OK to be like that, equals what I really think about myself. Clearly this is an oversimplification, but a constructive one, I hope.

Consequently we have a challenge on our hands. The *images* that students build up of themselves are the result of the feedback they get, over time, from sources we can't control, such as family, friends, and neighbors, and sources we can, such as ourselves and other students. The subtle messages we give through tone of voice, body language, being available, and having a laugh are as powerful as the explicit messages we give through encouragement, assessment comments, reprimands, and acknowledgments. They all tell students what we think of them. Imagine, for example, the effect of saying, "You're not like your older sister, are you? She didn't need things repeated umpteen times." Likewise, imagine the positive effect of smiling at a student every time you see him in the hall. Messages from other students come through all sorts of situations. Imagine as a student the positive experience of classmates wanting you to be part of their group, listening while you speak, not making fun, asking your opinion, congratulating you on your achievement, letting you go first, and so on.

In developing a healthy *self-image,* students also benefit from receiving accurate information about their learning progress, their learning potential, and their learning styles. Their images can remain positive if they receive the constant message that each of them is, in fact, a potentially successful learner. To believe this, they will need many experiences of actual success, mixed in among the moments of mistake, struggle, and relative failure.

Artificial success is no good. Giving students watered-down tasks that a donkey could do, or praising them for work that is clearly substandard because you feel it will boost their confidence, is actually counterproductive. For a start, most students see through it. Also, it builds a dangerously shaky foundation for the future by giving students a false impression of their capabilities. Later in life, when the shattering truth becomes clear, the blow is bitter. This has implications for they way we design learning experiences. Differentiation and variety are minimum requirements. Differentiation provides all learners with challenging but achievable learning activities so that *genuine* success can be experienced. Variety ensures that different learning styles are provided for, so success is more likely.

In regard to *self-esteem,* students' value of themselves is largely a product of how much they *feel* valued. Consequently it's important to create an acceptant, inclusive classroom with firm ground rules that eliminate put-downs and guarantee listening. Likewise, as teachers, we can signal unconditional regard by remaining upbeat with students even when there are some serious behaviors and learning skills to be improved. Don't allow behavior and performance to define the student. No one is "bad," "stupid," "unteachable," "lazy," or "no good at math," at least not entirely! Remain optimistic about the person and her potential for learning. This fundamental orientation will come through in all your dealings with her. Similarly, students are expert at detecting truthfulness and integrity—it's impossible to pull the wool over their eyes. When we treat them as adults, being willing to let them know when we feel stuck, giving them the real reasons for a change in the plan, for instance, they grow taller inwardly.

Asking students for their opinions, asking them to make choices, asking them to negotiate and arrive at decisions with you, rather than just follow the decisions you have made for them, all signal that you trust and value their judgments. Being prepared to break the icy barrier that often exists between students and teacher—by chatting informally, sharing a joke, listening to their music, and playing a game—again signals acceptance. Equally, it's important that students are not let off the hook, that they understand how certain actions bring certain consequences. This is all part of their learning about personal responsibility, personal style, and choice, which in turn enables each student increasingly to shape his life.

Naïvely, schools tend to assume that self-esteem can be raised by awarding merit badges, stickers, prizes, medals, and even financial incentives. Nothing could be further from the truth. In fact, when self-esteem is taken seriously, the issues to be addressed strike at the heart of school routines and organization, and at the delicate area of teachers' personal style.

Bettie B. Youngs (1992), in her book *Six Vital Ingredients of Self-Esteem: How to Develop Them in Your Students*, lists the following ingredients that, if present, empower us, and if absent, detract from our lives. Self-esteem is fed by all of them:

1. Physical safety: freedom from physical harm
2. Emotional safety: the absence of intimidation and fear
3. Identity: the "who am I?" question
4. Affiliation: a sense of belonging
5. Competence: a sense of feeling capable
6. Mission: the feeling that one's life has meaning and direction

How many of these do schools deliver? Some would argue that typical American schools, as institutions, are anti–self-esteem. On the whole they are built like factories and run like prisons. What messages does your organization give? If we go down this path, we quickly arrive at the need for schools to reconstruct themselves entirely. Although there are many examples of schools doing just that (Ted Sizer's Coalition of Effective Schools, for example), the current political climate in the United States will not tolerate such a fundamental rethink. For a fuller discussion of these points, see section 1 (pages 5–10)

So it's time for an honest assessment. Translating desired esteem-raising qualities into hard behaviors and procedures is not easy, but let's give it a shot. Take an honest look at yourself, your department or team, and your school. Use the following inventory on the one hand to identify areas you need to strengthen and on the other to spot behaviors and procedures you need to drop. There are five domains to scrutinize.

The items listed in the charts that follow are interrelated. Some of them may seem extreme or impossible, and in isolation they probably are. For example, "Do away with threats and bribes"—most schools depend on them. Yet with several other strands in place—such as "Teach students how and when to be assertive with each other," "Create and maintain classroom ground rules," "Train and use peer mediators," and "Always follow through with the consequence you have described"—doing away with threats and bribes becomes a realistic prospect.

Enhancing self-esteem is like weaving a spider's web. Every strand is individually strong and important, but only when many strands are interconnected will the web do its job. This takes time, but then, spiders are remarkably patient creatures.

Impact on Student Self-Esteem Checklist

Decide on the subjects of the audit. For example A = yourself, B = your department or team, C = the school, D = the school district. Then use a five-point scale to give honest and accurate assessments of each skill or quality: 5 means "perfectly" or "totally in place" or "always"; 1 means "not at all."

A. Underlying issues—what goes on inside your head	A	B	C	D
1. Believe that all your students are capable. Have high expectations of students based on modern notions of intelligence and potential, rooted in a scientific understanding of the brain's capacity. Realize that your expectations of students influence their expectations of themselves.				
2. Reflect on the psychology and philosophy underpinning your teaching. Rarely operate from expediency. Consistently work from humanistic and democratic principles, rather than behavioristic and authoritarian ones. Keep long-term goals in mind.				
3. Retain a generally positive approach to teaching and nourish it with an understanding of recent brain research. Consequently, bring energy and optimism into the classroom, and learn how to work with, rather than against, the grain of the brain.				
4. See students as individuals. Accept that each human brain is as unique as a fingerprint. Understand and use at least one learning-style model.				
5. Open yourself to self-reflection and self-examination. Model the learning process yourself, which means showing your students that you are prepared to experiment, take risks, and learn from disappointments and mistakes.				
6. Be aware that your demeanor has a profound impact on students. Work to demonstrate genuineness, empathy, and unconditional positive regard. The minimum is basically to like students and have a warm disposition toward them.				
7. Believe that every student has the right to be included in a success culture and has the right to achieve to the highest levels of which each is currently capable.				
Totals				

B. Teachers' personal skills and behaviors—the way you come across to students	A	B	C	D
1. Eliminate sarcasm and all other forms of put-downs, even in fun, from your communications with students.				
2. Challenge damaging talk about students by colleagues, in the teachers' lounge, for example. It's easy to perpetuate a culture of negativity. This needs to be reversed.				
3. Use language with students that promotes personal responsibility.				
4. Be aware that when students feel wrong, they feel small—use alternative means of challenging students who have inaccurate or incomplete ideas. For example, ask students to prove their answer, check with other students, or go back to the book and rethink. Turn mistakes into learning points. Give specific, executable suggestions for improvement.				
5. Approach students as grown-ups. Use reason and expect reason. Tell the truth, remain calm, listen. Model these behaviors to students. Show how a crisis can be dealt with without turning it into a drama.				
6. Approach students in an "I'm OK, you're OK" frame of mind. Clear your mental slate of anything that's gone on before. Make each lesson a new start. Expect things to go well.				
7. Listen actively to students, especially when there is a difference of opinion, a conflict, or strong emotion. When busy, let them know that you realize they have something important to say and that you'll catch them later, during or after the lesson. Don't make promises you can't keep.				
8. Use assertiveness with students as an alternative to behaviorist techniques. Do not use rewards and punishments, bribes and threats. Instead be clear about rules; explain and offer choices. Speak of consequences, rather than rewards and punishments. Always follow through with the consequence you have described.				
9. Acknowledge students often, both in private and in public. Let students know that you have noticed their achievement and their efforts. Thank students. Do not use artificial praise.				
10. Avoid communicating judgments and labeling students. Especially risky are throw-away comments such as "You'll never be a musician," "You're not like your brother," "Well, that's a surprise coming from someone who . . ."				
11. Use the skills of giving and receiving feedback. Be willing to receive constructive feedback from students about your teaching and style. Model how to give positive and negative feedback in the way you assess and comment on students' learning.				
12. Bring energy and optimism into the classroom. Be lively. Use humor, but never at anyone's expense.				
13. Make it a priority to learn and use all students' first names.				
14. Teach students how to use self-affirming language. Use affirmations yourself: for example, "I have all the skills I need to be an excellent teacher."				
15. Seek the students' opinions as often as possible about the order in which things should be tackled, learning strategies, timeframes, assessment procedures, problems they're facing, solutions, improvements to the classroom, behavior issues, conflicting priorities, and so forth.				
Totals				

C. Classroom environment—what it's like to be in your class	A	B	C	D
1. Teach students to listen actively to each other and expect it of them in class. Challenge students who don't listen. Ask students who have not been heard properly to repeat what they are saying and ask someone else to summarize.				
2. Create and maintain ground rules that eliminate put-downs and guarantee emotional safety. These need to be made with each class. Review these rules every now and then with students.				
3. Teach students how and when to be assertive with each other. Expect assertiveness instead of aggression or weakness.				
4. Play esteem-enhancing and cooperative games. These can be done at orientation, on the first day of school, or at the start or end of class.				
5. Make the classroom aesthetically pleasing. Attend to color, display, carpet, plants, and aroma, as well as the basics of oxygen and temperature.				
6. Make resources available. Teach students where to get, and how to use economically, consumable resources such as paper, felt-tip pens, glue, cardboard, crayons, paper clips, and staplers. Ensure that text and reference books, CD-ROMs, worksheets, videotapes, and audio-cassettes are openly available in the classroom, or that students know where they are located in the school resource center.				
7. Play varieties of music, perhaps at the beginning and end of class, and sometimes during. Value different tastes.				
8. Give students access to quality drinking water. Ideally, have a chilled-water dispenser in the classroom.				
9. Welcome students to class, preferably by greeting them at the door.				
Totals				

D. Learning strategies—the teaching techniques you use	A	B	C	D
1. Let students in on your thinking about learning objectives, learning strategies, and progress. Keep reminding them of the big picture of their learning. Have timeframes, deadlines, and progress charts on the wall. At a minimum, share lesson objectives with students.				
2. Challenge yourself to share with students more responsibility for learning. Offer choices, negotiate, make decisions democratically. Discuss and decide with students the learning strategies, deadlines, and means of recording and assessing outcomes. Plan *with* them rather than *for* them.				
3. Organize learning activities to take into account a full range of learning styles. The minimum is to vary teaching techniques so that all learning styles are honored over, say, four lessons. Beyond this, offer different ways of doing things simultaneously.				
4. Monitor learning tasks to ensure that they are sufficiently challenging. No one should be "dumbed down" by coloring in, doing word searches, or copying a text. On the other hand, tasks should be achievable even though they will require effort, thought, and perhaps support from peers or you.				
5. Give prompts and regular feedback about learning progress. Give lots of on-the-spot feedback. Replace grades with constructive and practical tips for improvement. Suggest personalized targets. Do not use norm-referencing. Use criterion-referenced assessment only.				
6. Teach students how to assess their learning realistically, how to use criteria, and look for evidence. Teach them how to set their own goals for improvement.				
7. Acknowledge, celebrate, and display all relative success. Frequently hold up pieces of work for everyone to see and explain the achievement. Never hold work up for ridicule. Do not select only the best work for display. Have plenty of space for work to be pinned up casually for short periods of time. Teach students how to mount work for longer-lasting displays.				
Totals				

E. Whole-school issues—things to think about with your colleagues	A	B	C	D
1. Develop the student council, if you have one, so that it functions effectively within the school's communication and decision-making structure. Ensure that it has a voice in staff meetings, parent-teacher meetings, and so forth.				
2. Set up a sizable budget for the student council.				
3. Create frequent opportunities for individual, and groups of, students to be heard. Ask them for feedback on teaching, consult them on major policy decisions, have a complaints procedure, have a suggestions box, with updates to students in assembly or home room.				
4. Seek to give groups of students their own physical space. If space permits, give each grade level a common room. Don't lock students out.				
5. Attend to the aesthetics, safety, and comfort of the physical environment. Carpets are essential. Provide lots of plants and art, and good ventilation and lighting. Use color and fabrics to soften the utilitarian nature of school interiors.				
6. Check that the students' restrooms are dignifying and have paper. Minimize time students spend in line at lunch. Make sure there's plenty of healthy food and lots of choice. Take students' advice on how to improve these facilities.				
7. Reappraise the behavior policy from a nonbehaviorist point of view. Do away with threats and bribes. Abandon behaviorist psychology. Negotiate a set of clear rules with students. Agree on positive and negative consequences with students. Place a premium on assertiveness. Offer choices. Emphasize personal responsibility. Use trained counselors. Train and use peer mediators. Make nonpunitive contracts with students about changes to their behavior.				
8. Allow students to move around the building without permission slips—to use the resource center, for example, during class.				
9. Group students in a way that supports self-esteem. Hold discussions with students, parents, and staff about mixed-ability grouping. Make self-esteem the deciding criterion. Take into account your ability to differentiate. Make a joint decision.				
10. Consult with students, staff, and parents to create a whole-school policy on self-esteem. Uphold the policy through reminders, modeling the behaviors, and challenging inappropriate behaviors.				
11. Make the enhancement of self-esteem a major plank of the school's mission statement and development plan. Explain what self-esteem is and why it's so important. Encourage reading about self-esteem and hold seminars and training events. Talk about self-esteem openly. Seek to achieve a common understanding and common sense of priority.				
Totals				
Grand Totals				

Check Your Delivery of Independent Learning Skills

It's no wonder that thinking skills and independent learning are major agendas in schools. Students need the attitudes and skills of independence for long-term success. National and state standards, homework, and requirements for passing a grade and for graduation all require qualities such as perseverance and a willingness to defer gratification along with planning, time-management, and research skills, and summarizing, memorizing, and presentation techniques. Together, these create the foundation of lifelong learning. In this day and age people can expect to change jobs and have to retrain several times within a working lifetime.

John Dewey, the father of experiential learning, often said, essentially, that children don't do what they learn, they learn what they do (1938). If he was right, the skills and attitudes of independence can be acquired only experientially. They can be introduced, but not internalized, through dedicated study-skills courses. To stick, they have to be practiced and rehearsed many times. In fact, psychologists tell us that behaviors become habits only after 40 or so repetitions, which suggests the need for cross-curricular delivery. Clearly, no one teacher or department can make it happen single-handedly. Such learning requires all teachers to accept a share of the responsibility and play their part in delivering the messages; otherwise the desired outcomes will fall through the cracks of the curriculum.

The natural place to focus attention on teaching independence is middle school, when the skills of independent learning are least emphasized in our schools. And a natural way to begin the process of development is to look at what happens in elementary schools and plan for continuity and progression with elementary school teachers.

What would you do as a middle school teacher to build on elementary school learning? What skills and attitudes do our students lack in high school? What, therefore, do we need to do in middle school to make sure that those qualities are developed before it's too late?

To get you going, here are two examples of secondary schools that have recently begun to lay out learning-to-learn skills in a systematic way. These lists refer only to grade six. The skills will be taught through ordinary lessons. All the teachers in both schools have committed themselves to designing lessons that deliver these skills through certain types of activities and methods. Their subject-specific content will be covered at the same pace but through learning-to-learn methodologies.

The first school, Villiers High School, is ethnically and culturally diverse and has a learning-to-learn curriculum made up of 15 elements. These are broken down into precise learning outcomes, which are too detailed to list here, but here is the list of the 15 skill sets:

1. Processing material
2. Locating and selecting resources
3. Interrogating resources
4. Planning
5. Thinking
6. Presenting
7. Being self-sufficient
8. Learning with others
9. Managing time
10. Memorizing
11. Connecting ideas and information
12. Being self-aware as a learner
13. Assessing self and others
14. Celebrating success and managing disappointment
15. Managing personal relationships

Underpinning these skills are five attitudes, or dispositions, that are required for the skills to flourish. These will be developed through the culture of classrooms, the manner and modeling of the teachers, school policies, and so on. They are largely taken from Professor Guy Claxton and his excellent book *Building Learning Power* (2002):

- reciprocity
- resourcefulness
- reflectiveness
- resilience
- responsibility

The second example is adapted from a chart used at an all-male private middle and high school, De La Salle College. A working party of teachers from various subjects have defined five skill areas that they want students to develop in their first year at the school in order to create a foundation for effective self-sufficient learning later on (see pages 215–17).

De La Salle College Skill Areas Chart

		Foundation Level	Intermediate Level	Advanced Level
Collaboration	1	a) I am willing to work in a variety of different groups.	b) I am able to give out and accept different roles and tasks within the group, and I make sure I complete my own task well.	c) I help to promote good group work by including everyone in the task and working out any problems quickly and pleasantly.
	2	a) I am quiet when others are talking.	b) I listen to whomever is speaking and show that I am paying attention.	c) I show that I have listened well by summing up and explaining the views of the speaker to others.
	3	a) I am able to take turns to speak.	b) I am able to explain my own ideas and opinions very clearly so that others understand them.	c) I am able to change some of my views if others offer different and more suitable ideas.
	4	a) I do not make fun of other people in the group by making unkind comments, facial expressions, or gestures.	b) I am able to give positive and encouraging comments to others when they do something well and I can accept praise from others when I do well.	c) I am able to see which ideas will work better than others and help the group to agree on the best way of completing the task.
		Foundation Level	**Intermediate Level**	**Advanced Level**
Oral Communication	1	a) I am able to give a presentation to an audience using notes and prompts.	b) I am able to interact with my audience by accepting comments and questions from them as well as just speaking to them.	c) I am able to change or add to my presentation on the spot if I need to.
	2	a) I am able to spot and understand the needs of a particular audience, whatever its size.	b) I am able to keep my audience's interest and attention.	c) I am able to judge how successful my presentation is by checking how much my audience has learned and understood.
	3	a) I am able to speak loudly and slowly enough for everyone to hear.	b) I am able to use and explain subject-specific vocabulary.	c) I am able to give my presentation in an expressive and interesting way.
	4	a) The information in my presentation is relevant.	b) I am able to select the most important information for my presentation and make decisions about the best order in which to present it.	c) I am able to offer my own judgments and draw my own conclusions about the information I am using.

De La Salle College Skill Areas Chart (continued)

Organization		Foundation Level	Intermediate Level	Advanced Level
	1	a) I can find and choose the most suitable resource or piece of equipment for the task I am doing.	b) I can use the resource or equipment safely, independently, and imaginatively to complete my task.	c) I can judge how useful and suitable the resource or equipment has been once my task has been completed.
	2	a) I can understand and explain the information from the resources I am using.	b) I can draw conclusions from the information in the resources that I am using.	c) I can explain the conclusions I have reached, find patterns, and apply those ideas to other work.
	3	a) I can read for a particular purpose, recognizing information that is and is not relevant.	b) I can pick out the most important words and phrases and recognize that some information is more important than other information.	c) I can take and revise notes in a variety of ways and choose which method will display the information the most clearly.
	4	a) I can complete my work and hand it in on time.	b) I can plan my time carefully so that I space out my work and meet a deadline comfortably.	c) I can plan my time in class and outside of school carefully so that I meet several deadlines for different tasks.

Problem Solving		Foundation Level	Intermediate Level	Advanced Level
	1	a) I can recognize and understand a problem that has been given to me.	b) I can think of and choose the methods I need to use to solve the problem.	c) I can judge how successful my methods have been at solving the problem and suggest other methods that could also have solved the problem.
	2	a) I can think of the right questions to ask for a particular task.	b) I can choose the best questions and place them in order of importance in order to complete a particular task.	c) I can judge how effective and useful my questions were once the task has been completed.
	3	a) I can describe the results we have found once the problem has been solved.	b) I can explain the results, and the methods used to reach those results, once the problem has been solved.	c) I can study the results and find patterns or explain how these results can be useful in solving similar problems.
	4	a) I can identify key patterns, relationships, and connections.	b) I can present a range of data in different ways and show their relationships.	c) I can interpret patterns and relationships and use them to make judgments about how to progress.

De La Salle College Skill Areas Chart (continued)

		Foundation Level	Intermediate Level	Advanced Level
Evaluation	1	a) I am able to pick out strengths (good points) or weaknesses (bad points) about my work.	b) I am able to pick out both strengths and weaknesses in my work accurately.	c) I am able to explain my strengths and weaknesses to others.
	2	a) I can read and understand assessment criteria (such as a matrix) for a particular piece of work.	b) I can use assessment criteria to grade my own work or the work of others accurately.	c) I can use assessment criteria to figure out what skills I, or others, need to improve in order to get the higher grades.
	3	a) I know what skills I need to learn or improve in order to make my work better.	b) I can explain what I need to do to learn or improve those skills.	c) I can put my ideas into action so that I improve those skills.
	4	a) I am prepared to allow others to grade my work.	b) I am prepared to listen to other people's opinions about my work.	c) I am prepared to discuss with others how my work could be improved.

Adapted from De La Salle "Skill Areas Chart." Used with permission of De La Salle College, St. Saviour, Jersey, Channel Islands.

Now consider high school and concentrate on the skills and attitudes required both during high school courses and in the preparation for final exams and college entrance exams. The chart on pages 219–23 presents them as a series of messages to get across to students. What do you think? This is only for starters. Add your own messages and bullet points.

I'm arguing that it's possible to see the independent-learning curriculum, or the study-skills curriculum, as a series of crucial messages that need to be repeated time and time again, messages that contain both skills and attitudes. Naturally, they need to be delivered from middle school on and be built up over the years with lots and lots of opportunities to practice skills and internalize attitudes. Remember, we're talking about habit formation. The campaign will work best if the messages are made explicit and explained to students up front, so that they know the agenda and its rationale. Then the messages have to be delivered through a range of activities, both in and out of the classroom. For maximum effect, students have to be debriefed after these activities to make the "learning about learning" outcomes explicit.

There are many opportunities in school to deliver these messages. Just as the messages have to be repeated time and again, so they have to come from many angles, through many different channels. Use the chart that follows to plot current practice and plan further coverage for each grade. Don't just check off each item: Write in detail. For instance, exactly how will student planners be used to get across time management (Message 9)? Only when the detail is secure will changes start to happen. It's easy to assume that, because planners are being used, time management is being handled. No, it depends on *how* the planners are being used, what coaching students get from their teachers, and how much fuss the school makes about, and how much it models, good planning.

Message	Implications for teachers	Implications for students
1. Don't just sit there. Learning requires the brain to be active—engage it.	• Use active learning techniques. • Don't give ready-made information, such as lecturing, having students copy from another source, or duplicated notes. • Require students to find things out and figure things out via research, problem solving, peer teaching, hypothesis testing, and so forth. • Require them to ask you rather than expect you to tell them. • When students ask for help, structure their thinking by asking them questions and giving them prompts so that they figure it out for themselves.	• Keep asking questions of yourself—"How does this fit with . . . ?" • Don't just passively read text—annotate, highlight, Mind Map. • Keep comparing what's new with what you know already: "What have I learned today?" • Keep testing yourself. • Keep connecting with the exam—"Where does this fit in the unit? What kinds of questions on this topic have come up in the past?" • Check your understanding with the teacher.
2. Get organized. There is no short cut: Your brain learns by figuring things out for itself, so give it a chance.	• Ask open-ended questions such as how, what if, why? • Ask students to make connections, for example "how is this different from . . . ?" • Assign tasks that involve translating material from one format into another—list into pie chart, text into keyword plan, storyboard into bulleted list, and so forth. • Ask students to summarize often—draw Mind Maps of whole topics, make personal summary cards, and so forth. • Require students to articulate their learning to others—peers, parents, a tape recorder. • Require students to keep moving in their heads from whole to parts and from parts to whole: "What's this an example of . . . ?" or "What's the principle behind this?" • Get the students to signal to you the moment they don't understand what you are saying.	• Turn the given material into another format—your own words, Mind Map, flowchart, keyword plan, bulleted list, storyboard, and so forth. • Don't pretend that you understand if you don't. Ask the teacher for clarification. • Accept the difference between doing the work and actually learning the material—don't con yourself into thinking that you will have learned something just because you have completed the exercise. Check your understanding. • When you read text, ask yourself, "What does this mean?" or "What is this saying?" • Explain what you have learned to others. If they can understand it, it proves that you have.

Message	Implications for teachers	Implications for students
3. Stress, "you're capable." The natural response to stress is to close down. Use techniques to minimize the problem.	• Teach and use self-affirming language: "I have all the skills I need to do well in this exam," and "I can get all the knowledge I need to pass; my past is not my potential." • Teach relaxation techniques—diaphragmatic breathing; muscle relaxation; and use of music, color, and aromas. • Teach envisioning—"In ten years' time, I see myself running my own small business," "I see myself in the exam feeling calm and thinking clearly," and "I see myself in college." • Teach about the potential and functioning of the brain. Students have all the brainpower they need. • Avoid threats and punishments such as statements that begin with "If you . . ." • Enhance self-esteem. Give lots of acknowledgment, recognition, and encouragement. • Take time to talk with, and especially listen to, students.	• Recognize reptilian-brain behavior—that is, when you feel panic and want to give up and run away—and take time out. • Use relaxation techniques. • Use self-affirmations: Talk to yourself! • Remind yourself of your long-term goals. • Break learning into small steps. • Record your achievements step by step and feel proud of what you achieve—a piece at a time. • Focus on what you have done, not what you have still have to do—the glass is half full, not half empty. • Keep talking to people who will encourage you. • Get away from your work—take breaks often, call a friend, listen to music, watch TV, go for a walk, read a book.
4. It's all your own work. Yes, it is. You have only yourself to blame, or thank.	• Get students into the habit of making choices—about learning method, deadlines, resources, assessment, modes of recording, and so forth. • Ask students to set their own goals and deadlines. • Let students face consequences and encourage them to recognize the options they had. • Ask students to come up with learning methods for themselves. • Debrief about the learning process with students on a regular basis. • Support them with a "students' toolkit" that gives lots of guidelines for working independently. • Model responsible language. • Show students the big picture often, so that they know where they stand in relation to the coursework and exam requirements. • Support them with adequate resources. • Avoid using rewards. They keep people dependent on external motivators.	• Make sure you know what you need to learn and the requirements of the exam. Always check what you are doing against the big picture. Have a clear idea of what you have done and what you have to do. • Own the learning—it's yours, not your teacher's. It's up to you to master it. • Reflect on missed deadlines and goals. Ask yourself what you will do differently next time. • Remember, in the exam, you can usually use only what's in your head. • Remember, only you can put stuff in there in advance. • Remember that everything you do (and don't do) is a choice. • There are no excuses, only choices. • Remember that you are doing this for yourself, not for your parents or the school.

Message	Implications for teachers	Implications for students
5. What's the difference? All brains are wired differently. Do it your way.	• Use lots of varied teaching and learning methods and debrief students about them. • Offer a choice of different tasks to suit different styles and ask students to make choices. • Be explicit about learning styles with students—explain the styles, demonstrate them, and use learning-styles terminology. • Ask students to accept increasing responsibility for learning. Enable them to study, record, and present learning in their own way. • Over time, require students to build a bank of personal learning techniques and encourage them to reflect on the suitability of various methods for their natural style.	• Understand about learning styles and recognize your own natural ways of learning. • Try lots of different study techniques so that you can find the ones that suit you best. • Use your preferred methods and practice them so that they become easy and natural. • Be willing to try new ways—you never know.
6. Take note! Learn to take notes; take notes to learn.	• Teach speed reading, scanning, and skimming techniques. • Teach the idea of hierarchies in text, ranging from headlines to details (most explicit in newspapers, but present in all nonfiction text)—this is the basis of notetaking. • Teach key-point identification. • Teach keyword identification. • Teach notetaking and summarizing formats, such as keyword plans, tables, Mind Maps, timelines, storyboards, flowcharts, concentric circles, target notes, bulleted lists, and so forth. • Assign notetaking homework. • Build identification of key points and succinct presentation into your assessment policy. • As time goes on, ask students to summarize summaries.	• Force yourself *not* to copy. • Cut down on reading time—practice scanning text for the relevant parts. • Cut down on reading time—practice skimming for the key points. • See if you can write points down in the fewest possible words. • Use sketches, diagrams, cartoons, and symbols instead of words. • Try lots of different notetaking techniques so that you know which ones suit you best. • Use colors. • Get into the habit of highlighting notes in your exercise book or notebook—even in textbooks if you own them. • Get into the habit of taking notes on the work you are covering, even if your teacher doesn't ask you to. • As you approach a test or exam, summarize your summaries.

Message	Implications for teachers	Implications for students
7. Remember to remember. You have two types of memory. Learn how to store things long term.	• Make learning multisensory—discuss the effects with students and teach them how to do multisensory learning at home. • Teach about short- and long-term memory skills. • Teach the Ebbinghaus effect—that retention fades over time unless material is revisited frequently. • Revisit and review previous learning as part of ordinary lessons. • Assign summarizing homework. • Give lots of minitests. • Have Mind Map summaries of topics on the classroom walls. Encourage students to do the same at home. • Teach memorizing techniques, such as "Now You See It . . ." (page 106).	• Accept the importance of revisiting previous learning. • Write lots and lots of summaries. • Use "Now You See It . . ." (page 106)—a basic technique. • Use physical memory methods. Use gestures. Put key points on cards and place them around the room and walk around. • Listen to the sound of your own voice to aid memory—speak and make recordings. • Use mnemonics, number words, recordings, listings, adhesive notes, and posters. • Prove what you know—test yourself or get others to test you.
8. Do yourself a favor. Your brain works best under certain conditions. Give it what it needs.	• Make sure your classroom models favorable learning conditions: good light; plenty of oxygen; appropriate color; and peripherals conducive to learning. • Encourage students to drink plenty of pure, chilled water instead of soda and other sugary or caffeinated drinks. • Change learning activities often in lessons. • Teach about concentration span, that it is usually minutes equal to chronological age plus two years (up to 14!). • Teach that it's important to break learning into small chunks to fit concentration span, and to have short breaks between chunks. • Model this in the classroom.	• Drink lots of water—avoid soda and other sugary or caffeinated drinks. • Eat small portions and often. • Make sure you have enough fresh air in the room and enough light. • Take frequent short breaks. • Eliminate distractions. Have the discipline to get away from the TV and ask your family not to disturb you. • Make the most of peripheral learning: Put key points on large paper and stick them around the house—behind the bathroom door, for example.

Message	Implications for teachers	Implications for students
9. There's plenty of time. Yes, there is plenty of time to learn everything—as long as you manage it well.	• Give plenty of practice working to non-negotiable deadlines. • Give plenty of practice setting realistic deadlines. • Keep referring to different timeframes for learning: short, medium, and long term. Have charts and calendars on the wall. • Have a large clock in the classroom and keep drawing attention to the pace of learning. • Model good time management. Let the students know the plan you made for the lesson, course, grading, or project work, and tell them about the replanning you do as you go along. • Give enough time for students to use their planners to record homework and deadlines and to identify potential clashes. • Remind students that every action, every word, is a choice, every moment of every day. Challenge students when they try to blame other people or external factors for choices they have made.	• Accept that life is a series of choices. You manage time; it does not manage you. • Make choices in advance; plan ahead—get a wall calendar or a planner. • Set short- and medium-term goals to guide your choices. • Put "things to do" in different categories to help you make choices: what I have to do; what I'm asked to do; what I want to do. • Involve your family—negotiate study time and ask them to support you by protecting the time. • When planning, follow the rules about reviewing—allow for time to go back over things. • When planning, follow the rules about concentration spans—take into account the need for breaks. • Replan when things don't go according to plan. • Do the worst first!

Recommended Resources

Organizations, Networks, and Projects

21st Century Learning Initiative: www.21learn.org

Alite—Accelerated Learning in Training and Education: www.alite.co.uk

Alternative Education Resource Organization: www.educationrevolution.org

BPI Advocating and Supporting Small Schools: www.bpichicago.org/pe/asss.html

Brain Gym: www.braingym.org

Campaign for Learning: www.campaign-for-learning.org.uk

Centre for Studies on Inclusive Education: http://inclusion.uwe.ac.uk

Citizenship Foundation: www.citfou.org.uk

Coalition of Essential Schools: www.essentialschools.org

Consortium for Research on Emotional Intelligence in Organizations: www.eiconsortium.org

The Cooperative Learning Center: www.co-operation.org

Creating Learning Communities Online Resource Center: www.creatinglearningcommunities.org

Education Now (Educational Heretics Press): www.educationnow.gr.apc.org/

Family Village—A Global Community of Disability-Related Resources: www.familyvillage.wisc.edu

Human Scale Education: www.hse.org.uk

Institute for Critical Thinking: www.chss.montclair.edu/ict

International Alliance for Learning: www.ialearn.org

International Council of Philosophical Inquiry with Children: www.simnet.is/heimspekiskolinn/icpic.html

Philosophy for Children: www.p4c.net

Project Zero: http://pzweb.harvard.edu

RSA Education: www.thersa.org/newcurriculum/home.html

Society for Effective Affective Learning: www.seal.org.uk

Teaching and Learning Research Programme: www.tlrp.org

Learning Theory and Research with Lots of Links

For synopses of 50 major learning theories: http://tip.psychology.org

12 key learning theories summarized: www.funderstanding.com/about_learning.cfm

An easy introduction to the science of the brain with lots of pathways for further investigation: http://faculty.washington.edu/chudler/neurok.html

Technical information about the structure of the brain, with lots of photographs and diagrams: www.vh.org/adult/provider/anatomy/BrainAnatomy/BrainAnatomy.html

The site of the book *The Learning Revolution* (Dryden and Vos 1999): www.thelearningweb.net

Good starting point for brain-based learning: www.loloville.com/brain_based_learning.htm

An amazing set of links about the structure and function of the brain: www.brainresearch.com

More brain information: www.brainconnection.com

A gateway to lots of modern teaching and learning ideas: http://academic.wsc.edu/redl/classes/tami/braintechwsc.html

Another excellent set of links: www.newhorizons.org

More interesting links: www.uwsp.edu/education/lwilson/learning

A wide range of topics summarized and linked: www.teach-nology.com/currenttrends

A great catalog of articles and links: www.emtech.net/brain_based_learning.html

Links to many interesting articles: www.middleweb.com/MWLresources/brain1.html

Links to a wide range of theories: http://dmoz.org/Reference/Education/Methods_and_Theories/ Learning_Theories

Lots of links to a range of teaching and learning topics: http://snow.utoronto.ca/Learn2/ resources.html

An impressive bibliography: www.excel-ability.com/Bib/Bib-BrainBasedL.html

Excellent starting point for learning-styles research: www.learningstyles.org

Some Leading Educational Lights

Thomas Armstrong: www.thomasarmstrong.com

Nathaniel Branden: www.nathanielbranden.net

Tony Buzan: www.mind-map.com

Renate and Geoffrey Caine: www.cainelearning.com

Edward Deci and Richard Ryan: www.psych.rochester.edu/SDT/faculty.html

Howard Gardner: www.pz.harvard.edu/PIs/HG.htm

Anthony Gregorc: www.gregorc.com

Eric Jensen: http://jlcbrain.com

Martha Kaufeldt: www.beginwiththebrain.com

Alfie Kohn: www.alfiekohn.org

Nancy Margulies: www.nancymargulies.com

David Perkins: www.pz.harvard.edu/PIs/DP.htm

Barbara Prashnig: www.clc.co.nz

Robert J. Sternberg: www.yale.edu/pace/teammembers/personalpages/bob.html

Pat Wolfe: www.patwolfe.com

Run searches on Daniel Goleman, Robert Sylwester, Carl Rogers

Learning-Style Instruments

Online Learning-Style Analyses for Adults (Free)

VAK (visual, auditory, kinesthetic)

www.chaminade.org/inspire/learnstl.htm

www.wiley.com/legacy/college/weygandt5e/32.htm

VARK (visual, auditory, read/write, kinesthetic)

www.vark-learn.com/english/page.asp?p=questionnaire

Multiple Intelligences

www.personal.psu.edu/staff/b/x/bxb11/MI/MIQuiz.htm

Miscellaneous

http://it-resources.icsa.ch/Pedagogie/Questionnaires/LSQuestE.html (a personality-based questionnaire)

www.efa.nl/onderwijs/2000/addictEUN/addictweb/Kolb&Vermunt.htm (Kolb and beyond)

Online Learning-Style Analyses for Adults (Not Free)

The Creative Learning Company (Barbara Prashnig): www.clc.co.nz/products.asp

Cymeon Research Learning Styles Profiler (intended for use in commercial businesses): www.cymeon.com/lss2.asp

The Dunn and Dunn Learning Styles Instrument: www.geocities.com/CollegePark/Union/2106/lsi.html

The Gregorc Style Delineator: www.gregorc.com/instrume.html

The Herrmann Brain Dominance Instrument: http://hopellc.com/bdsi.html

Honey & Mumford Learning Styles Questionnaire: www.peterhoney.co.uk/product/brochure

Johnston and Orwig's Learning Type Test: www.sil.org/LinguaLinks/LanguageLearning/OtherResources/YorLrnngStylAndLnggLrnng/TheLearningTypeTest.htm

The Keirsey Temperament Sorter II: www.advisorteam.com/user/ktsintro.asp

The Myers-Briggs Type Indicator: www.knowyourtype.com

Miscellaneous

From the Center for New Discoveries in Learning: www.howtolearn.com/personal.html

A substantial instrument from the Creative Learning Company: www.creativelearningcentre.com/products.asp?page=LSA&lang=&cs=NZ%24&cr=1

The Dunn, Dunn, and Price Learning Style Inventory: http://learn.humanesources.com

Further Dunn and Dunn questionnaires to purchase: www.learningstyles.net

DVC Learning Style Survey for College: www.metamath.com/lsweb/dvclearn.htm

The Paragon Learning Style Inventory: www.oswego.edu/~shindler/plsi

Soloman and Felder's analysis from NC State University: www2.ncsu.edu/unity/lockers//users/f/felder/public/ILSdir/ilsweb.html

Adult Questionnaires in Books

Details of all the books are in the bibliography (page 229).

Accelerated Learning for the 21st Century (1998), by Colin Rose and Malcolm J. Nicholl: multiple intelligence quiz

Emotional Intelligence in the Classroom (2001), by Michael Brearley: thinking-styles questionnaire

Learning about Learning (2000), by Chris Watkins et al.: questionnaire based on Honey and Mumford

The Learning Revolution (1999), by Gordon Dryden and Jeannette Vos: an adaptation of Gregorc's analysis

OutSmart Yourself (2004), by David Lazear: multiple intelligences self survey

Teaching for Success (2000), by Mark Fletcher: a VAK questionnaire

Online Learning-Styles Analyses for Students

Some of the following items are free; others have to be bought. They vary enormously in quality and also in the sophistication of the language, the concepts, the contexts they use, and the extent to which they have been scientifically tested, so please don't hold me responsible for the choices you make! Check them out, consider their underlying principles, and make sure you believe that they will be beneficial before you use them. If you decide to use a students' questionnaire, please consider all the cautions discussed on pages 197–98.

VAK

http://lookingahead.heinle.com/filing/l-styles.htm

www.usd.edu/trio/tut/ts/style.html

www.howtolearn.com/personal.html

Multiple Intelligences

www.surfaquarium.com/MI/inventory.htm

www.personal.psu.edu/staff/b/x/bxb11/MI/MIQuiz.htm

Right-Left Hemispheres

http://brain.web-us.com/brain/braindominance.htm

www.mathpower.com/brain.htm

Miscellaneous

www.learningstyle.com (the Dunn, Dunn, and Price Inventory)

www.learningstyles.net (further Dunn and Dunn questionnaires to purchase)

www.oswego.edu/~shindler/plsi (the Paragon Learning Style Inventory)

www.outsider.co-uk.com (a British analysis designed for use with students over 16 years of age)

www.engr.ncsu.edu/learningstyles/ilsweb.html (Soloman's and Felder's analysis from North Carolina State University)

www.metamath.com/lsweb/dvclearn.htm (DVC Learning Style Survey for College)

www.creativelearningcentre.com/products.asp?page=LSA&lang=&cs=NZ%24&cr=1 (a substantial instrument from the Creative Learning Company, available in junior and senior versions)

www.learnmoreindiana.org/careers/inventories/MSPI.cgi

Student Questionnaires in Books

Accelerated Learning in the Classroom (1996), by Alistair Smith: VAK prompt chart

Accelerated Learning in Practice (1998), by Alistair Smith: multiple intelligences questionnaire

Multiple Intelligence Approaches to Assessment (1998b), by David Lazear: multiple intelligences profiles

Strategies for Closing the Learning Gap (2001), by Mike Hughes with Andy Vass: VAK questionnaire

Also take a look at the questionnaires designed for adults. Some of them might work with older students, and others could possibly be adapted.

Bibliography

21st Century Learning Initiative. 2004. "The 21st Century Learning Initiative: Promoting a Vision, Knowledge, Experience and a Network." www.21learn.org (accessed June 1, 2004).

Abbott, John. 1993. *Learning Makes Sense: Recreating Education for a Changing Future*. Surrey, UK: Education 2000.

Abbott, John, and Terry Ryan. 1999a. "Constructing Knowledge, Reconstructing Schooling." *Educational Leadership* 57 (3): 66–69.

———. 1999b. "Constructing Knowledge and Shaping Brains." 21st Century Learning Initiative. www.21learn.org (accessed December 1999). Also available in reworked form in appendix 2 to *The Unfinished Revolution*.

———. 2000. *The Unfinished Revolution: Learning, Human Behavior, Community, and Political Paradox*. Stafford, UK: Network Educational Press.

———. 2001. "An Emergent Science of Learning for the 21st Century." In *The Unfinished Revolution: Learning, Human Behavior, Community, and Political Paradox*. Alexandria, Va: Association for Supervision and Curriculum Development. www.ascd.org/publications/books/2001abbott/ chapter2.html (accessed September 1, 2004).

Alexander, Titus. 2000. *Citizenship Schools: A Practical Guide to Education for Citizenship and Personal Development*. London: Campaign for Learning.

Anderson, Roy. 1999. *First Steps to a Physical Basis of Concentration*. Bancyfelin, Wales: Crown House Publishing.*

Armstrong, Thomas. 1987. *In Their Own Way: Discovering and Encouraging Your Child's Personal Learning Style*. New York: Putnam.

Arnold, Ellen. 1999. *The MI Strategy Bank*. Tucson, Ariz.: Zephyr Press.

Baldaro, James. 1995. "The Benefits of Student Participation." *Education Now News and Review Feature Supplement* (Summer): 1–2.

Ball, Sir Christopher. 1995. "Sophie's World—A Learning Society." *RSA Journal* 145 (December): 6.

Bayliss, Valerie. 1999. "In My View." *Insight* (Autumn): 18–19.

Beaver, Diana. 1994. *Lazy Learning: Making the Most of the Brains You Were Born With*. Shaftesbury, Dorset, UK: Element Books Limited.

Bellanca, James. 1990. *Keep Them Thinking: A Handbook of Model Lessons*. Arlington Heights, Ill.: IRI/Skylight Training and Publishing.

———. 1994. *Active Learning Handbook for the Multiple Intelligences Classroom*. Arlington Heights, Ill.: IRI/Skylight Training and Publishing.

Bellanca, James, Carolyn Chapman, and Elizabeth Swartz. 1994. *Multiple Assessments for Multiple Intelligences*. Arlington Heights, Ill.: IRI/Skylight Training and Publishing.

Bellanca, James, and Robin Fogarty. 1991. *Blueprints for Thinking in the Cooperative Classroom*. Arlington Heights, Ill.: IRI/Skylight Training and Publishing.

———. 1993. *Catch Them Thinking: A Handbook of Classroom Strategies*. 2nd ed. Arlington Heights, Ill.: IRI/Skylight Training and Publishing.

Bentley, Tom. 2000. "Creativity, Community and a New Approach to Schooling." In *Schools in the Learning Age,* ed. Bill Lucas and Toby Greany, 57–64. London: Campaign for Learning.

Berman, Sally. 1995. *A Multiple Intelligences Road to a Quality Classroom.* Palatine, Ill.: IRI/Skylight Training and Publishing.

Bloom, Benjamin, ed. 1956. *Taxonomy of Educational Objectives: The Classification of Educational Goals.* New York: Longmans, Green.

Bodenhamer, Bob G., and L. Michael Hall. 1999. *The User's Manual for the Brain.* Bancyfelin, Wales: Crown House Publishing.*

Bowkett, Stephen. 1999. *Self-Intelligence: A Handbook for Developing Confidence, Self-Esteem and Interpersonal Skills.* Stafford, UK: Network Educational Press.

Bowring-Carr, Christopher, and John West-Burnham. 1997. *Effective Learning in Schools: How to Integrate Learning and Leadership for a Successful School.* London: Pitman.

Branden, Nathaniel. 1994. *The Six Pillars of Self-Esteem.* New York: Bantam Books.

———. 2001. Nathaniel Branden. http://www.nathanielbranden.net/ (accessed July 10, 2001).

Brandes, Donna, and Paul Ginnis. 1986. *A Guide to Student-Centred Learning.* Cheltenham, UK: Stanley Thornes.

———. 1992. *The Student-Centred School.* Hemel Hempstead, UK: Simon and Schuster.

Brearley, Michael. 2001. *Emotional Intelligence in the Classroom: Creative Learning Strategies for 11–18 Year Olds.* Bancyfelin, Wales: Crown House Publishing.*

Browne, Lesley. 1995. "Setting Up a Democratic Classroom." In *Developing Democratic Education,* ed. Clive Harber, 61–72. Nottingham, UK: Education Now Books.

Bruer, John T. 1993. *Schools for Thought: A Science of Learning in the Classroom.* Cambridge, Mass.: MIT Press.

Bruner, Jerome. 1996. *The Culture of Education.* Cambridge, Mass.: Harvard University Press.

Burke, Kay. 1992. *What to Do with the Kid Who . . .: Developing Cooperation, Self Discipline, and Responsibility in the Classroom.* Arlington Heights, Ill.: IRI/SkyLight Training and Publishing.

Burnett, Gary. 2002. *Learning to Learn: Making Learning Work for All Students.* Bancyfelin, Wales: Crown House Publishing.*

Butler, Kathleen. 1986. *Learning and Teaching Style: In Theory and Practice.* Columbia, Conn.: The Learner's Dimension.

Butterworth, Brian. 1999. *The Mathematical Brain.* London: Macmillan. (Reprinted as *What Counts: How Every Brain Is Hardwired for Math.* New York: The Free Press, 1999.)

Buzan, Tony. 1986. *Use Your Memory.* London: BBC Worldwide Publishing.

———. 1993. *The Mindmap Book: How to Use Your Radiant Thinking to Maximize Your Brain's Untapped Potential.* London: BBC Worldwide Publishing. (Reprinted New York: Plume, 1996.)

Caine, Renate Nummela, and Geoffrey Caine. 1997. *Unleashing the Power of Perceptual Change: The Potential of Brain-Based Teaching.* Alexandria, Va.: Association for Supervision and Curriculum Development.

Calvin, William. 1996. *How Brains Think: Evolving Intelligence Then and Now.* New York: Basic Books.

Carbo, Marie. 1980. "An Analysis of the Relationship between the Modality Preferences of Kindergartners and the Selected Reading Treatments as They Affect the Learning of a Basic Sight-Word Vocabulary." Dissertation, St. John's University, New York.

Carbo, Marie, Rita Dunn, and Kenneth Dunn 1986. *Teaching Students to Read through Their Individual Learning Styles.* New York: Prentice Hall.

Chapman, Carolyn. 1993. *If the Shoe Fits . . .: How to Develop Multiple Intelligences in the Classroom.* Arlington Heights, Ill.: IRI/Skylight Training and Publishing.

Churchland, Paul. 1995. *The Engine of Reason, the Seat of the Soul: A Philosophical Journey into the Brain.* Cambridge, Mass.: A Bradford Book / MIT Press.

Clarke, Fiona. 2000. "Democracy Has to Be Lived to Be Learned." *Times Educational Supplement,* October 20, 2000. Available online at www.tes.co.uk/search/search_display.asp?section=Archive&sub_section=News+%26+opinion&id=339744&Type=0

Claxton, Guy. 1999. *Wise Up: The Challenge of Lifelong Learning.* New York: Bloomsbury.

———. 2002. *Building Learning Power: Helping Young People Become Better Learners.* Bristol, UK: TLO (available from www.buildinglearningpower.co.uk).

Coles, Robert. 1997. *The Moral Intelligence of Children: How to Raise a Moral Child.* New York: Random House.

Costa, Arthur. 1995. *Teaching for Intelligent Behavior: Outstanding Strategies for Strengthening Your Students' Thinking Skills.* Bellevue, Wa.: Bureau of Education and Research.

Covey, Stephen R. 1989a. *The Seven Habits of Highly Effective People.* London: Simon and Schuster. (Reprinted New York: Simon and Schuster, 1990.)

———. 1989b. *The Seven Habits of Highly Effective People.* New York: Simon and Schuster. Audiocassette (abridged).

Craft, A. 1997. "Proceedings of Creativity in Education Colloquium on Multiple Intelligences and Creativity with Howard Gardner." Colloquium held in July 1997, Open University School of Education, London.

Damasio, Antonio. 1994. *Descartes' Error: Emotion, Reason and the Human Brain.* New York: Grosset/Putnam.

DeAmicis, Bonita. 1997. *Multiple Intelligences Made Easy: Strategies for Your Curriculum.* Tucson, Ariz.: Zephyr Press.

De Bello, T. 1985. "A Critical Analysis of the Achievement and Attitude Effects of Administrative Assignments to Social Studies Writing Instruction Based on Identified, Eighth Grade Students' Learning Style Preferences for Learning Alone, with Peers, or with Teachers." Dissertation, St. John's University, New York.

Deci, Edward, Rosemary Hodges, Louisa Pierson, and Joseph Tomassone. 1992. "Autonomy and Competence as Motivational Factors in Students with Learning Disabilities and Emotional Handicaps." *Journal of Learning Disabilities* 25:457–71.

Deci, Edward, and Richard M. Ryan. 1985. *Intrinsic Motivation and Self-Determination in Human Behavior.* New York: Plenum.

———. 2002a. "The Paradox of Achievement: The Harder You Push, the Worse It Gets." In *Improving Academic Achievement: Contributions of Social Psychology,* ed. J. Aronson, 59–85. New York: Academic Press.

Deci, Edward, and Richard M. Ryan, eds. 2002b. *Handbook of Self-Determination Research.* Rochester, N.Y.: University of Rochester Press.

Deci, Edward, Robert Vallerand, Luc Pelletier, and Richard M. Ryan. 1991. "Motivation and Education: The Self-Determination Perspective." *Educational Psychologist* 26:325–46.

Della Valle, Joan 1984. "An Experimental Investigation of the Relationships between Preference for Mobility and the Word Recognition Scores of Seventh Grade Students to Provide Supervisory and Administrative Guidelines for the Organization of Effective Instructional Environments." Dissertation, St. John's University, New York.

Della Valle, Joan, Kenneth Dunn, Rita Dunn, G. Geisert, and R. Sinatra. 1986. "The Effects of Matching and Mismatching Students' Mobility Preferences on Recognition and Memory Tasks." *Journal of Educational Research* 79 (5): 267–72.

Denney, Nancy W. 1985. "A Review of Life Span Research with the Twenty Questions Task: A Study of Problem-Solving Ability." *The International Journal of Aging and Human Development* 21 (3): 161–73.

Dennison, Paul E., and Gail E. Dennison. 1988. *Brain Gym.* Teacher's ed. Ventura, Calif.: Edu-Kinesthetics.

Devlin, Keith. 2000. *The Math Gene: Why Everyone Has It, but Most People Don't Use It.* London: Phoenix. (Reprinted as *The Math Gene: How Mathematical Thinking Evolved and Why Numbers Are Like Gossip.* Collingdale, Pa.: Diane Publishing Company, 2000.)

Dewey, John. 1916. *Democracy and Education.* New York: Macmillan.

———. 1938. *Experience and Education.* New York: Macmillan.

Doll, William E., Jr. 1989. "Complexity in the Classroom." *Educational Leadership* 47 (1): 65–70.

Dryden, Gordon, and Jeannette Vos. 1999. *The Learning Revolution: To Change the Way the World Learns.* Updated international ed. Torrance, Calif.: The Learning Web.

Dunn, Rita, Jeffrey S. Beaudry, and Angela Klavas. 1989. "Survey of Research on Learning Styles." *Educational Leadership* 46 (6): 50–58.

Dunn, Rita, Kenneth Dunn, and Gary Price. 1996. *Learning Styles Inventory.* Lawrence, Kans.: Price Systems.

Ekwall, Eldon E., and Shanker, James L. 1988. *Diagnosis and Remediation of the Disabled Reader.* 3rd ed. Boston: Allyn and Bacon.

Fletcher, Mark. 2000. *Teaching for Success: The Brain-Friendly Revolution in Action.* Folkstone, UK: English Experience.

Fogarty, Robin. 1994. *How to Teach for Metacognitive Reflection.* The Mindful School. Palatine, Ill.: IRI/Skylight Training and Publishing.

———. 1997. *Brain Compatible Classrooms.* Arlington Heights, Ill.: SkyLight Professional Development.

Fogarty, Robin, and James Bellanca. 1986. *Teach Them Thinking.* Arlington Heights, Ill.: IRI/Skylight Training and Publishing.

Freire, Paulo. 1970. *Pedagogy of the Oppressed.* New York: Seabury Press.

Fry, Ron. 1996. *Improve Your Memory.* Franklin Lakes, N.J.: The Career Press.

Fry, William F. 1997. "Spanish Humour, a Hypotheory: A Report on Initiation of Research." *Humour: International Journal of Humour Research* 10 (2): 165–72.

———. 1998. Thriveonline interview. http://thriveonline.oxygen.com/serenity/humor/wfrychat.html (accessed January 1998).

Gammage, Philip. 1999. "After Five, Your Brain Is Cooked." *Education Now News and Review* no. 24 (Summer): 1–2.

Gardner, Howard. 1983. *Frames of Mind: The Theory of Multiple Intelligences*. New York: Basic Books.

———. 1993a. *Multiple Intelligences: The Theory in Practice*. New York: Basic Books.

———. 1993b. *The Unschooled Mind: How Children Think and How Schools Should Teach*. London: Fontana Press. (Orig. pub. New York: Basic Books, 1991.)

———. 1997. *Extraordinary Minds: Portraits of 4 Exceptional Individuals and an Examination of Our Own Extraordinariness*. London: Weidenfield & Nicolson. (Orig. pub. New York: Basic Books, 1997.)

———. 1999. *Intelligence Reframed: Multiple Intelligences for the 21st Century*. New York: Basic Books.

Gazzaniga, Michael. 1996. *Conversations in Cognitive Neuroscience*. Cambridge, Mass.: MIT Press.

———. 1998. *The Mind's Past*. Berkeley: University of California Press.

Ginnis, Paul, ed. 1998. *The Trailblazers*. Nottingham, UK: Education Now Books.

Givens, Barbara. 2000. *Learning Styles: A Guide for Teachers and Parents*. Rev. ed. Oceanside, Calif.: Learning Forum Publications.

Glasser, William. 1986. *Control Theory in the Classroom*. New York: HarperCollins.

Gleick, James. 1987. *Chaos: Making a New Science*. New York: Viking.

Glines, Don. 1989. "Can Schools Today Survive Very Far into the 21st Century?" *National Association of Secondary School Principals Bulletin* (February): 49–56.

Goleman, Daniel. 1996. *Emotional Intelligence: Why It Can Matter More Than IQ*. London: Bloomsbury. (Orig. pub. New York: Bantam, 1995.)

———. 1998. *Working with Emotional Intelligence*. London: Bloomsbury. (Orig. pub. New York: Bantam, 2000.)

Greenfield, Susan. 1994. "Journey to the Centre of the Brain." Royal Institution Christmas Lectures. London: Royal Institution of Great Britain.

———. 1998. *The Human Brain: A Guided Tour*. London: Phoenix. (Orig. pub. New York: Basic Books, 1998.)

———. 2000a. *Brain Story: Unlocking Our Inner World of Emotions, Memories, Ideas, and Desires*. London: BBC Worldwide. (Reprinted New York: DK Publishing, 2001.)

———. 2000b. *The Private Life of the Brain: Emotions, Consciousness, and the Secret Life of the Self*. London: Penguin Books. (Reprinted Hoboken, N.J.: John Wiley & Sons, 2001.)

Gregorc, Anthony F. 1982. *An Adult's Guide to Style*. Columbia, Conn.: Gregorc Associates. (Reprinted 2001.)

———. 1998. *The Mind Styles Model: Theory, Principles and Practice*. Columbia, Conn.: Gregorc Associates.

———. 2000–2001. Personal correspondence with the author by e-mail, April 2000–December 2001.

———. 2001. *Mind Styles FAQs Book*. Columbia, Conn.: Gregorc Associates.

———. 2004. "Mind Styles Presentations, Speeches and Keynotes." Gregorc Associates, Inc. www.gregorc.com/presenta.html (accessed June 1, 2004).

———. 2005. "FAQ." Gregorc Associates. www.gregorc.com/faq.html (accessed January 7, 2005).

Gregorc, Diane F. 1997. *Relating with Style*. Columbia, Conn.: Gregorc Associates.

Gregory, Gayle H., and Carolyn Chapman. 2002. *Differentiated Instructional Strategies: One Size Doesn't Fit All*. Thousand Oaks, Calif.: Corwin Press.

Handy, Charles. 1996. *Beyond Certainty: The Changing Worlds of Organizations.* Cambridge, Mass.: Harvard Business School Press.

Hannaford, Carla. 1995. *Smart Moves: Why Learning Is Not All in Your Head.* Atlanta, Ga.: Great Ocean Publishers.

Harber, Clive. 1998. "Paulo Freire." In *The Trailblazers,* ed. Paul Ginnis, 11. Nottingham, UK: Education Now Books.

Hart, Leslie. 1983. *Human Brain and Human Learning.* White Plains, N.Y.: Longman.

Herrnstein, Richard J., and Charles Murray. 1994. *The Bell Curve: Intelligence and Class Structure in American Life.* New York: Free Press.

Higham, Anita. 1997–1998. "Something Significantly Different. . . ." *Education Now News and Review* 18 (Winter): 1

Hobson, J. Allan. 1994. *The Chemistry of Conscious States: How the Brain Changes Its Mind.* New York: Little and Brown.

———. 1998. *Consciousness.* New York: Scientific American Library.

———. 1999. *Dreaming as Delirium: How the Brain Goes Out of Its Mind.* Cambridge, Mass.: MIT Press.

Hodges, H. 1985. "An Analysis of the Relationships among Preferences for a Formal/Informal Design, One Element of Learning Style, Academic Achievement, and Attitudes of Seventh and Eighth Grade Students in Remedial Mathematics Classes in a New York City Alternative Junior High School." Dissertation, St. John's University, New York.

Hoff, Erika. 2003. "The Specificity of Environmental Influence: Socioeconomic Status Affects Early Vocabulary Development via Maternal Speech." *Child Development* 74, no. 5 (October): 1368–78.

Holt, John. 1969. *How Children Fail.* London: Penguin. (Reprinted New York: Perseus, 1995.)

Howard, Pierce J. 2000. *The Owner's Manual for the Brain: Everyday Applications from Mind-Brain Research.* Austin, Tex.: Bard Press.

Howe, Michael J. A. 1997. *IQ in Question: The Truth about Intelligence.* London: Sage Publications.

Hughes, Mike. 1999. *Closing the Learning Gap.* Stafford, UK: Network Educational Press.*

Hughes, Mike, with Andy Vass. 2001. *Strategies for Closing the Learning Gap.* Stafford, UK: Network Educational Press.*

Humphreys, Tony. 1998. *Self-Esteem: The Key to Your Child's Education.* Dublin: Gill and MacMillan.

Illich, Ivan. 1971. *Deschooling Society.* New York: Harper and Row.

Jensen, Eric. 1993. *Learning Styles for the Nineties.* Del Mar, Calif.: The Brain Store. 3 audiocassettes.

———. 1995a. *The Learning Brain.* San Diego, Calif.: The Brain Store.

———. 1995b. *Super Teaching.* San Diego, Calif.: The Brain Store.

———. 1996. *Completing the Puzzle: The Brain-Compatible Approach to Learning.* Del Mar, Calif.: The Brain Store.

———. 1998. *Teaching with the Brain in Mind.* Alexandria, Va.: Association for Supervision and Curriculum Development.

———. 2000a. *Brain-Based Learning: The New Science of Teaching and Training.* Rev. ed. San Diego, Calif.: The Brain Store.

———. 2000b. *Different Brains, Different Learners: How to Reach the Hard to Reach.* San Diego, Calif.: The Brain Store.

———. 2000c. *Learning with the Body in Mind*. San Diego, Calif.: The Brain Store.

———. 2001. *Unleashing the Awesome Power of Your Brain*. San Diego, Calif.: The Brain Store. E-book.

———. 2003. *Environments for Learning*. San Diego, Calif.: The Brain Store.

Johnson, David R., Roger T. Johnson, and Edythe Johnson Holubec. 1984. *Circles of Learning: Co-operation in the Classroom*. Alexandria, Va.: Association for Supervision and Curriculum Development.

Johnson, David R., and Roger T. Johnson. 2005. The Cooperative Learning Center at the University of Minnesota. www.co-operation.org/ (accessed January 8, 2005).

Kagan, Spencer. 2004. Kagan Cooperative Learning. www.kaganonline.com (accessed June 1, 2004).

Kaufeldt, Martha. 1999. *Begin with the Brain: Orchestrating the Learner-Centered Classroom*. Tucson, Ariz.: Zephyr Press.

———. 2005. *Teachers, Change Your Bait! Brain-Compatible Differentiated Instruction*. Williston, VT : Crown House.

Keefe, J. W. 1979. "Learning Style: An Overview." In *Student Learning Styles: Diagnosing and Prescribing Programs*, ed. J. W. Keefe, 1–17. Reston, Va.: National Association of Secondary School Principals.

King, Edith. 1998. "Ivan Illich." In *The Trailblazers*, ed. Paul Ginnis, 10. Nottingham, UK: Education Now Books

Kirschenbaum, Howard, and Valerie Land Nenderson, eds. 1990. *The Carl Rogers Reader*. London: Constable. (Orig. pub. Boston: Houghton Mifflin, 1989.)

Kohn, Alfie. 1993. *Punished by Rewards: The Trouble with Gold Stars, Incentive Plans, A's, Praise, and Other Bribes*. Boston: Houghton Mifflin.

Kolb, David A. 1984. *Experiential Learning: Experience as the Source of Learning and Development*. Englewood Cliffs, N.J.: Prentice-Hall.

Kosslyn, S. M., and O. Koenig. 1995. *Wet Mind: The New Cognitive Neuroscience*. New York: Free Press.

Kuhl, Patricia, K. 2004. "Early Language Acquisition: Computational Strategies, Social Influences, and Neural Commitment in the Developing Brain." *Nature Reviews Neuroscience* 5: 831–43.

Lashley, Conrad. 1995. *Improving Study Skills: A Competence Approach*. London: Cassell. (Reprinted Stamford, Conn.: Thomson Learning, 1996.)

Lazear, David. 1991. *Seven Ways of Knowing: Teaching for Multiple Intelligences*. Arlington Heights, Ill.: IRI/Skylight Training and Publishing.

———. 1994. *Pathways of Learning: Teaching Students and Parents about Multiple Intelligences*. Tucson, Ariz.: Zephyr Press.

———. 1998a. *Intelligence Builders for Every Student: 44 Exercises to Expand Multiple Intelligences in Your Classroom*. Tucson, Ariz.: Zephyr Press.

———. 1998b. *Multiple Intelligence Approaches to Assessment: Solving the Assessment Conundrum*. Tucson, Ariz.: Zephyr Press.

———. 2004. *OutSmart Yourself: 16 Proven Strategies for Becoming Smarter Than You Think You Are*. Maui: David Lazear Group.

Lewkowicz, Adina Bloom. 1999. *Teaching Emotional Intelligence: Making Informed Choices*. Arlington Heights, Ill.: Skylight Training and Publishing.

Lucas, Bill, and Toby Greany, eds. 2000. *Schools in the Learning Age.* London: Campaign for Learning.

MacLean, Paul D. 1973. *A Triune Concept of the Brain and Behaviour.* Toronto, ON: University of Toronto Press, published for the Ontario Mental Health Foundation.

Malleret, Gael, Ursula Haditsch, David Genoux, Matthew W. Jones, Tim V. P. Bliss, Amanda M. Vanhoose, Carl Weitlauf, Eric R. Kandel, Danny G. Winder, and Isabelle M. Mansuy. 2001. "Inducible and Reversible Enhancement of Learning, Memory, and Long-Term Potentiation by Genetic Inhibition of Calcineurin." *Cell* 104: 675–86.

Margulies, Nancy, with Nusa Maal. 2002. *Mapping Inner Space: Learning and Teaching Visual Mapping.* 2nd ed. Tucson, Ariz.: Zephyr Press.

Margulies, Nancy, and Christine Valenza. 2005. *Visual Thinking: Tools for Mapping Your Ideas.* Norwalk, Conn.: Crown House Publishing.

Maxted, Peter. 1999. *Understanding Barriers to Learning.* London: Campaign for Learning.

McCarthy, Bernice. 1980. *The 4Mat System: Teaching and Learning Styles with Right/Left Mode Techniques.* Barrington, Ill.: EXCEL.

McCrone, John. 1999. *Going Inside: A Tour Round a Single Moment of Consciousness.* London: Faber and Faber. (Reprinted New York: Fromm International, 2001.)

McGaugh, James L. 1989. "Dissociating Learning and Performance: Drug Hormone Enhancement of Memory Storage." *Brain Research Bulletin* 23 (4/5): 339–45.

———. 2000 "Memory: A Century of Consolidation." *Science* 287: 248–51

McKay, Matthew, and Patrick Fanning. 2000. *Self-Esteem: A Proven Program of Cognitive Techniques for Assessing, Improving, and Maintaining Your Self-Esteem.* Oakland, Calif.: New Harbinger Publications.

Meighan, Roland. 2001. *Natural Learning and the National Curriculum.* Nottingham UK: Educational Heretics Press in association with Natural Parent.

Meighan, Roland, and Iram Siraj-Blatchford. 1997. *A Sociology of Educating.* London: Cassell. (Reprinted New York: Continuum, 2004.)

Miller, Ron, ed. 2000. *Creating Learning Communities: Models, Resources and New Ways of Thinking about Teaching and Learning.* Brandon, Vt.: The Foundation for Educational Renewal.

Mills, R. C. 1987. "Relationship between School Motivational Climate, Teacher Attitudes, Student Mental Health, School Failure and Health Damaging Behavior." Paper presented at the Annual Conference of the American Educational Research Association, April 1987, Washington D.C.

Nadel, Lynn. 1990. "Varieties of Spatial Cognition: Psychobiological Considerations." *Annals of the New York Academy of Sciences* 608:613–26.

Nadel, Lynn, J. Wilmer, and E. M. Kurz. 1984. "Cognitive Maps and Environmental Context." In *Context and Learning,* ed P. D. Balsam and A. Tomi, 385–406. Hillsdale, N.J.: Lawrence Erlbaum.

Neelands, Jonothan. 1984. *Making Sense of Drama: A Guide to Classroom Practice.* London: Heinemann.

———. 1990. *Structuring Drama Work: A Handbook of Available Forms in Theatre and Drama.* Cambridge, UK: Cambridge University Press.

Neimark, Jill. 1995. "It's Magical. It's Malleable . . . It's Memory." *Psychology Today* (January–February): 44–49, 80, 85.

O'Keefe, John, and Lynn Nadel. 1978. *The Hippocampus as a Cognitive Map*. Oxford, UK: Clarendon Press.

Ornstein, Robert. 1991. *The Evolution of Consciousness*. New York: Simon and Schuster.

———. 1997. *The Right Mind: A Cutting Edge Picture of How the Two Sides of the Brain Work*. Orlando, Fla.: Harcourt Brace and Company.

Parry, Terence, and Gayle Gregory. 1998. *Designing Brain-Compatible Learning*. Arlington Heights, Ill.: Skylight Professional Development.

Patterson, Marilyn Nikimaa. 1997. *Every Body Can Learn: Engaging the Bodily-Kinesthetic Intelligence in the Everyday Classroom*. Tucson, Ariz.: Zephyr Press.

Perkins, David. 1995. *Outsmarting IQ: The Emerging Science of Learnable Intelligence*. New York: The Free Press.

Piaget, Jean. 2001. *The Psychology of Intelligence*. New York: Routledge.

Plomin, Robert. 1983. "Developmental Behavioral Genetics." *Child Development* 54 (2): 253–59.

Postle, Denis. 1989. *The Mind Gymnasium*. London: Gaia Books.

Postman, Neil, and Charles Weingartner. 1969. *Teaching as a Subversive Activity*. New York: Delacorte.

Powell, Robert. 2001. *The Danish Free School Tradition: A Lesson in Democracy*. Kelso, Scotland: Curlew Productions.

Prashnig, Barbara. 1998. *The Power of Diversity: New Ways of Learning and Teaching*. Auckland, New Zealand: David Bateman.

Prigogine, Ilya, and Isabelle Stengers. 1984. *Order Out of Chaos: Man's New Dialogue with Nature*. New York: Bantam.

QCA [Qualifications and Curriculum Authority]. 2005. National Curriculum Online. www.nc.uk.net/index.html (accessed January 8, 2005).

Race, Phil. 1995. *Who Learns Wins: Positive Steps to the Enjoyment and Rediscovery of Learning*. London: Penguin Group and BBC Enterprises.

Ratey, John. 2002. *A User's Guide to the Brain: Perception, Attention, and the Four Theaters of the Brain*. New York: Vintage Books.

Reardon, Mark, and Rob Abernathy. 2002. *HotTips for Teachers: 30 Steps to Student Engagement*. Tucson, Ariz.: Zephyr Press.

Reardon, Mark, and Seth Derner. 2004. *Strategies for Great Teaching: Maximize Learning Moments*. Chicago, Ill.: Zephyr Press.

Reif, Sandra F., and Julie A. Heimburge. 1996. *How to Reach and Teach All Students in the Inclusive Classroom*. West Nyack, N.Y.: The Center for Applied Research in Education.

Restak, Richard. 1993. "Brain by Design." *The Sciences* 33 (5): 27–33.

Roberts, Mike. 1994. *Skills for Self-Managed Learning, Autonomous Learning by Research Projects*. Nottingham, UK: Education Now Books.

Rogers, Carl R. 1951. *Client-Centred Therapy: Its Current Practice, Implications and Theory*. London: Constable. (Orig. pub. Boston: Houghton Mifflin, 1951.)

———. 1961. *On Becoming a Person: A Therapist's View of Psychotherapy*. London: Constable. (Reprinted Boston: Mariner Books, 1995.)

———. 1983. *Freedom to Learn for the 80's*. Columbus, Ohio: Charles E. Merrill.

Rose, Colin, and Louise Goll. 1992. *Accelerate Your Learning*. Aylesbury, UK: Accelerated Learning Systems.

Rose, Colin, and Malcolm J. Nicholl. 1997. *Accelerated Learning for the 21st Century: The 6-Step Plan to Unlock Your Master-Mind*. London: Piatkus. (Reprinted New York: Dell, 1998.)

Rosenthal, Robert, and Leonore Jacobson. 2003. *Pygmalion in the Classroom*. Bancyfelin, Wales: Crown House Publishing.* (Orig. pub. New York: Holt, Rinehart and Winston, 1968.)

Rowntree, Derek. 1970. *Learn How to Study: A Guide for Students of All Ages*. London: Warner Books.

Ryan, Richard M., and Edward Deci. 2000. "Self-Determination Theory and the Facilitation of Intrinsic Motivation, Social Development, and Well-Being." *American Psychologist* 55: 68–78.

Ryan, Richard M., and J. G. La Guardia. 1999. "Achievement Motivation within a Pressured Society: Intrinsic and Extrinsic Motivations to Learn and the Politics of School Reform." In *Advances in Motivation and Achievement,* vol. 11, ed. T. Urdan, 45–85. Greenwich Conn.: JAI Press.

Salovey, Peter, and Mayer, John D. 1990. *Emotional Intelligence: Imagination, Cognition, and Personality*. New York: Harper.

Scarr, Sandra. 1992. "Developmental Theories for the 1990's: Development and Individual Differences." *Child Development* 63: 1–19.

———. 1993. "Biological and Cultural Diversity: The Legacy of Darwin for Development." *Child Development* 64: 1333–53.

Scottish Consultative Council on the Curriculum 1996. "Teaching for Effective Learning: A Paper for Discussion and Development." Dundee, Scotland: Scottish Consultative Council on the Curriculum. (This group now calls itself Learning and Teaching Scotland, and the second edition of the paper appears under the new name. Visit at www.LTScotland.com.)

Shea, T. C. 1983. "An Investigation of the Relationship among Preferences for the Learning Style Element of Design, Selected Instructional Environments, and Reading Achievement of Ninth Grade Students to Improve Administrative Determinations Concerning Effective Educational Facilities." Dissertation, St. John's University, New York.

Shipman, Virginia, and F. Shipman. 1983. "Cognitive Styles: Some Conceptual, Methodological and Applied Issues." In *Review of Research in Education,* vol. 12, ed. E.W. Gordon, ed., 229–91. Washington, DC: American Educational Research Association.

Shute, Chris. 1994. *Alice Miller: The Unkind Society, Parenting and Schooling*. Nottingham, UK: Educational Heretics Press.

Slavin, Robert. 2003. *Educational Psychology*. 7th ed. Boston: Allyn and Bacon.

Smith, Alistair. 1996. *Accelerated Learning in the Classroom*. Stafford, UK: Network Educational Press.*

———. 1998. *Accelerated Learning in Practice: Brain-Based Methods for Accelerating Motivation and Achievement*. Stafford, UK: Network Educational Press.*

———. 2005a. *Accelerated Learning: A User's Guide*. Norwalk, Conn.: Crown House Publishing.

———. 2005b. *The Brain's Behind It: New Knowledge about the Brain and Learning*. Norwalk, Conn.: Crown House Publishing.

SDT. 2004. "The Theory." *Self-Determination Theory: An Approach to Human Motivation and Personality*. www.psych.rochester.edu/SDT/theory.html (accessed December 5, 2004).

Sternberg, Robert, ed. 1994. *Encyclopedia of Human Intelligence.* New York: Macmillan; Toronto: Maxwell Macmillan Canada.

Stine, Jean Marie. 1997. *Double Your Brain Power: Increase Your Memory by Using All of Your Brain All of the Time.* Paramus, N.J.: Prentice Hall.

Stratton, Peter, and Nicky Hayes. 1993. *A Student's Dictionary of Psychology.* 2nd ed. London: Edward Arnold.

Sylwester, Robert. 1993–1994. "What the Biology of the Brain Tells Us about Learning." *Educational Leadership* 51 (4): 46.

————. 1998. "The Downshifting Dilemma." Unpubl. paper.

————. 2003. *A Biological Brain in a Cultural Classroom: Enhancing Cognitive Development through Collaborative Classroom Management.* 2nd ed. Thousand Oaks, Calif.: Corwin Press.

————. 2005. *How to Explain a Brain: An Educator's Handbook of Brain Terms and Cognitive Processes.* Thousand Oaks, Calif.: Corwin Press.

Sylwester, Robert, and Joo-Yun Cho. 1993. "What Brain Research Says about Paying Attention." *Educational Leadership* 50 (4): 71–75.

Teare, Barry. 1997. *Effective Resources for Able and Talented Children.* Stafford UK: Network Educational Press.*

————. 2001. *More Effective Resources for Able and Talented Children.* Stafford UK: Network Educational Press.*

Thompson, Richard F. 1985. *The Brain: A Neuroscience Primer.* New York: W. H. Freeman and Company.

Tobias, Cynthia Ulrich. 1994. *The Way They Learn: How to Discover and Teach to Your Child's Strengths.* Colorado Springs: Focus on the Family Publishing.

Tomlinson, Carol Ann. 1999. *The Differentiated Classroom: Responding to the Needs of All Learners.* Alexandria, Va.: Association for Supervision and Curriculum Development.

————. 2001. *How to Differentiate Instruction in Mixed-Ability Classrooms.* Alexandria, Va.: Association for Supervision and Curriculum Development.

————. 2003. *Fulfilling the Promise of the Differentiated Classroom: Strategies and Tools for Responsive Teaching.* Alexandria, Va.: Association for Supervision and Curriculum Development.

Tomlinson, Carol, Ann, ed. 2004. *Differentiation for Gifted and Talented Students.* Thousand Oaks, Calif.: Corwin Press.

Toppo, Greg. 2002. "Schools Use High-Tech Tools, Personal Touch to Get Truants Back to Classroom." *Chicago Sun-Times,* August 18, 2002. Available at www.suntimes.com/special_sections/skul/old/bc-schools-truancy.html (accessed June 1, 2004).

Torrance, E. P., and O. E. Ball. 1984. *Torrance Tests of Creative Thinking: Streamlined.* Bensenville, Ill.: Scholastic Testing Service.

Tsien, J. Z., D. F. Chen, D. Gerber; C. Tom, E. H. Mercer, D. J. Anderson, M. Mayford, E. R. Kandel, and S. Tonegawa, S. 1996. "Subregion– and Cell Type–Restricted Gene Knockout in Mouse Brain." *Cell* 87:1317–26.

Vail, Priscilla L. 1992. *Learning Styles: Food for Thought and 130 Practical Tips for Teachers K–4.* Rosemont, N.J.: Modern Learning Press.

Virostko, J. 1983. "An Analysis of the Relationships among Academic Achievement in Mathematics and Reading, Assigned Instructional Schedules, and the Learning Style Time Preferences of Third, Fourth, Fifth and Sixth Grade Students." Dissertation, St. John's University, New York.

Watkins, Chris, Eileen Carnell, Caroline Lodge, Patsy Wagner, and Caroline Whalley. 2000. *Learning about Learning: Resources for Supporting Effective Learning.* London; New York: Routledge.

Weber, Ellen. 1997. *Roundtable Learning: Building Understanding through Enhanced MI Strategies.* Tucson, Ariz.: Zephyr Press.

White, Alan. 1989. "Student-Centred Learning." Unpublished paper.

White, R. T. 1980. "An Investigation of the Relationship between Selected Instructional Methods and Selected Elements of Emotional Learning Style upon Student Achievement in Seventh Grade Social Studies." Dissertation, St. John's University, New York.

Winebrenner, Susan. 1992. *Teaching Gifted Kids in the Regular Classroom: Stategies and Techniques Every Teacher Can Use to Meet the Academic Needs of the Gifted and Talented.* Minneapolis, Minn.: Free Spirit Publishing.

Wolfe, Patricia. 2001. *Brain Matters: Translating Research into Classroom Practice.* Alexandria, Va.: Association for Supervision and Curriculum Development.

Youngs, Bettie B. 1992. *Six Vital Ingredients of Self-Esteem: How to Develop Them in Your Students.* Rolling Hills Estates, Calif.: Jalmar Press.

Zack, Linda R. 1995. *Building Self-Esteem through the Museum of I: 25 Original Projects That Explore and Celebrate the Self.* Minneapolis, Minn.: Free Spirit Publishing.

Zohar, Danah, and Ian Marshall. 2001. *SQ: Spiritual Intelligence: The Ultimate Intelligence.* London: Bloomsbury.

* Available at www.chpus.com

Index